Identity Re-creation in Global African Encounters

The Africana Experience
and Critical Leadership Studies

Series Editors

Abul Pitre, PhD
North Carolina A&T State University

Comfort Okpala, PhD
North Carolina A&T State University

Series Titles

Identity Re-creation in Global African Encounters

Edited by
John Ayotunde Isola Bewaji
and Adedoyin Aguoru

LEXINGTON BOOKS
Lanham • Boulder • New York • London

Published by Lexington Books
An imprint of The Rowman & Littlefield Publishing Group, Inc.
4501 Forbes Boulevard, Suite 200, Lanham, Maryland 20706
www.rowman.com

6 Tinworth Street, London SE11 5AL

British Library Cataloguing in Publication Information Available

Library of Congress Cataloging-in-Publication Data Available

ISBN: 978-1-4985-9813-2 (cloth)
ISBN: 978-1-4985-9814-9 (electronic)

Contents

Introduction

Adedoyin Aguoru and John Ayotunde Isola Bewaji

The kernel of the essays brought together in this volume was planted at the Toyin Falola Africa Conference in 2013, the edition of which was as ambitious as it was expansive in terms of thematic coverage, a trademark of these annual gatherings in the name of one of Africa's foremost historians. The ambitiousness and expansiveness was not only matched by the enthusiasm and intellectual rigor brought to bear on the various aspects of the issues by the array of outstanding scholars who presented seminal essays at the conference, the discussants and the general audience engagement were phenomenal. This spurred the editors of this volume to commit to bringing these essays to a global audience, working under the aegis of the dire need to appreciate global Africa holistically, especially in the decade of Peoples of African Descent proclaimed by United Nations. Hence, while ethnicity has long been a staple analytical category of scholarly engagements on Africa and Africa-descended worlds, sparking rich, variegated conversations on its many referents and meanings, scholars of Africa and its vast Diaspora have rarely conceptualized race as a stand-alone unit of Africanist analysis outside the familiar templates of colonial and neo-colonial binaries, and outside of oppressive Euro-American racial formations such as apartheid, plantation slavery, and Jim Crow. Nor have they seriously considered how the emerging grid of place as a physical, imagined, and aspirational representation of "self" and the "other" might complicate notions of ethnic identity and racial awareness.

Clearly, ethnicity is an expansive category. It encompasses a plethora of representational practices, textual productions, material cultures, symbols, aspirations, cultural retentions and mixtures, religious belief, and forms of political negotiation. These elements are individually or collectively mobilized to articulate a coherent narrative of identity and solidarity, however transient such a narrative may be. Taken together or unpacked for separate engagement, these constitutive elements of ethnicity offer the space for rich multidisciplinary analyses. They can foreground, and can be applied to, empirical and conceptual inquiries in many fields in the social sciences and the humanities.

This conception was very prescient as, indeed, the essays collected in this volume paid careful attention to the nuanced ways and patterns of ethnicity as manifested in the cross-disciplinarity and intersections of various paradigms of scholarships. The fact that it is conference in acknowledgment and honour of the scholarship of Toyin Falola, who himself has contributed in no small measure to this scholarship in Africana academy on ethnicity presages pathbreaking contributions from transcontinental Africanists and intellectual leaders. Even more significant is the recognition of the patterns of locations and dislocations which have spawned ideas across spaces and places in global Africa. In the true spirit of the honouree, there manifests less grandstanding or pontification in the essays collected here, and even less settling of scores about who is right or wrong.

There is a general recognition of the at once homogeneity and equal diversity scholars of Africa and of the African Diaspora spawned by autochthony, continental indigeneity, slavery, colonialism, trade, exile, economic hardship, opportunity, adventure, and postcolonial migration, need to systematically grapple with the place of race, distance, shared ancestry, race consciousness, and constructions of racial communities across numerous boundaries and attributes in the evolution of African and African Diaspora cultures and experiences around the world. Yet racial ideas, the raciation and de-raciation of groups and identities, not just reactive ideas about racial solidarity, but proactively constructed notions of intra-racial difference have proliferated in the texts and conversations of global black elites, intellectuals, and black communities around the world. This development has in turn given political and social valence to ideas and debates about black authenticity, race treachery, racial integration and separatism, compromise and resistance, and even the philosophical implications of skin lightening, hair straightening, and other bodily practices among black folk. Differing understandings of racial destiny, black victimhood, black racial purity, and the intertwinement of authenticity and place of origin have become subjects of discussion in global black intellectual circles. Moreover, beyond the analysis of the complex and at times difficult legacies of European-African, Asian-African, and Arab-African encounters and miscegenation in Africa, Asia, the Middle East, Europe, and the New World, recent studies have begun to unearth elaborate racial claims and narratives of racial differentiation within "African" communities and in "African" zones of contact previously narrated homogeneously into an African racial formation.

One thing that has become clearer to global African scholars remain the need for tenacity in the interrogation of ideas on, about and regarding human communities birthed globally through the agency of Africa, even as peoples dispersed voluntarily and otherwise over many millennia. Even while disagreeing in interpretations of text, genuine respect for the other's right to a different interpretation is acknowledged in the essays collected here. This is a mark of the humility of the conveners of the conference, embraced by all, as reflective of African traditions practiced in the Setswana *Kgotla* or Yoruba *Apejo* or *Igbimo*, where every person, young or old, male or female, rich or poor, abled or disabled are entitled to a hearing and airing of their views, because *omode gbon, agba gbon, ni isedale Ife* (transliterated as "children have their wisdom, adults have their wisdom; that is the foundation on which the cradle of Yoruba society, Ile-Ife, is built"). And where there is need for clarification, no one goes on to act or pursue a unidirectional line of view, without attention to the original ideas of the protagonists being interrogated (Bewaji, 2012).

The Truth and Reconciliation programme of post-Apartheid South Africa is a sterling example of African jurisprudence and social engineering at its best. Even while differences of opinions may warrant elucidation, there is always room for honest disagreement. And once space, place, or avenue is provided for clarification, where there remain differences of opinion, such would not constitute ground for unending feud or animosity. Without trending in the path of global apocalypse, it seems clear that the global community has now come to recognize the need to take seriously the values of indigenous cultures of Africa and its Diaspora, as the atomization and reclusivity of economic brigandage permeates into the recesses of today's multipolar world.

In this regard, the essays brought together here are singularly germane in the perspectives they present for the engagement of dire situations of reclusive ethnicities in the face of collapsing exceptionalisms and identities. Even more significant is the realization that there is no need to want to be like the other, where the other has shown clearly markers of inhumanity or intellectual arrogance of know it all. The stories about *Ijapa t'Iroko, Oko Yanibo*, who presumed that he could put all the wisdom of the world in a basket/gourd and carry it up a palm tree, to prevent other people from gaining any part of the content, and to become the sole purveyor of wisdom shows the weakness of perverted egoism (Bewaji, 2003). This un-African characteristic may resonate with the triadic of co-capitalist IMF, World Bank, and WTO, as agents of global dislocation and deprivation of the masses from the wealth derived from their backyard. In *The Man, The Mask, The Muse,* we see the strands of humanism beyond boundaries, and the effect of beneficence spread transcontinentally (Afolabi, 2010). Compared with the idea of some agencies of oppression and domination, framed as advocates of global order, holding onto some ephemeral technological superiority while the rest are prevented in the name of global security, the discussions that permeate the essays collected in this volume show why it is impossible for one individual or group to hold the rest of humanity to ransom—not just impossible, but self-defeating, because even *Ijapa* soon found, to his chagrin, that such a venture is beyond anyone.

In human community, there is always the need to exercise the principle of charity, which is to allow the other a perspective, albeit different, disagreeable, or even dissonant. The eventual consequence of the tapestry of colors painted on the canvass of humanity is the conjoining of our greatness through the advancement of plurality of ideas and essence. In *Encyclopedia of the Yoruba,* Adegbidin (2016) eloquently enumerated the importance of the paraphernalia of *Ifa* divination. This, contrary to a skewed view expressed by Oluwole (2014), recognizes the fact that *Ifa* literary corpus cannot just be taken as literature, read as an intellectual disquisition, without attending to the divination activities that it purveys. It is this error of taking the literature, which is just a part, for the whole of what *Ifa* means, which led Oluwole to the hasty conclusion of assuming that those who refuse to score cheap discovery channel points in equating *Ifa* with Plato's *Republic* do not value Yoruba heritage to the same extent as she does. All that Plato did was philosophize, from the context of Greek socio-political experience; not, in anyway, supposing that his effort contained more by way of religion; by contrast with *Ifa* and the Hebrew bible, which are not just literary texts but philosophical and religious, lending themselves to healing, protection, divination, and counselling, among others.

Thus, some questions were already framing discussions of the role of race and racial constructs in the study of African communities around the world; questions about whether the Sahara, Indian Ocean, Atlantic Ocean, the Mediterranean, and certain sectors of the Red Sea constitute a racial divide that disturb the geographical continuum of Africa; whether Africa is a byword for "black" and if so what "black" means in light of its obvious exclusion of "white" Africans; whether the field of play between race and ethnicity is narrow or wide; whether we can posit intra-black racism as a phenomenon; whether a black racial essence exists that connects Africa to its Diaspora and produces trans-oceanic communities of solidarity; whether continental Africans and Diaspora Africans relate to race and racism differently and/or have different racial imaginations that may engender intra-racial tensions; whether xenophobia and native/immigrant tensions are sustained by popular racial and ethnic stereotypes or are grounded in real differences within black communities; whether immigrant and native-born blacks can work together to pursue agendas specific to their common interests in white-dominated power structures like the United States; whether the fault lines of some conflicts in Africa correspond to a clichéd understanding of racial difference between Africans and Arabs; and whether intra-African racial claims are stand-ins for other aspirations or deserve to be understood on their own racial merits.

The essays brought together in this volume explore race, racial politics, and racial transformation in the context of Africa's encounter with the world outside, in the context of oppression, in the context of the racialization of ethnic difference, in the context of dislocation, in the context of distanciation, in the context of migrations and alienation, in the context of marginalization, in the context of misplacement, in the context of dehumanization, in the context of post-slavery and emancipation, in the context of epistemicide, and in the context of identity deconstruction, destruction, and reconstruction in response to colonial and postcolonial policies of differentiation and privilege.

For this simple reason, in the essays that address place and location, our conception of place ties in with the provocative outlines articulated above on race and ethnicity. We understand place to be a physical, mental, and ideological location or situation in which significant socio-political, economic, and emotional investments have been made; they are sites of economic, religious, cultural, and humanity othering. These divestments and investments often define the contours of identity, humanity, humanism, and humaneness, serving as anchors and referents for a variety of identity practices, including racial and ethnic self-representation. We acknowledge, however, that "place," its connotations, and the semiotic burdens it is often called upon to bear are always changing. These have given birth to essays that radically redefine "place," "home," "location," "origin," and related idioms of affiliation and affinity.

While some of these matters are well worn within global academy, the perspectives introduced by the essays here harvested are fresh, perceptive and very germane to the evolving trends in contemporary global geopolitics and economics. There is no doubt that Africa, and indeed the world, is faced with challenges of centrifugal forces emanating from parochial sentiments with entrenched self-interests. The way and manner in which the two Middle Eastern–originated religions have bifurcated Africa for division and antagonisms, under exclusionary generic fundamentalisms with primordial fears of each other, and the continued vilification of indigenous religions of Africa, while extracting economic benefits for the ancestral homes of these religions, continue to attract intellectual discourse. For these reasons, even the incomes derived from migrations are not immune from the reaches of the recursive influences of ethnicity, nationality, and religion, as presented by the essays in this section. At the same time, our authors engage with critical issues of African identity, self and group awareness, battling stereotypes globally and understanding the original historicity of human emergence from Africa, from where humanity dispersed globally, both historically and contemporaneously, without being reductive in the annotation of the colonial past and postcolonial present with eminently researched essays utilizing carefully dug out precedents, antecedents, and consequences of colonialism on the global African space-scape.

To deal with the ontology and epistemology of global gender discourse, we bring critical reflections on the challenges faced by global Africa where these matters are concerned. We explore issues that are ignored in the academy relating to socio-cultural practices, which often fall below the radar. Thus, by opening up layers of the themes that constitute the central ideas engaged in the seventeen-chapter volume, there is no doubt that it will provoke not just attention but engagement. The importance of putting the essays together in an accessible format is both to preserve for researchers the essays, but also to help stimulate further research which will continue to chart new vistas in the search for integrative and elevating formulas for global Africa as we continue to waddle through the labyrinths of globalization and depreciating capitalism.

BIBLIOGRAPHY

Afolabi, N. (2010). *The Man, The Mask, The Muse*. Durham, NC: Carolina Academic Press.

Bewaji, J. A. I. (2003). *Beauty and Culture*. Ibadan, Nigeria: Spectrum Books Ltd.

———. (2007). *An Introduction to Theory of Knowledge*. Ibadan, Nigeria: Hope Publications.

———. (2012). *Narratives of Struggle*. Durham, NC: Carolina Academic Press.

———. (2013). *Black Aesthetics*. Trenton, NY: Africa World Press.

———. and Imafidon, E. (Eds.). (2014). *Ontologized Ethics*. Lanham, MD: Lexington Books.

———. (2016). and Babatunde, A. P. (2017). *Media Theory, Practice and Ethics*. Ibadan, Nigeria: BWright Integrated Publishers.

———. (2017). (Eds.) *The Humanities and the Dynamics of African Culture in the 21st Century*. London: Cambridge Academic Scholars Publishers.

———. (2016). *The Rule of Law and Governance in Indigenous Yoruba Society*. Lanham, MD: Lexington Books.

Falola, T. and Akinyemi, A. (2016). *Encyclopedia of The Yoruba*. Bloomington: Indiana University Press.

Oluwole, S. (2014). *Socrates and Orunmila*. Lagos: Ark Publishers.

Chapter One

Race and Ethnicity

Irreducible Categories in Black Peoples' Encounters

Kunirum Osia

There is so much diversity in the world in terms of race and ethnicity than is readily affirmed by some who continue to discriminate against others on that basis. The continued claim of race as an irreducible biological category that is understood as the nature and embodiment of humans exacerbates the problems of racism in its various manifestations. Social construction of race means that, for a variety of reasons, humans invent the category and assign meanings to it as well as to racial hierarchies. Such construction has tended to provide permanency to racism with its multiple manifestations of prejudice, discrimination, and stereotypes.

Racism creates distance between, and inequality among, peoples, thus generating conflicts. It assumes that traits and abilities are biologically determined by race and postulates the inherent superiority of one race and its right to dominate others. History notes that groups use ethnicity as a protective shield against racial hostility. We will define the concepts of race, ethnicity, culture, racism, prejudice, and stereotype as these will guide our reevaluation of human and cultural diversity in today's world. However, attention would be paid to the concepts of "ethnicity" with its conceptual difficulties, the reality of "racism" with its strains of prejudice, discrimination and stereotype, and "race" with its irreducibility in constructing humanity into fixed categories.

We argue that unless there is a collective change in humanity's evaluation of diversity and interpretation of race, black people's negative encounters with peoples of other climes would continue, if not overtly, but in their insidious subtlety, which will continue to mask negative prejudices. Under such circumstances, it will become even more difficult to objectively appre-

ciate the varieties of unwarranted subordinations of peoples of different cultural and phenotypical strains globally, thereby perpetrating the falsehood of
natural differences between peoples from different parts of the world just
from mere variations of appearances.

It would appear that culture defines a set of shared assumptions derived
from group experiences over time, whereby people can predict others' actions as members of the group in a given circumstance and react accordingly.
It is the totality of behaviour patterns, arts, beliefs, institutions, values and all
other products of human work or thought *typical* of a population or community at a *given time* (Bewaji, 2003, 2012, 2013). In this definition, what is
typical, defining, or normative for a particular group is the key. So, to understand any group's culture, one must understand what is *typical* of that cultural group (Lee, 1999). This makes the definition of culture as a learned
behaviour preferred. It is not genetically determined. Culture is not an easy
concept since so many rituals, symbolisms, and practices contribute to its
shaping. Its ramifications are sweeping, subtle, and often unarticulated. Its
effects upon us often lie below the threshold of words or even consciousness.
Social anthropology teaches us that culture is dynamic and not static.

Race, applied to human beings, is a local geographical or global human
population, distinguished as, a more or less, distinct group by genetically
transmitted physical characteristics. Often it is used to categorize a group of
people united or classified together on the basis of common history, nationality, or geographic distribution (Lee, 1999). It is the mixture of physiological
and non-physiological characteristics which make race such a slippery concept to apprehend and discuss. The definition would be further elaborated
below in our full analysis of *race.*

Ethnicity is described as a sense of commonality that is as seriously
embraced as race, religion or national origin. Conscious and unconscious
processes contribute to a sense of identity and historical continuity in formu-
lating ethnicity. It is often derived from a perceived common ancestry,
whether real or fictitious. In this sense there are several broad ethnic groups
within several countries of our civilization. Greater elaboration is provided
below under understanding ethnicity.

Racism's definition includes two components: first, the assumption that
all traits and abilities are biologically determined by race, and second, the
belief in the inherent superiority of one race and its right to dominate other
races. Given these definitions, which combine an a*ssumption*, and an ensuing
belief, it is not surprising that racism is so prevalent. The assumption that
abilities are biologically determined is very controversial. Another definition
of racism involves unjustified negative treatment resulting from individual
prejudice and discrimination or institutional policies and procedures. This
definition includes institutional racism, or the use of established laws, cus-

toms, and practices or norms that produce racial inequalities, thus it makes it subtle and difficult to detect (Jones, 1972).

Prejudice is an antipathy based on a faulty and inflexible generalization. It may be felt or expressed. It may be directed toward a group as a whole or toward an individual because he or she is a member of a group (Allport, 1954, 9). The word *prejudice* comes from the Latin words *prae*, meaning before, and *judicium*, meaning judgment. In other words, prejudice occurs, for example, when someone is prejudged before any real knowledge of that person is known (Okolo, 1974).

According to social comparison theory, people tend to make judgments about themselves by comparing themselves to a similar group of people, or *reference group*. If the comparisons are positive, they feel better about themselves. Prejudice occurs when a person takes his or her own group as the positive reference point from which to judge other people *negatively* (Festinger, 1954). In this regard it is coextensive with racism and its effects on races are the same.

Discrimination takes place when actions are taken that favor one group or individual at the expense of another group or individual. An example of this would be if a person thinks of his or her own ethnic group as his or her primary reference group, to the extent that he or she feels he or she is succeeding, in comparison to others in the reference group, his or her self-esteem may increase. However, if he or she judges people from other groups as unfit or inadequate compared to his or her own ethnic group, he or she is exercising prejudice. If he or she takes actions to favor his or her ethnic group at the expense of another group, for example, if he or she passes laws that do not allow members of another group to own property or vote, this constitutes discrimination (Lee, 1999).

A *stereotype* is a generalized description of a group of people that has developed over time on the basis of cross-cultural interactions. In this age of media exposure, it is very easy to take what we see as true cross-cultural interaction. If you have never met someone from another ethnic background, you may have a stereotype of that culture based on what you read or saw but not based on real personal interaction with others from that ethnicity. Our views of other groups are often guided by stereotypes, which can form on the shakiest bits of information. Our views of other groups very frequently are based on fictitious events, hearsays, or simple-case encounters with out-group members, without any very scientific evidence. Unfortunately, most people care less about being accurate in their social perceptions than they do about coming to a quick evaluation of another person or group (Nelson, 2006).

One of the major sources of stereotypes and prejudices are our parents. Children learn the values and beliefs of their parents and tend to internalize those same beliefs. In this way, stereotypes and prejudices often are transmitted within families, from generation to generation. Conversely, victims of prejudices transmit their experiences to their children from generation to generation. For example, Japanese Americans would transmit their experiences during the internment for five years without due process during the WWII to generations of their children. African Americans would transmit their centuries of enslavement, Jim Crow, and ethnic suppression to generations of their children. Similarly, Native Americans would transmit their encounter with the white man and the United States government to generations of their children (Nelson 2006). Having internalized what was learned from childhood, people grow up viewing groups as different and thus, begin discussing relationships in terms of differences in race categories.

UNDERSTANDING RACE

The continued claim of race as an irreducible biological category that equates with culture, which is understood as the nature and embodiment of humans that are to be found in a timeless history, exacerbates the problems of racism. Social construction of race means that, for a variety of reasons, humans invent the category of race and assign meanings to it and to racial hierarchies. Modern forms of race and racism acquire meaning within social, political, and economic relations that reflect inequality. State policies of segregation, such as Jim Crow in the United States and apartheid in the old South Africa, gave particular meanings to race and racism. Race works through different claims, for example, ancestry, blood, color, and a number of retrospective illusions that help to frame right, fright, status, and privilege for some at the expense of others (Watson, 2001).

Notions of racial purity are as false as notions of racial impurity. There is no such thing, though much of human history has been frittered away by people trying to legitimize race as the defining element in what passes for civilization. Both science and history have debunked the attributions of *phenotypical* and *genotypical* traits in humans of superiority over inferiority and superordination over subordination. We are aided not only by history but also by science in the affirmation that human beings have more similarities than dissimilarities. The "out-of-Africa" migration of humans has held sway despite continued challenges, showing that Africa was the original home of human beings before the dispersals to the further extremities of the earth, where millennia of adaptation has produced the diversities that we witness in human groups.

OUT-OF-AFRICA THEORIES OF HUMAN ORIGIN

In 1986, researchers published papers suggesting that everyone alive on earth today descended from a small number of individuals, men and women who migrated from Africa not later than 50,000 years ago (Booth, 1991). The most compelling scientific support yet for a theory that traces the roots of modern human beings to Africa is evidence extracted from a study of a material of human inheritance passed from mother to child. The study suggests that most recent human ancestors lived in Africa 171,500 years ago and from there began their epochal migration. An analysis of mitochondrial deoxyribo nucleic acid (DNA), the genetic material of the mitochondria, the cells powerhouse, from fifty-three ethnically diverse humans, provides cogent support for the "out-of-Africa" origin of human species.

Ulf Gyllensten and his research team of scientists, from the University of Uppsala in Sweden, have gone a step further by obtaining complete sequences—the order of chemical "letters" that make up the recipe of life—of the mitochondria DNA. These scientists sequenced the entire mitochondria genome—16,500 bases pairs in 53 humans of different races and geographic regions. The results were statistically significant and support an African origin for our species.

Additionally, biologists from the University of California at Berkley took the "out-of-Africa" proposition even further by presenting the genetic evidence to suggest that the entire modern human population is descended from a single woman who lived in sub-Saharan Africa about 200,000 years ago (Brown, 2008). Even fossils found in Asia indicate that members of the human evolutionary line known as homo erectus, who predate homo sapiens, migrated out of Africa at least 800,000 years ago (UPI, 2000). While these hypotheses continue to be refined, they reflect a truth that is gradually beginning to dawn on humankind; that regardless of the apparent differences of race, colour, language and religion, the people of the world have much more in common than was formerly supposed. Genetic differences among humans can be explained by the distribution of genetic variables and do not correspond with any useful category of race defined genetically, by skin color or any other physical attributes. That has not stopped many from believing that distinct races exist and from trying to use scientific language to buttress their arguments, and thereby gain credence for their warped prejudices and discriminations.

There was a complex and dynamic interplay between the popular conception of race and the scientific categories, neither of which was grounded in physiological or biological reality, but both of which carried greater emotional import to white people and very devastating consequences to black people and peoples of color generally, regardless of how these categories were being defined. There is likewise no scientific (biological or genetic) basis to support the concept of whiteness or the concept of blackness. There is nothing scientifically distinctive about either except skin color and that is greatly variable. The skin color of a person tells us nothing about his or her culture, country of origin, character, or personal habits. Because there is nothing biological about whiteness or blackness, it ends up being defined by contrast to other groups, and in the process becoming confused with ideas of nationality, religion, and ethnicity (Kivel, 1995).

CONCEPTUAL DIFFICULTIES OF ETHNICITY

Analysts conversant with the discourse on ethnicity can attest to the quantity of studies produced which have been astounding especially considering the paucity of such studies just a few generations ago. The concept of ethnicity that emerges from these studies is somewhat perplexing and too frequently there has been little agreement on what constitutes an ethnic group or an ethnic issue. Nonetheless, ethnicity has become an important intellectual concept, if the number of people writing on the subject could be taken as a measure of significance. It has also become an important focal point for the formulation of public policy in most societies, and even if there was little agreement about the meaning of the concept, it is recognized as being of importance and warrants classification.

It is not necessary to review all of the definitions of the concept of ethnicity that have been given; this has been done by a variety of researchers (Gitter, 1977). More important for our purposes are three interrelated problems that are common to most of these definitions and thus hindering the concept's analytical utility. The first difficulty is the breadth associated with the concept. There is little consensus on what types of distinctions should be regarded as ethnic in nature. Some analysts wish to include social distinctions based on racial or physiological characteristics, religion, language, culture, historical traditions, nationality groups, or various aggregations of these factors. Others desire to see the concept used in a more restrictive manner, particularly separating out racial and nationality groupings (Thompson and Ronen, 1986).

The difficulties with these approaches are obvious. The broad and inclusive approach raises questions about analytical rigor. It seems so inclusive that it is difficult to conceive of what is not, or cannot be, an ethnic characteristic. If that is the case then the older concepts of race, nation, and so forth, may be more useful analytically. Furthermore, an all-inclusive approach to the concept makes it difficult to integrate the less recent research with the new, given an incomparability of terms.

Yet the more exclusive approach is not without its problems. When the concept is used restrictively to denote distinctions between such concepts as racial and ethnic groups, then one is forced to overlook the fact that the boundaries between the distinctions have been intellectually and historically obfuscated. Seldom does any example of an ethnic group possess a clear set of these traits, particularly given the fact that the importance of group distinctiveness is derived from its ascribed qualities. The usual pattern is for a group to possess an overlapping set of traits, such as language, religion, and culture, while sharing others with the rest of the society, with group distinctiveness becoming manifest only in various forms of social, economic, and political interaction. Likewise, the stereotypes and prejudices commonly associated with racial conflicts are not restricted to such cases, as the British, Irish, Poles, and Jews, among many others, can testify. Thus, neither approach provides the necessary clarity required for adequate comparison (Thompson and Ronen, 1986, 27).

The second problem involving the concept of ethnicity pertains to the difficulty of comparing various types of ethnicity to one another. There is a tendency for analysts to deal almost exclusively with a single type of ethnic conflict and frequently a single case or related set of similar cases. Yet the definition of ethnicity clearly suggests a set of interrelationships between such types as native populations, immigrant groups, religious minorities, linguistic minorities, and heterogeneous nationalities that are the issues in a number of countries, especially those formed from colonial past. We need to know more precisely what sociological and political distinctions, if any, exist between these categories and how they interact with one another. The concept will be of little use if analysts were not able to be clearer in distinguishing the interactions that exist among the concept's component categories.

The third problem that relates to the concept of ethnicity is its relationship with other forms of identification and conflict. Just as different types of ethnic conflict may overlap with one another, so, for example, do ethnic and social-class conflicts. Regional issues may coincide with ethnic issues. It is not clear whether ethnic movements are comparable to other movements. Do policy processes treat ethnic issues as a variety of and in the same manner as cultural issues, or socio-economic issues? In order to understand ethnicity, we must also comprehend the interrelationships between it and other forms of identity conflicts and organizations.

These three identified problems do not suggest rejection of the literatures dealing with ethnicity. They may just highlight the fact that scholars of ethnicity are from multidisciplinary backgrounds and thus provide multidisciplinary approach. It is not uncommon for them to cite sociologists, anthropologists, historians, religious scholars, linguists, political scientists and psychologists. Given this diversity of intellectual traditions, analytical and research perspectives, it should not be surprising that there is little agreement over the content of ethnicity as a concept.

Because of the aforementioned difficulties that the concept of ethnicity has exhibited according to analysts, we would prefer interpreting it in a similar and simpler way as Chua (2003) did, that ethnicity will refer to a kind of group identification, a sense of belonging to a people that is experienced as a greatly extended form of kinship. This understanding makes ethnicity broad, while noting the importance of subjective perceptions. It encompasses differences along racial lines, (for example, blacks and whites in the United States), lines of geographic origin (for example, Malays, Chinese, and Indians in Malaysia), as well as linguistic, religious, tribal, or other cultural lines (for example Kikuyu and Kalenji peoples in Kenya or Jews and Muslims in the Middle East). Ethnic identity is not static but shifting and highly malleable. In Rwanda, for example, the 14 percent Tutsi minority dominated the Hutu majority economically and politically for four centuries, as a kind of cattle-owning aristocracy. For most of this period the lines between Hutus and Tutsi were permeable. The two groups spoke the same language, intermarried. That was no longer true after the Belgians arrived, and seeped in specious theories of racial superiority, issued ethnic identity cards on the basis of nose length and cranial circumference.

The resulting much sharper ethnic divisions were exploited by the leaders of Hutu Power. Along similar lines, all over Latin America, where it is often said that there are no ethnic divisions because everyone is mixed-blooded, large numbers of impoverished Bolivians, Chileans, and Peruvians were suddenly being told that they were Aymaras, Incas, or just *Indios*, or whatever identity best resonated and mobilized. These indigenization movements are not necessarily good or bad, but they are contagiously potent. What it all means is that individuals would withdraw into their ethnic shield as a safe mode of defence and any attempt to encroach on this posture would meet with resistance and conflicts inevitably would ensue.

At the same time ethnic identity is rarely constructed out of thin air. Subjective perceptions of identity often depend on more objective traits assigned to individuals based on, for example, perceived morphological characteristics, language differences, or ancestry. Attempt to tell black and white Zimbabweans that they are only imagining their ethnic differences or that ethnicity is a social construct would be met with scorn. They would agree that you are not helpful. Much more concretely relevant is the reality that there is roughly zero intermarriage between blacks and whites in Zimbabwe, just as there is virtually no intermarriage between Chinese and Malays in Malaysia or between Arabs and Israelis in the Middle East. That ethnicity can be at once an artifact of human imagination and rooted in the darkest history, fluid and could be manipulated yet important enough to kill for, is what makes an understanding of the impetus of ethnicity extremely essential if we can contain the burgeoning strife of our civilization (Chua, 2003).

UNDERSTANDING ETHNICITY

Everywhere in the world today, men and women are reaffirming their local particularities, their national, ethnic, or religious identity (Walzer, 1992). People witness the general affirmation of particular identities and the implications for social and political coexistence and cohesive nation building. In extremely different contexts, one finds a doubt, even an anxiety concerning identity, and it is tempting to seek common denominators for such a phenomena that as diverse as hitherto violent conflicts among the Serb, Croat, and Muslim communities in Bosnia, between Catholics and Protestants in Northern Ireland, between Hindus and Muslims in India, the break-up of Czechoslovakia, between the Kurds in Iraq and the government of Turkey, between the Arab Janjaweed militia and Africans in Darfur, between the Basque movement and the government of Spain, just to name a few. Much of the strife has an undercurrent of groups of individuals seeking to ward off hostilities that threaten their ethnic cleavages or identities. Because such incidents are often couched in political terms as *self-determination*, the impetus of ethnicity is subsumed.

Ethnicity is a matter of ascription. There is a propensity to interact with human beings who speak the same language, share common religion and historic memories, and so forth—all of which are commonly considered to be the attributes of ethnicity. Such groups provide certain specifics needed in the circumstances that engender a sense of security, a need for familiarity, a sense of continuity. It is politicized into ethnic factor when an ethnic group is in conflict with the political elite over such issues as the use of limited resources or the allocation of benefits. The greater the stakes involved, the greater the ethnic factor with which the central government must deal. Ethnicity is, of course, not a new term nor is the phenomenon new or unrecognized. It is merely labeled differently. Karl Deutsch (1969) devoted his seminal work to the study of ethnicity in its entirety, although he uses the terms "nationality," "national diversity," and "differentiation" in place of ethnicity.

What may have contributed to the emergence (or, more correctly, the re-emergence) of the term "ethnicity" is that a familiar phenomenon, for which the new term was to be used, emerged in circumstances different from the circumstances that existed prior to the mid-1960s. This familiar phenomenon was a nationalistic awakening or movement. However, from the mid-1960s on, this phenomenon of ethnicity emerged in sovereign, independent, modern, even democratic states both in developed and developing countries, where national awakening was not a legitimate phenomenon as it had been prior to World War II, when various nationalities were incorporated into the political framework of the modern state. Now there was the unexpected emergence of a phenomenon within existing, internationally recognized modern political entities.

The phenomenon of ethnicity reemerged at the time when the disruption of the functioning of modern states in the West and in the Western camp was very much evaluated within the context of East-West relations. Ethnicity was seen as a possible indication that Western ideology, policies, and developmental efforts were failing. Ethnicity tended to be viewed as a destabilizing force that threatened to disintegrate states or at least to disrupt their smooth functioning. Ethnicity appeared no longer as a term for a folkloric or a primordial phenomenon, the manifestation of tribal feelings, but as a term applied as a political force with which to be reckoned.

Since social mobility reduced the salience of a rigid class identity in Europe, and since modern class distinctions were not yet institutionalized in the Third World (especially in sub-Saharan Africa), ethnic identity presented itself as a convenient rallying point to be utilized as a political instrument for developmental gains. Ethnic identity by the mid-1960s had become an organizational form, a weapon, a tool, and or a means for the attainment of goals, just as integrative national identity often was in the nineteenth century and at the beginning of the twentieth century. Ethnicity therefore has appeared as a political phenomenon which has been no more disintegrative than political party formation. But what it actually represents is a social, cultural and, if the need arises, political community, which provides the roles and narratives enabling individuals to develop or construct themselves and make sense of their place in the world, as well as their view of the good life and their shared principles and norms.

UNDERSTANDING RACISM

Racism is a long-standing characteristic of many human societies. Justifying exploitation and violence against other peoples because they are "inferior" or different has a long history in European traditions. The important distinction, for example, in the United States has always been binary—between those who counted as white and those who did not. Drawing on already popular classifications, whiteness was delineated more clearly in the United States in the 18th century, as slavery was introduced and distinguished from various forms of shorter term servitude. The victims of slavery were mostly black, and the slave masters were mostly white.

Although a racial hierarchy was in place from the time of earliest European settlers, racism was only defined "scientifically" as a biological/genetic characteristic about 150 years ago with Darwin's publication of species modification and Linnaeus' system of classification. These ideas were combined by others into a pseudoscientific theory, eventually called Social Darwinism, which attempted to classify human population into distinct categories or races and put them on an evolutionary scale with white on top.

The original classifications consisted of three categories: Caucasoid, Negroid, and Mongoloid. These were not based on genetic differences but on differences that Europeans and European Americans perceived to be important. They were, in fact, based on stereotypes of cultural differences and faulty measures of physiological characteristics, such as skull size (Gould, 1981).

There was a complex and dynamic interplay between the popular conception of race and the scientific categories, neither of which was grounded on physiological or biological reality, but both of which carried great emotional import to white people and devastating consequences to people of color, regardless of how they were being defined. Further elaboration reveals racism as an ideology that invariably connects between cultural behaviour and physical type. Hence it exemplifies specific groups as having characteristic traits (usually detestable or in some way inferior) that are inherent outgrowths of their biological constitution (Schermerhorn, 1970). We can infer that the most common form of racism is a doctrine of group supremacy or superiority couched in physical terms as Ruth Benedict puts it, "the dogma that one ethnic group is condemned by Nature to hereditary inferiority and another group is destined to hereditary superiority" (Benedict, 1943, 98).

Because of this type of categorization of humanity, humankind has ended up with a set of opposing qualities or attributes, which are said to define people either as white or as not white. The tendency, therefore, to see the world in sets of opposites, *either/or* categories, is itself a core pattern of thinking developed in elite settings in Western Europe and the United States. Many other cultures do not divide the world into opposing camps. The English phrase *black-and-white* reflects the desire to divide things into opposites even though everyday reality is rarely clearly defined or neatly categorized. Classical Greek *either/or* logic and Christian theology of *good versus evil* were combined to impose a *good/bad* set of values based on selected categories of racial difference.

Since the 1970s, a number of literatures have begun to demonstrate a shift of emphasis from attitudes to behavior—from prejudice to racism. This change was prompted by the growing demand for a reversal of obvious inequities in societies due to racism. It is also quite clear from both scientific analyses and social action, that scholars of race relations have moved from simplistic conceptualizations of race problems to more sophisticated, multidimensional formulations. This is clear from earlier growth of definitional distinctions regarding racism and the concomitant emphasis on viewing racial questions within social systems framework (Friedman, 1975; Jones, 1972; McConahay and Hough, 1976).

Social scientists agree that the effects of social transactions have wide ramifications. This understanding provides the basis for the systems approach to social phenomena. In such system, everything is correlated with everything else. Actors in psychosocial systems are interdependent, namely, they influence one another, they affect the nature of the system and are affected by it, and they affect themselves by their own actions Thinking in this mode enables us to clearly understand the adverse effects of racism in our civilization.

Why is our discussion of *prejudice* and *stereotyping* important? Aside from the need to understand the negative influence such thinking has on the thoughts, feelings, and behaviours of people in their daily lives, and how they relate to the targets of their prejudice, it is important to understand that such negative attitudes form the basis for the subsequent negative inter-group behaviour that give rise to racism.

Virtually much of histories' wars, battles, and other acts of group violence have been driven by some form of prejudice, stereotyping, and/or discrimination. There are those who believe and indeed assert that prejudice and stereotyping are no longer of consequence because of laws in many countries. While it is the case that overt expressions of racial prejudice and intergroup hatred have declined dramatically in some countries, racial prejudice and stereotypes have by no means disappeared. In fact racial hostilities exist in many countries of our civilization. During the last world football competition in 2010, some newspapers carried articles questioning whether or not the French team was really French. Why, because there were a good number of people of colour playing for France.

We witnessed the British star player, David Beckham condemning, before the world cup, the infiltration of attitudes of racism into football. We witnessed some fans taunt black players by throwing banana peels into the field of play to remind the black players that monkeys eat banana. These are not hoodlums. They are individuals acting out what they have learned. One needs to read the newspapers, listen to the news for examples of intergroup violence that are driven by prejudice. We can still remember the several days of rioting in Southern France, as a result of the police killing of two unarmed youths who had escaped from their custody? People of color, who lived around the neighborhood from where the youths came set that part of France ablaze for days. In recent times, and in not too distant past, according to Nelson (2005), we experienced the following incidents from the United States, which typify effects of prejudice that resulted in violence against black people:

a. In 2007, four black youths were charged to court for beating a white fellow student mercilessly. The incident was dubbed Jena 6, which resulted from the hanging of noose by white high school students in Jena, Louisiana.
b. Also in 2007, the hanging of noose on the campus of the University of Maryland College Park created an uproar and sadness.

c. In October 2007, a noose was hung on the door of the office of an African American professor at Columbia University, New York.

d. In 2006, several houses owned by African American families in Charles County, Maryland, were burned. These incidents have fostered soul-searching.

e. In 1998, in Jasper, Texas, three white men offered a ride to James Byrd Jr., an unsuspecting black man, who was walking on the side of the road. The men drove Byrd to a remote location, where they severely beat him, tied his feet to a logging chain, and tied the chain to the back end of their pick-up truck. They then dragged the still-conscious Byrd behind their truck down a remote country road, when Byrd's body quickly disintegrated, and he was decapitated as his body hit a storm drain in a ditch near the road.

People know the history of the noose and its connection to lynching. For it to be hoisted in full view in the 21st century smacks of intentional provocation. The question is not why people use it or display it. The answer is simple: to churn up hate, to dehumanize, to feel powerful. Such feelings ultimately give rise to violence. These are the seeds of strife that must be incinerated lest our civilization continue to be in crisis.

Other forms of racial violence and hatred against black people are well known in other parts of the world where people of color are not in majority and do not appear to have power or support to fight back. According to Leinwand (1972), the situation of race relations, indeed the violence meted on black people and the seeming persistence of racism, has been aptly captured by analysts. Racial hostility runs deep. We are not born racists; we learn to be racists from our parents, friends, and teachers, from our educational, religious, political, and social institutions. Yet, there is no way to pass a law eliminating racism, for the right to one's thoughts is beyond the reach of any government. It is only when one's racial thoughts are expressed in acts of discrimination that the government can attempt to eradicate racism. A government can pass laws only about what one does, not about what one believes. But to pass and enforce laws against discrimination without at the same time, attempting to change the bigot's attitude is delusional. Since it is almost impossible to change attitudes overnight, bigotry persists.

REEVALUATING DIVERSITY

Based on what history and science have demonstrated, it is clear that, despite differences and diversities, humanity is the same. It would have to take a relearning of the truth and disabusing ourselves of attitudes which all-too-often tend to cast aspersion at others because of physical dissimilarities that

have nothing to do with ability and capability. The pervasiveness of prejudice demonstrates lack of informed knowledge about the groups towards
whom it is directed. Racism is the systematic institutionalized mistreatment
of one group of people by another based on racial heritage (Andersen and
Collins, 1995). It is the institutionalization of injustice based on skin colour,
other physical characteristics, as well as on differences in culture and religions.

Culture is an important concept we referred to earlier. There are cultural
norms within every society or community. Culture is not static but forms
around specific identities, geographies, beliefs, and daily practices. It becomes necessary that individuals take interest in understanding the culture of
other groups in addition to their own. There should be emphasis on cultural
competency not only in the academic institutions but within and among
human interactions. To learn to be sensitive to other group's cultural norms
and expressions is not difficult. It does not require too much time and energy.
It is important to learn, observe, and appreciate other people's ways of doing
things. An understanding of other people's ways of doing, perceiving and
responding to the quotidian realities would go a long way to diminish, if not
eliminate, stereotyping, which inflames racial hostility. Much of what is said
of culture equally applies to history. We must learn the history of other
groups to understand the foundations of their society. Our present civilization
is one of diversity, therefore people must make the effort to learn, understand
and foster relationships that do not denigrate but enhance the dignity of the
individual. We can make a difference because each of us is already part of a
community, society, and nation where racism exists and thrives. In these
tumultuous times it would appear difficult what to do. We must pay attention
to what actual difference that race makes today in societies.

POLICY IMPLICATIONS OF UNRESOLVED RACISM

Certainly, if nothing more concrete and permanent is done all over the world,
the human cost in terms of fostering hatred, suspicions, and distance between
the races would incrementally exacerbate. The configuration of economic,
political and social power and privilege on which racial injustice is based
should systematically be dismantled. The key to eliminating racism are held
primarily by racists, not by the victims of racists (Bennet, 1970). Constructive change in the field of race relations has been impeded in many societies
by persistent failure to deal directly with structural aspects of racism. Those
at the receiving end of racism also have an obligation to continue to affirm
their own equality of humanity.

By conceptualizing racism as mainly a "minority problem," efforts to
eliminate it is subsumed under matters of little consequence until violence

erupts. What people of color and white people have done in the past to make a difference must be highlighted and reintroduced. How people of color are building communities and resisting racism should be studied and encouraged and used as templates in other geographic areas of the world where people of color are still being treated as dregs of humanity. What black people say they need from white people should be articulated. What tactics white people are using to resist equality should be exposed and expunged. In the final analysis, the problem is all about racial injustice. White people in particular must begin to unlearn prejudice and begin to learn to recognize racist acts (Kivel, 1996). Eliminating racism's structural supports may appear dysfunctional to some because of the omnipresence of racism in most societies, but over the long run it must result in generally beneficial social change.

The United States has taken the lead more than many nations to frontally confront the incidences of racial hostility in the 1950s and 1960s by its response with the enactment of decision of Brown versus Board of Education and affirmative action. However, increasingly invidious institutional systems rooted in Euro-American values, that tend to lead to the devaluing of Third World cultures and consequently to disadvantage their peoples, are reemerging. Nations, based on their peculiar situations, must seek to formulate and implement policies that eliminate racism or racial hostility that create strife in the world. Expressing his anguish and anger Albert Einstein has this to say he does not believe there is a way in which this deeply entrenched evil can be quickly healed. But, for him, until this goal is reached there is no greater satisfaction for a just and well-meaning person than the knowledge that he has devoted his best energies to the services of the good cause (Einstein, 1950). Every society establishes institutions to perpetuate its values and traditions. It should be important public policy to replace societal values and traditions that hitherto had fostered racism with those that enhance values that recognize and respect the dignity of individuals regardless of their race, country of origin, religion, and ethnicity.

CONCLUSION

Each of us is part of several groups. Being part of a group defines who we are as individuals, and we derive our self-esteem in part from our membership in groups. However, groups also lead us to look more favorably on our other group members than on those who are not in our groups. The logic of racial oppression/hostility denies members of the subjugated group the full range of human possibility that exists within societies and cultures. From this perspective racism is an historical and social project aimed at reducing or diminishing the humanity of the racially oppressed. The continued use of race and ethnicity as irreducible categories for relating to individuals must be eliminated from human interactions worldwide. All the roles, places, and stereotypes that are forced upon the dominated share a common feature: they function to define the black person within frameworks that are less than, or opposed to, the status of full adult humanhood. It is hard to understand both the long history of racism on the one hand and its continued existence on the other. What could be done about it is difficult to say, answers may be found in societies and their institutions, however, the battle against racism and the social construction of humanity into irreducible categories on the basis of race and ethnicity must be waged within the individual.

BIBLIOGRAPHY

Allport, G. W. (1954). *The Nature of Prejudice*. Reading, MA: Addison-Wesley.
Andersen, M. L., and Collins, P. (1995). (Eds). *Race, Class and Gender: An Anthology*. New York: Wadsworth Publishing Company.
Benedict, R. (1943). *Race, Science, and Politics*. New York: Viking
Bennett, L. Jr. (1970). "The White Problems in America," in *White Racism: Its History, Pathology, and Practice*. Eds. B. N. Schwartz and R. Disch. New York: Dell. 251–263
Blauner, Robert. (1972). *Racial Oppression in America*. New York: Harper & Row Publishers
Booth, W. (1991). "New Evidence of 'Eve': Theory of Humans' African Roots Defended,"*The Washington Post*, September 27, A1
Bowser, B. P., and Hunt, R. G. (1981). *Impacts of Racism on White Americans*. Beverly Hills: Sage Publications.
Brown, D. (2008). "Genetic Mutations Offer Insights on Human Diversity," *The Washington Post*, February 22, A5.
Chua, A. (2003). *World On Fire: How Exporting Free Market Democracy Breeds Ethnic Hatred and Global Insecurity*. London: Random House.
Deutsch, K. (1969). *Nationalism and Social Communication: An Inquiry into the Foundations of Nationality*, Cambridge, MA: MIT Press
Einstein, A. (1950). *Out of My Later Years*. New York: Philosophical Library. 132–134.
Festinger, L. (1954). "A Theory of Social Comparison Process," *Human Relations* 7: 117–140.
Friedman, R. (1975). "Institutional Racism: How to Discriminate without Really Trying" in *Racial Discrimination in the United States*. Ed. T. Pettigrew. New York: Harper & Row. 384–407.
Gitter, Joseph B. (1977). "Towards Defining an Ethnic Minority." *International Journal of Group Tensions*, 7: 4–119.
Gould, Stephen J. (1981). *The Measure of Man*. New York: W. W. Norton.
Jones, J. M. (1972). *Prejudice and Racism*. Reading: MA: Addison-Wesley.
Kivel, P. (1995). *Uprooting Racism: How White People Can Work for Racial Justice*. Gabrola, BC: New Society Publishers.
Lapides, F., and Burrows, D. (1971). (Eds.) *Racism: A Case Book*. New York and London: Wadsworth Publishing Company.
Lee, W. M. (1999). *Introduction to Multicultural Counseling*. Austin, TX: Accelerated Development, Inc.
Leinwand, G. (1972). (Ed.). *Racism: An Examination of a Destructive Force which Has Been Ripping Our Country Apart*. New York: Simon & Schuster, Inc.
McConahay, J. B., and Hough, J. C., Jr., "Symbolic Racism", *Journal of Social Issues*, 32: 23-451976
Nelson, T. D. (2005). *The Psychology of Prejudice*. Boston: Pearson Educational, Inc.
Okolo, C. B. (1974). *Racism: A Philosophic Probe*. New York: Exposition Press.

Thompson, D. L., and Ronen, D. (1986). (Eds.). *Ethnicity, Politics, and Development*. Boulder, CO: Lynne Rienner Publishers.

Schermerhorn, R. A. (1970). *Comparative Ethic Relations: A Framework for Theory and Research*. New York: Random House.

United Press International. (2000). "Genetic Evidence for Man's African Roots."

Walzer, M.. (1992). "The New Tribalism," *Esprit*, November, 44.

Watson, H. (2001). "Theorizing the Racialization of Global Politics and the Caribbean Experience," in *Alternatives: Global, Local, Political*, 26: 449–483.

Chapter Two

The Concept of Common Origin and the Question of Racism

Moses Oludare Aderibigbe

The aim of this chapter is to assess the concept of common origin of human beings in relation to the question of racism in the society.[1] The chapter attempts to examine the two dominant theories that explain common origin, which are monogenesis and polygenesis. Just as the former posits a common descent for all human races, the later asserts that different human races descended from different ancestral roots. Following this, the chapter proceeds to analyse the ideology of racism, which was invented on the belief that human races were not just different from one another, but that some were superior to others.

However, attempt is made to examine postulations on racial differences. The argument seems to lack moral respect for humankind and deny the rule of equality from the universal point of view. To this end, the chapter concludes that since rationality is central to all mankind, the question of racism then becomes untenable.

THE CONCEPT OF COMMON ORIGIN

There are two dominant theories that explain the concept of common origin; these are monogenesis and polygenesis. Monogenesis is the theory of human origin that posits a common descent for all human races. It adhered, on the one hand, to the scriptural creation story in asserting that all humans descended from a common ancestor, perhaps Adam, and this belief in all human descendants of Adam is central to traditional Judaism, Christianity, and Islam. On the other hand, it considers human evolution from a single couple of ancestors, following Darwin who convinced the scientific community that humans had a single ancestral origin. This common origin to Darwin is essential for evolutionary theory and thus known as the single-origin hypothesis.

The traditional Christian preference for monogenism is established on two grounds. For some Christians, the defense of the thesis is based directly on certain passages of the scripture. In the Catholic tradition, however, much more emphasis has been placed on monogenism as the only view consistent with the doctrine of the Original Sin. There are passages in both the Old and the New Testaments that suggest a monogenetic origin for the human race. The story of *Genesis* 2–4 depicts the record of the first two human beings. In the same view, Paul's sermon to the Athenians (*Acts* 17:26) further establish monogenetic claim of common origin; "from one man," "one blood," and "one stock." However, Catholic theology, in its traditional support of monogenesis maintains a consistent view with the doctrine of the Original Sin. Pope Pius XII (1950), in his encyclical *Humani Generis,* wrote, as quoted by Kenneth W. Kemp (2011),

> For the Christian faithful cannot maintain the thesis which holds that either after Adam there existed on this earth true men who did not take their origin through natural generation from him as from the first parent of all, or that "Adam" signifies a number of first parents. Now it is in no way apparent how such an opinion can be reconciled with that which the sources of revealed truth and the documents of the magisterium of the church proceeds from a sin actually committed by an individual Adam and which, through generation is passed on to all and is in everyone as his own. (218–219)

The above reveals the account of the origin of human race and explains the state of the Original Sin, which afflicts each human being from his first moment of existence. However, natural science speak more precisely on genetics, which leads to the conclusion that although man probably came into being at "one place," the size of that place is only probably a relatively small place and could be as large as the entire old world, the population size might be relatively small but surely not a single couple. It seems, therefore, unlikely on the basis of scientific evidence that there was a single first couple that emerged alone from a biologically pre-human population to become the ancestors of all human beings. Neo-Darwinism also lends support in favour of polygenism.

Moreover, polygenesis is a theory of human origins positing that the human races are of different lineages. In other words, different races of human beings had evolved from different apes. Polygenists reject the argument that human races must belong to a single species because they can interbreed. Polygenism describes all alternative explanations for the origin of humankind that involved more than two individual "first people." Following this, there are three main arguments posed against the biblical account of common origin; these include: pre-Adamism, co-Adamism, and incompleteness of the Table of Nations in *Genesis* 10.

Pre-Adamism claims that there were already races of humans living before the creation of Adam. This position was strongly rejected in Christian terms and considered heretical. Co-Adamism argues that there was more than one Adam or small groups of men, created at the same time in different places across the earth, and therefore that the different races were separately created. The Garden of Eden, to them, is believed to be more than one. The contention of this polygenist on the Table of Nations is that many of the races on earth, such as Negros and Asians, were not featured in Genesis 10 and that the author's knowledge was limited to their own region; hence, to them the bible does not concern the whole of earth's population. Given the above, polygenesis was criticized in the twentieth-century Roman Catholic Church by Pope Pius XII, on the grounds that it is incompatible with the doctrine of the Original Sin as quoted in the above passage.

By way of summary, the theories of monogenesis and polygenesis discussed above has made scholars to view these two concepts as a mixture of biblical and scientific thoughts in ways that made scriptural exegesis a scientific activity. Also, it has devised two modes of knowing; one is based on the data of revelation favouring monogenesis and the other on the data of observation favoring a polygenetic account of human origin.

RACISM

A precise definition of racism is a bit controversial, because there is just little scholarly agreement about the meaning of the concept race. Extant literature suggests that the term is applied differentially, with a focus on such prejudices by whites and defining mere observations of racial differences as racism. However, racism is usually defined as views, practices, and actions reflecting the belief that humanity is divided into distinct biological groups called races and that members of a certain race share certain attributes that make that group as a whole less desirable, inferior or superior.

Similarly, racism is seen as the theory or idea that there is a causal link between inherited physical traits and certain traits of personality, intellect, or culture and combined with it, the notion that some races are inherently superior to others. In this regard, racism has to do with unfair treatment of people and violence against people that belong to a different race other than your own; also it is the belief that different races of people have different character and abilities and that the qualities of your own race are the best.

Tracing the beginning of racism, according to Moore, it is not mere coincidence that racism was invented during the time that tens of thousands of Africans were being captured, enslaved, and transported in chains to the

Americas, to work as field hands and manual workers for European owners. It is interesting and important to note that the institution of chattel slavery, in which human beings were considered as mere property, was put into place before scientific racism was invented. The point here is that racism is a recent invention, with its assertions about inherent human inequality, whereas slavery was a very old institution in the Mediterranean region of the old world. Following Moore's view, therefore, blackness in ancient times was not equated with the status of slaves, citing the example of Rome where prominent black men, like Emperor Septimius Severus, Consul Lusius Quietus, and a Roman general who became Saint Maurice, the patron saint of medieval chivalry. The only invisible, inherent differences among men, which led some to be kings and others to be slaves, according to Plato, is the only supposed inequalities among men, which Stephen Chorover called "the most frightening document in European history" (Moore, 2008, xii).

RACISM AND COMMON ORIGIN

Having defined racism and the concept of common origin, an attempt is made here to critically examine some arguments that form the basis of racism. Voltaire, in his 1734 book, *Traite de metaphysique,* wrote, "whites . . . negros . . . the yellow races are not descended from the same man" (Keane, 2007, 89). In his later work, he further found biblical monogenism laughable as he expressed it that "it is a serious question among them whether the Africans are descended from monkeys or whether the monkeys come from them. Our wise men have said that man was created in the image of God. Now here is a lovely image of the divine maker: a flat and black nose with little or hardly any intelligence. A time will doubtless come when these animals will know how to cultivate the land well, beautify their houses and gardens, and know the paths of the stars: one needs time for everything."

As a follow-up to the above view, Voltaire, when comparing Caucasians to Negroes claimed that they are different species as the Negro race is a species of men different from ours as the breed of spaniels is from that of greyhounds. The mucous membrane, or network, which nature has spread between the muscles and the skin, is white in us and black or copper–colored in them.

The argument of Voltaire against the black race is quite derogatory to humanity. His conviction on polygenesis as a theory of human origin led to his hasty conclusion about the black race. David Hume, in the same vein, exhibited his contempt and aversion for the black race. He placed his argument on the premise that a person's intellectual ability or otherwise is a function of his or her nativity or racial descent. Hume held that the African is incapable of logical thinking and is therefore intellectually unproductive among other inadequacies. Hume believed strongly in the idea that Europe is the model for humanity, culture, and history itself. It is this notion of his that led him to conclude that he was apt to suspect the Negroes to be naturally inferior to the whites. There scarcely ever was a civilized notion of that complexion; or even any individual eminent in action or speculation.

From the above, it is clear that Hume attaches great importance to complexion and accords it a prominent role in the determination of a person's rationality or irrationality. It may not be a mistake to conclude that Hume is a racist and racial prejudice has greatly influenced his philosophical insight. Likewise, Immanuel Kant in his early work, shares the same thought with Hume and ascribed rationality to skin color (white and black); he avers that since this fellow was quite black from head to foot, it was a clear proof that what he said was stupid.

Kant here was not making an empirical hypothesis as Hume had, but was offering a "transcendental" basis for the distinction between whites and blacks. And in so doing Kant established a racial dichotomy between the whites and other people of different skin colors. He went further to divide the human race into four groups. First race, Northern Europe; second race, copper red (America); third race, black (Senegambia); fourth race, olive yellow, Indians. Given the above, Kant falls into the same racial prejudice and narrow-mindedness that characterized Hume's writing and exposes their lack of genuine philosophical attitude of open-minded and objective way of seeing things beyond self.

Hegel, in contradiction to Aristotle, stated that of all races, only the Caucasian race (white Europeans and the descendants) have this inherent capability for rationality. According to Hegel, the African, Indians, and other races lacked the capability for rationality. Thus, they cannot be classified as human; at best they are to be treated as sub-humans.

The summary of the views of these philosophers, whose work might have brought enlightenment to understanding nature, are racially sentimental to describe some set of people as incapable of reasoning, primitive, just because they are of different race or origin. Thus, there is no moral, rational, and logical justification for such derogatory conclusion or thinking. If, for instance, one may ask, to what extent can this claim be true, since the race, which Hegel excludes from the class of rational beings, has been part of the great civilizations and center of learning since time immemorial, looking at the example of Egypt? By implication, Hume appeared to have committed fallacy of appeal to ignorance.

PHILOSOPHICAL APPRAISAL

Philosophical discussions on the concept of race are divided into three schools of thought, following the disagreement on the possible ontological status of different conceptions of race. According to Mallon, there are three metaphysical camps, these are: racial scepticism, racial constructivism, and racial population naturalism; these are in conjunction with two other normative camps (eliminative and conservationism). Racial scepticism holds that because racial naturalism is false, and races of any type do not exist. Thus, they contend that, the term race cannot refer to anything in this world, since biological races have been proven not to exist. Prominent in this school of thought are Anthony Appiah and Naomi Zack, who adopt normative racial eliminativism, which recommends discarding the concept of race entirely because of its historical genealogy and logical incoherence.

Racial constructivism refers to the argument that, even if biological race is false, races have come into existence and continue to exist through "human culture and human decisions." Race constructivists accept the sceptics' dismissal of biological race but argue that the term still meaningfully refers to the widespread grouping of individuals into certain categories by society, indeed often by the very members of such racial ascriptions.

The third school of thought regarding the ontology of race is racial population naturalism. This camp suggests that, although racial naturalism falsely attributed cultural, mental, and physical characters to discrete racial groups, it is possible that genetically significant biological groupings could exist that would merit the term races. Importantly, these biological racial groupings would not be essentialist or discrete: there is no set of genetic or other biological traits that all and only all members of a racial group share that would then provide a natural biological boundary between racial groups. Thus, these thinkers confirm the strong scientific consensus that discrete, essentialist races do not exist.

Given the above, the views of each school of thought have its own merits and demerits, and by implication, there is none of them that are absolutely error free. It is against this background that the question of morality becomes relevant in line with the issue of racism in focus. Lawrence Blum, in addressing the moral status of the concept of race and the problem of racism, argues that "racism" be restricted to two referents: *inferiorization*, or the denigration of a group due to its putative biological inferiority, and *antipathy*, or the "bigotry, hostility and hatred" toward another group defined by its putatively inherited physical traits.[17] The point here is that, it should be noted that racism in the light of morality deserves condemnation; this is because it violates moral norms of respect, equality and dignity and also it is historically connected to extreme and overt forms of racial oppression.

The historical connection between racism and extreme oppression from time immemorial has made some scholars to argue against using the term "race" to distinguish certain groups of people from the others. Blum is one of those who advocates using the term "racialized group," instead of the term "race," to denote those socially constructed identities whose supposedly inherited common physical fruits are used to impose social, political and economic costs. To Blum, "racialized group" creates distance from the biological conception of race and it admits other individuals according to their racialized identities.

Anthony Appiah, in his own metaphysical racial skepticism, appears to maintain the normative position of *eliminativisms*; he is "against races" but for "racial identities."[18] He maintained that there is a wide social consensus that race exists; individuals are ascribed to races regardless of their individual choices or desires. This being the case, racial identity remains far more salient and costly than ethnic identity, thus mobilization along racial lines is justifiable, in order to combat racism. But even at this point, Appiah still fears that racial identification may constrain individual autonomy by requiring members of racial groups to behave according to certain cultural norms or "scripts." Hence, he concludes, that racial identity can be the basis of resistance to racism and that even as we struggle against racism we should not let our racial identities subject us to new tyrannies, which will constitute tropes of oppression to others.

The metaphysical view presented by Appiah in this context is observed by some critics that Appiah remains an eliminativist rather than a racial constructivist. He prefers to be free of all residual constraints entailed by socially constructed races, and as such he is therefore not a radical critic of race. The point to note here is that the position maintained by Appiah is to buttress further the idea that race or racism should better be perceived from the sense of being a marker of identities, which should not constrain individual autonomy. To this end, the extent to which this can be realized without constraint is the concern of his critique.

On this note, the arguments of the racialist philosophers, as pointed out earlier, appears untenable, as they lack moral respect for humankind and deny the rule of equality and as well dehumanize human race from the universal point of view. To this end, central at the heart of humanism are two key ideas. First, humanists hold that human beings, while an inherent part of nature and subject to its laws, nevertheless have an exceptional status in nature, because of the unique ability arising out of human rationality and sociability to overcome the constraints placed upon them by nature. Second, humanists believe in the unity of humankind, holding that all humans possess something in common, a something that is often described as a common "human nature."

Following these two key ideas, the concept of common origin invariably can be established on the premise of human rationality and common human nature. Thus, the question of superiority or inferiority, which racism brought to the fore, cannot hold beyond all reasonable doubt. And it has been universally established that common to all humans, irrespective of the skin color are the twin fundamental attributes of rationality and common human nature. The point here is that the singular fact that all human persons are rational is enough a logical reason to establish the claim that all human beings at a minimum have at least two common features: human rationality and human nature. What differentiates them (one human being from another human being) is not more of internal (nature), rather it tends toward other factors that are external.

CONCLUSION

In this chapter we have clarified basic concept of common origin of human beings. In doing this, an effort was made to define the two dominant theories which are monogenesis and polygenesis. The question of racism, which is central to our examination of human homogeneity of existence, was discussed and the extant views of thinkers who embrace the existence of race categories were analyzed. The three main schools of thought in philosophy of race were brought to the fore, with a critical view to providing a careful examination of the morality of the whole issue. The conclusion reached in our discussion hinged on the fact that most arguments raised in favor of racism lack moral respect for humankind and negate the two undeniable common features possessed by humankind, which are rationality and nature; the first intellectual, and the second physiological.

BIBLIOGRAPHY

Benton, W. (1980). *Encyclopaedia Britannica*, vol. 15, London: Sage. 258.
Bolaffi, Guido, et al. (2003).*Dictionary of Race, Ethnicity and Culture.* London: Sage. 242.
Eloise, H. M. (1994). "Race and Ethnicity: An Anthropological Perspective," in Jean Ait Belkhir, *Race, Gender & Class Journal*, 1(2): 138.
Keane, D. (2007). *Caste-based Discrimination in International Human Rights Law.* London: Routledge.
Kemp, Kenneth W. (2011). *American Catholic Philosophical Quarterly*, 85(2): 218.
Moore, J. H. (2008). *Encyclopaedia of Race and Racism*, vol. 2. New York: Macmillan.
Popkin, R. (1999). *The Columbia History of Western Philosophy*. New York: Columbia University Press. http://en.race. *Stanford Encyclopaedia of philosophy.* Accessed on June 24, 2013.

NOTE

1. An earlier draft version of this chapter was published in Open Journal of Philosophy, 5, 25-30. 10.4236/ojpp.2015.51003.

Chapter Three

Apartheid and Beyond

An Exploration of South African Drama

Bosede Funke Afolayan

In this chapter, we would like to begin our discussion with the following passage from the perceptive Athol Fugard, when in an interview with David Richards, he says,

> The huge changes that have taken place have obviously involved an extraordinary liberation for South Africans, and as an ordinary South African, I have been dealt into that liberation. . . . But as a writer, there has also been the most extraordinary payoff. I feel free to take on the telling of personal stories, which I would have considered a gross indulgence, in the older South Africa. There was a moral imperative then that someone bear witness to what the hell was going on in that society and you would not ignore it, but now I'm free. (Wertheim, 2001, 227)

The above prefatory statement captures the sense of freedom as an individual and as a writer that Fugard felt with the dismantling of apartheid system—a reign of terror that has been visited on non-whites in South Africa since 1948. Now, Fugard could write about what he likes as against the silent compulsion and tacit law that compels writers to employ their art as a weapon in the struggle for liberation.

Hitherto, drama has been in the forefront of non-whites emancipation from the oppressive rule of the minority: whites in South Africa. Fugard, a leading playwright in South Africa, like other playwrights, has used his plays to expose the harsh conditions in which non-whites live. Apartheid means separateness. It is a political, social and economic system that encourages segregation and promotes racial discrimination.

This system started in 1948 and was abolished in 1992. While it lasted, apartheid restricted the movement of non-whites. It was a system that formally identified one race as superior and another one as inferior. It put whites against blacks and propagates a state of oppression, suppression, and repression. This social, political and economic system bred the poverty and exploitation of blacks by the whites. Therefore, the literature of the period, especially by blacks and sympathetic and liberal white writers like Andre Brink, Nadine Gordimer, J. M. Coetzee, and Alan Paton, explored the inequalities and the fall-outs from the apartheid regimes.

However, when the system collapsed, and a just, humane and free system replaced it, the literature of South Africa must, out of necessity, show new themes. Eldred Jones, writing in *African Literature Today*, has this to say:

> The dismantling of legal apartheid has liberated the culture and with it the languages and literatures of South Africa into the outside world. It has also freed the country itself from a monumental block which limited the creative imagination by forcing it into a posture of reaction against an all-pervasive oppressive system. The dominating influence in South African literature, indeed, in all South African culture, has been apartheid. (2002, vii)

Jones' statement corroborates our view that the singular topic worth expressing during the apartheid regime was writers' reaction to it and how the writers show how their people react to it and its effects on their daily lives.

It is also the reason why some critics view South African literature as lacking artistic sensibilities, because the writers focus so much on the message, at the expense of using art to please. Jones further avers that this has made writers in South Africa to "produce a literature of protest which is limiting even in its compelling necessity" (vii).

Nevertheless, the collapse of apartheid is hoped to bring to literature a new vision, a new society and the injection of new insights. With democracy, the obvious question critics ask is what would now become the fate of South African drama, because its prominent and basic subject matter has been removed?

It is against this backdrop that this chapter explores the fate of South African drama after the end of apartheid in the works of Fugard. The choice of Fugard is motivated by the fact that he is a leading campaigner for freedom of the oppressed in his apartheid plays. It will, therefore, be interesting to see how he has been able to shift focus from attacking apartheid and its structures to other themes after apartheid. The problem is the examination of the place of apartheid in the drama of South Africans. Its ubiquitous nature needs to be critically examined now that it has been dismantled.

Lekan Oyegoke's (2002) statement on this matter illuminates our choice of Fugard. He says, "From the point of view of protest or social relevance, Fugard's plays score very high marks and are socially and politically relevant texts. His works have been eminently successful going by, if nothing else, the frequency of banning orders, arrests, prohibitions and other forms of state harassment of the citizen" (Oyegoke, 2002, 5). Athol Fugard, though a non-black writer, has been sympathetic to the plight of blacks and his plays were devoted to the treatment of this issue of exploitation and the inequalities between blacks and whites in South Africa.

THEORETICAL FRAMEWORK

The nature of this study demands the application of a critical theory that examines the relationship between the oppressed and the oppressor. Therefore, the theory of Marxism will aid our understanding and illuminate the selected plays. Marxism is a set of social, economic and political ideas meant to transform the world. It is a system that believes in the examination of the unequal economic structures in the society that breed conflict. In fact, it tries to repudiate capitalism through its revolutionary view of history.

Marxism began in the thought of Karl Marx, who lived between 1818–1883. Marx argued that it is the means of production that controls the society, its institutions and beliefs. To buttress this, he propounded the notion of dialectical materialism, a theory that argues for the idea of history as a struggle between contradictions which will eventually be synthesized.

A key point in Marxism is class struggle. Conflict is bound to occur in a highly stratified classed society and it is believed that the struggle will ultimately lead to a revolution in which the oppressed will overturn the capitalist bourgeoisie and take control of economic power. This change of events will culminate into a classless society where class structures will disappear totally. Marx believe that history is determined by economic power and he argued for the eradication of private ownership of production and services.

Ideology is another key concept in Marxism. The capitalist bourgeoisie has its own ideology, which suppresses the proletariat. This belief system must be upturned, such that the masses are not brainwashed to continue to see themselves as inferior. Literature must reflect society's consciousness towards the establishment of a new hegemony for the masses. Such literature must give vent to the oppression of the masses.

In the South African society, during the apartheid rule, a class system operated. Both Fugard's *Sizwe Bansi is Dead* (1973) and Nkosi's *Rhythm of Violence* (1964) exemplify this. Just like in all apartheid systems, be it racism, chosen people, white minority rule, apartheid in South Africa is based on economic power. A small white minority, who have access to economic power, seek to oppress others because of the colour of their skin. The whites impose themselves on the majority blacks, because they have economic power. They take their lands and restrict them to the arid areas. Deprived of economic power, the blacks become helpless. As capitalists, the white minority exploited the services of the blacks as manual labourers. The blacks, as seen in Fugard's and Nkosi's plays, are relegated to the background in their own land. They are peasants, having been deprived of their own natural resources. This deprivation that involves economic power leaves the blacks as the dregs of the society. In such a situation, there is bound to be class struggle. The blacks have risen against the oppression of the white in many cases as shown in the violent resistance put up by the young students in Nkosi's *Rhythm of Violence.*

APARTHEID DRAMA OF PROTEST AND RESISTANCE

Athol Fugard's *"Sizwe Bansi is Dead"* and Lewis Nkosi's *Rhythm of Violence*

Keorapetse Kgositsile (1981), in an interview with Theo Vincent during FESTAC 77, elucidates on the contribution of the dramatist (artist) to the liberation struggle in this way:

> If one realised the picking up a gun is not necessarily a revolutionary act, then it becomes clear that the intellectual or the ideological, the cultural content of the struggle is uppermost. Otherwise the one that picks up the gun without knowing clearly what he or she is fighting for, becomes just a common murderer even if that person killed Smith or Vorster. But in that sense, the importance of the work of the artist becomes, as I believe Achebe said, at some point, "education." (67–68)

Kgositsile aptly sums up the aim or philosophy of the writing of most South African playwrights during the apartheid period. Their aim is to expose the evils of apartheid and call for liberation.

Using Fugard's *Sizwe Bansi is Dead* (1973) and Nkosi's *Rhythm of Violence* (1964), there is a conscious effort by these dramatists to employ their art as instruments of protest and resistance. Life and living under John Vorster, P. W. Botha and F. W. de Klerk was hell and this hell was well documented in the writings of the period. The literature catalogued the unsavoury details of apartheid.

When these plays were written and staged, South African literature could not afford to indulge in any topic other than the theme of liberation. The thread that runs through the web of these two plays is anti-racism. The xenophobic ideas and practices of the white minority over the majority blacks were condemned. Fugard and Nkosi deliberately highlighted the harsh conditions under which blacks lived in apartheid South Africa. The black person lived a life of bitterness, running away from the long and cruel hands of the apartheid law. As a man or woman, his/her life was a constant reminder of the oppressive nature of the government as (s)he barely survived.

As exemplified by the black workers in *Sizwe Bansi is Dead*, blacks are portrayed as suffering. Their wages are meagre and, as Styles reads the newspaper and comments, more exploitative tendencies of the whites on the blacks are revealed. The white masters do not care about the welfare of their laborers. At the Ford factory, the black man is shown as a dehumanized being. He is inferior to the white and his life is of no consequence. He/she is Mr. Ford's property. Styles leaves the factory in anger and sets up a photographic studio. It is his way of reacting against the oppression of the white man.

The pass book is a metaphor for the limitation of the black man's movement. Oyegoke (2002) opines that *Sizwe Bansi is Dead* "captures the dire circumstances under which Blacks lived in the heyday of apartheid. The play is arresting not so much because of the action (there isn't much of this by Hollywood and Nollywood standards) but because of the sordid details and truths it reveals about apartheid" (5).

The play portrays the terrible times under which blacks lived their lives in South Africa at this time. The singular symbol of this time is the passbook. Through it, the black man's movement is restricted. He/she cannot go anywhere without it and the lack of it signifies imprisonment or death.

Sizwe Bansi leaves his family to get a job in Port Elizabeth and because he has no work permit, he is arrested as an illegal occupant. He is subsequently taken to court and sent back to King William's Town where he is from. He joins Buntu in his bid to survive. However, he cannot get employed because he has no pass. To do any other job such as hawking fruits, you need a hawker's licence, which he does not possess.

As a confused man, Sizwe goes drinking with his friend. On the way, they stumble on a dead man whose passbook was intact. Buntu encourages Sizwe to take up the dead man's identity, in order to live. Sizwe cannot live "as another man's ghost." His initial refusal to take up Robert Zwelinzima's identity brings out the profound statement from Buntu, quoted below, that explains that whether dead or alive the black man remains a "ghost to the white supremacists":

> when the white man looked at you at the Labour Bureau, what did he see? A man with dignity or a bloody passbook with an N.I Number? Isn't that a ghost? When the white man sees you walk down the street and calls out, "Hey, John! Come here" ... to you, Sizwe Bansi . . . isn't that a ghost? Or when his little child calls you "Boy" . . . you a man, circumcised with a wife and four children ... isn't that a ghost? Stop fooling yourself. All I'm saying is to be a real ghost, if that is what they want, what they've turned us into. (Fugard, 1973, 38)

The dead man's passbook has correct identification and all Sizwe needs to do is to affix his passport photograph on it, because a black man to the white man is just like any other. Without the passbook, the black man is insignificant and cannot function even as a labourer, hawker or gardener.

It is interesting to note that the passbook is not needed in the mines. In the mines, the population control does not affect the black workers, especially when they have to dig gold for the white man. The pass law is, thus, a major control measure of the whites to limit the blacks' movement and lives.

Fugard's *Sizwe Bansi is Dead* portrays the harrowing lifestyles of the black man in apartheid South Africa. It is his hope that the exposure of these evils will bring about a change of conscience and thereby lead to the abrogation of the evil laws underwriting apartheid. The pass law is the metaphor of this constricting lifestyle. Sizwe Bansi's travails symbolize the life of a typical black man in South Africa of that time. His life dramatizes the oppressive apartheid system. It is a life lived under destructive prejudices and xenophobia. The whites expressed an attitudinal hostility toward blacks, which guides social and political life in South Africa under apartheid rule.

While the protest in Fugard's *Sizwe Bansi is Dead* is mild, Nkosi's *Rhythm of Violence* is belligerent and revolutionary. The play dramatizes the action of a group of left-wing university students who are non-racial and pursuing an agenda to destroy the symbol of apartheid regime, which is the City Hall. Gama, the African student, is their leader. His white friend, Jimmy, and white girlfriend, Mary, are some of the other members of the group. The other members are of Jewish, Indian, and Afrikaner origins. This goes to show the multiracial demography of South Africa. Their members are united by one common identity and one common overarching aim, which is that they are university students and they have non-racial society as their goal for South Africa.

The story revolves around the activities of this group in their bid to sensitise others to join their group and destroy the vestiges of apartheid. To the policeman monitoring the actions of these students, the black students are a nuisance whose sole weapon to upturn the status quo is to talk. While to the black students, the sole advantage the whites have over the blacks and their supporter is their guns.

These students are left-wing. They are no longer interested in student-riots, marches, protests, and shouting of slogans. They decided to bomb the Johannesburg city hall. Their aim is to counter the evil at Sharpeville, where the whites butchered many Africans:

Gama: Did you see the bodies at Sharpeville? Did you see the shoulders of children rippled off by machine gun fire. . . . A butchery." (Fugard, 1973, 32).

There will be more violence if this government clings insanely to its apartheid policies. (35)

The students count down to the bomb explosion at the City Hall in their hideout. They drink, dance, make jokes and perform all forms of revelry until it is discovered that Sarie's father, a liberal Afrikaner, was going to be at the city hall. Sarie is a new convert and Tula's friend. Tula is bound by this new friendship to rescue Sarie's father. Unfortunately, he (Tula) is killed in the process.

These students are shown as belligerent and not willing to stand by while apartheid ruins their lives. As a socialist group, they believe in action that will bring about change. In fact, the policemen on patrol calls them communists.

Right from the meeting of the students at the beginning of the play, Gama shows himself fearless and uncompromising. Slogans, such as "Freedom in our lifetime," can be heard interrupting the conversation of the white policeman. One of the policemen becomes restless and enraged and wants to shoot the unarmed students, but he is restrained by his partner.

The white policemen engage in dialogue that reveals their hatred of, and their all-too-willing attitude to shoot, blacks. They both recount the first time they killed a black man. While Jan gets sick over blasting the head of a black person, Piet says he has learnt to kill blacks "academically," without displaying any emotion or his conscience pricking him.

They make fun of Tula, who has come to deliver the petitions of the students to them. Tula is constantly referred to as "kaffir," "animal," "ape," and "a goddam ape." These are derogatory names used for Africans. Jan is repulsed by the very presence of Tula. He says to him, "Jan: Don't come any closer, Kaffir. There's already an awful stink in here." Tula is reduced to a shadow of himself when he is made to respond to Jan and Piet as "Baas". The play exposes the negative effect of white domination, subjugation and repression on the blacks.

Even, among these interracial bohemian young students, there is the realisation that it is only in that room or in the university that they can meet, as laws have been put in place to restrain contact among them. Sarie articulates this view when she responds to Tula's wish to see her again: "Sarie: I just wish that it were not so difficult with all the laws controlling our lives" (Fugard, 1973, 55).

Despite the strong spirit of camaraderie among the group, the whites among them, especially Mary, Gama's girlfriend, clings to her sense of superiority. She says, "you think I'd risk all the laws of this country just for that [she means sex]. If I want to sleep with any man, I can find a white man tomorrow" (27). The Immorality Act forbids a white to have sex with a black or vice versa. This is also Jan and Piet's grouse with Sarie, as she leans and sobs over Tula's dead body. Although Tula dies, the aim of the group has been accomplished with the bomb explosion at city hall. Nkosi seems to say here that violence gives back violence and the rhythm of violence has just begun.

RECENT POST-APARTHEID PLAYS

Drama of Freedom and Choice in Fugard's *Captain's Tiger* and *Valley Song*

With the release of Nelson Mandela from prison in 1990, the lifting of the ban on ANC, the general election which the ANC won, and Mandela's inauguration as president in "a new South Africa," as coined by F. W. de Klerk, non-white South Africans could breathe a sigh of relief from police harassment, pass law restrictions, forced exile, repression, and generally from apartheid and its stifling measures. There is a general note and an air of hope and freedom, as expressed by non-whites.

Those destructive shackles of apartheid should give rise to freedom, as the nation undergoes "a renaissance"—a rebirth of some sort, whether psychologically, physically, politically, and socially. As part of its healing process, the Truth and Reconciliation Commission was set up not to haunt offenders, but to heal the wounds of past years. The change occasioned by the fall of apartheid should not just be psychological; it ought to show in the writings of this "new" period.

What then is the fate of South African drama after this time? Apartheid has been the focus of apartheid literature. Do post-apartheid plays still focus on apartheid? Or are plays now concerned with other themes? Are the gains of democracy in politics and social life visible in drama?

Andre Brink (1998), writing in the paper entitled "Interrogating Silence: New Possibilities faced by South African Literature," posits that:

> I will recognize the regenerative powers of South African literature: not sim-
> ply to escape from the inhibitions of Apartheid but to construct and decon-
> struct new possibilities; to activate the imagination in its exploration of those
> silences previously inaccessible; to play with the future on that needlepoint
> where it meets past and present and to be willing to risk everything in the
> leaping flame of the word as it turns into world. (27)

Although Brink makes a general opinion about South African post-apartheid plays, his assertion could be applied to the works of Fugard, who has, after apartheid, moved to those "silent" areas which were left unexplored during apartheid. Fugard has, in the words of Graham Pechey, moved from the "fixations upon suffering and the seizure of power into just such stories as this: stories of which then open out to transform the victory over apartheid into a gain for postmodern knowledge" (Brink, 1998, 58).

South Africa as a nation and its literature are trying to come to terms with its ugly past, so as to forge a new future. The idea of "a rainbow nation," coined by Desmond Tutu, and the effects of The Truth and Reconciliation Commission, also chaired by him, are steps in the right direction of integrating the different ideas and notions into one nation.

To believe that racism could be wiped off suddenly in political and social life in South Africa is wishful thinking. To elucidate, our focus will be on Fugard's *The Captain's Tiger* (1999) and *Valley Song* (1996). Fugard is integral to South African drama and his development from an anti-apartheid crusader to a post-apartheid writer is worth exploring. *The Captain's Tiger* is aptly subtitled "a memoir for the stage."

In this play, Fugard abandons his anti-apartheid crusade and focuses on his own growth as a writer. Just as the prefatory statement suggests, Fugard shows that the social and political change in South Africa affected him as an individual and as a writer. Now, he has freedom to explore areas neglected or left uncharted because of the urgency and immediate relevance of dismantling apartheid structure.

To put theory to practice, he explores the frontiers of drama in conveying an autobiographical piece like a memoir, a diary or a letter. He attempts to start a new drama where the author appears on stage not as a Brechtian aesthetics of alienation but in the tradition of Luigi Pirandello's *Six Characters in Search of an Author*. He becomes a medium through which the story is told. *The Captain's Tiger* is like a fusion of the arts of the theatre and the autobiography. Fugard becomes a young actor and narrates his beginnings and alternates between himself as a sixty-five-year-old man and his younger character who is the captain's tiger (a personal steward to the captain of the ship). As the captain's tiger, he is young and inexperienced, and he takes his journey on the SS Graigaur heading for Japan.

This journey motif explored in this play is reminiscent of works by Hemmingway's *The Old Man and the Sea* and Mark Twain's *The Adventures of Huckleberry Fin*. It is a journey taken in inexperience, innocence, and naivety, which ends in the young man becoming knowledgeable and experienced. The play traces the captain tiger's journey from naivety to experience. His role model at first was his mother whose picture as a young girl in her room is the muse for writing a novel that Tiger engages in on the ship. It is interesting to note that this photograph becomes real, as young Betty Le Roux and at several instances interrupts the flow of Tiger's writing, demanding the path that the story of her life should follow.

As earlier stated, there are many parallels between Tiger's story as a young man on a journey with that of Fugard as a young man. First, as Dennis Walder tells us, Fugard abandons school to hitchhike from South Africa to

Africa. Tiger too does the same. Second, Tiger in writing letters to his mother barely sends his greetings to his father. This also finds a parallel in the life of the young Fugard who is shown to be closer to his mother, who was a great influence on his life.

As a writer, the journey is meant to be a training ground for Tiger. Later, a black man called Donkeyman becomes Tiger's source of inspiration and an audience, as he listens to and encourages Tiger to continue his writing. As a friend and companion, Tiger benefits immensely from this "almost silent" audience. Through him Tiger is introduced to "adult life" as they visit Aiko, from whose relationship Tiger had his first sexual encounter with a female. This friendship with a black man and the willingness to come down to Donkeyman's level, first, to speak pidgin English and later Swahili, goes to show the liberal and human nature of Fugard, like all human beings, who, despite his white skin does not discriminate against the color of another man's skin. In fact, he refers to Donkeyman as "Big Brother," while he is the "small brother."

Liberating himself from his mother's hold, by revolting against the young Betty, who tries to control his thoughts, Tiger throws his manuscript into the sea. Betty's words, in referring to this break with the past, best articulate her "death" and loss of control over Tiger. By this act, Tiger discovers himself, first as an individual and second as a writer. He learns the secret of good writing, which is to "always be true."

In *The Captain's Tiger*, Fugard has shown that there is a great deal of stories to dramatize after the dismantling of apartheid. But it is significant that references are still made to apartheid period. The issue of the different races in South Africa is also a historical fact that cannot be wished away. There is also a Donkeyman (a black man) with whom Tiger (a white man) must relate. However, this is a contact that does not call for a master/servant relationship. Oyegoke claims that "by the admission of some South Africans of all shades there is as yet a wall of ignorance separating blacks, whites and other South Africans, the collapse of apartheid structures notwithstanding" (2002, 9).

In other words, there is a continuing relevance of apartheid, even after its structures have been dismantled. Apartheid, xenophobia, hostility, and de-structive anti-black opinions cannot be easily wished away just by the abro-gation of its laws and freedom of movement. It will definitely take some time for the mental healing to be effected. South Africa may not easily become the dreamed melting pot, as the presumed, even though rationally unsupported distinctive features of the different races are too outstanding; it may become a "salad bowl," allowing the different races to express itself or, as Desmond Tutu avers, it may remain "a rainbow nation."

Valley Song dramatizes the lives of ordinary people in South Africa after the end of apartheid. It has a small cast of Abraam Jonkers, an elderly "colored farmer" who symbolizes the "old in the new south Africa," Veronica, a young girl of seventeen who craves for a change and the author who is Fugard himself, and who has spent most of his life in the "bright light" of the theater but now wishes to settle down in the rural area. As shown here, Fugard is still interested in the relationships of the races in South Africa, the effects of the contact between the races; a point he has severally addressed in his apartheid plays.

The old man is a laborer on a white man's land. He is afraid of change, as he listens to his granddaughter craving to abandon the rural area for the urban area. Abraam Jonkers has every reason to loath the city, because Veronica's mother had earlier eloped to the city only to be told of her death and the birth of a baby (Veronica). Abraam does not want a repeat of what happened to Veronica's mother, who was lured to the city.

However, the Sneeuberg Valley, a Karro is not enough for Veronica. Veronica has been singing from birth. She sings at school, at church, and everywhere. She even sneaks out at night to watch television through the window of a white woman's house. She craves for the bright light. She wants to sing elsewhere, in a big city and be famous. To achieve this, she secretly makes moves to join her friend in the city. Abraam, her grandfather, is furious about this. Abraam's idea of a miracle is summed up in the seed that grows bountiful on the ground of the Karoo, but Veronica is the opposite. Life in the rural area is boring, uneventful, and monotonous and she desires "adventure and romance." She becomes restless, as she wants to travel and see big cities.

Her grandfather's fear is further compounded when a white man visits the land on which he is a laborer and inspects it. Abraam is afraid that he may be driven off the land he has known all his life by this new owner. Land is thus, shown as still a relevant topic in post-apartheid play. At last, the white man who is modelled after Fugard desires to come to the rural area, based on the generosity of Abraam who offers him the fruits of the land.

There are two different stories in this play. First is the story of Veronica, the young adventurous girl, who wants to abandon her grandfather in order to find herself. Second, is the story of the old white South African dramatist, who has seen all the glamour and glitz of his trade and of the city and craves peace by returning to his roots. These two stories are united by Abraam.

A major technique used in the play is soliloquy. All the characters: Abraam, the Author, and Veronica, talk straight to the audience or address imaginary figures. In these soliloquies, their character traits are shown better than it could have been if they engage in dialogue.

Significantly, these three characters also represent different perspectives on the contact situation among the races in the "new south Africa." In other words, they symbolize the different voices, and their ability to pursue to the end their dreams will reveal what the "new south Africa" will be like.

Again, the historical context of *Valley Song*, which hangs in the background, is the end of apartheid. This is a "new south Africa." How will the races, as shown in Abraam (colored), the author (the white man), and Veronica (the black young woman), fare in this new country depends on how they cooperate in the story.

CONCLUSION

This chapter has compared apartheid and post-apartheid themes in Fugard's *Sizwe Bansi is Dead* and Nkosi's *Rhythm of Violence* with Fugard's *Valley Song* and *The Captain's Tiger*. The analysis shows that although the apartheid system has crashed, it remains the recurring decimal in the dramas of both periods. The recent murder of the thirty-two protesting miners by policemen in a Jacob Zuma–ruled South Africa points to the fact that things are not yet right with the country. It is, definitely, not yet Uhuru. As a historical fact, the system cannot be easily wished away.

It forms the core of all the plays explored in this chapter. Direct references are made to it. As a matter of fact, it is in the background, it is the framework on which post-apartheid plays are based. There are instances where particular references are made to the reprehensible laws promulgated and practiced during the apartheid period in post-apartheid plays.

Valley Song also shows that despite the advent of democracy, land is still a big issue in the new South Africa. The choicest land areas have been taken by the whites, while blacks and colored people are servants on these lands. How do they fare?

Abraam must be willing to show genuine love to the likes of the white author who have come to possess the land and the author must extend the hand of friendship to the likes of Abraam if the new South Africa is to achieve its billing as a melting pot for the different peoples that make up the rainbow nation. There must be true and genuine reconciliation, in order to build the future. This represents Fugard's response to the changing political and social situation of South Africans. Our focus has been to show playwright's reaction to the end of apartheid since then; plays have been deployed to the exposition of the atrocious effects of apartheid. Now, as the prefatory statement states, the playwright has freedom to indulge in themes other than apartheid.

BIBLIOGRAPHY

Brink, André. (1998). "Interrogating Silence: New Possibilities Faced by South African Literature," in *Writing South Africa*. Eds. Attridge, D., and Jolly, R. Cambridge: Cambridge University Press.

Dobbie, A. B. (2009). *Theory to Practice: An Introduction to Literary Criticism*(2nd edition). Boston: Wadsworth Cencage Learning.

Fugard, A. (1973). *Sizwe Bansi is Dead*. London: Oxford University Press.

———. (1999). *The Captain's Tiger* New York: Theatre Com. Group.

———. (1996). *Valley Song*. London: Faber and Faber.

Jones, E. D. (2002). "South and Southern African Literature," *African Literature Today*, 23.

Jones, E. D., and Jones, M. (2002). (Eds.) *South and Southern African Literature*. Oxford: James Currey.

Kgositsile, K. (1981). "Interview with Theo Vincent," in *Seventeen Black and African Writers on Literature and Life*. Ed. Theo Vincent. Lagos: CBAAC, 67–68.

Nkosi, L. (1964). *Rhythm of Violence*. London: Oxford University Press.

Oyegoke, L. (2002). "Renaissance and South African Writing," in *South and Southern African Literature. African Literature Today,*vol. 23. Eds. Jones, E. D., and Jones, M. Oxford: James Currey.

Pechey, G. (1998). "The Post-Apartheid Sublime: Rediscovering the Extraordinary," in *Writing South Africa*. Eds. Attridge, D., and Rosemary J. Cambridge: Cambridge University Press.

Tyson, L. (1999). Critical Theory Today. New York: Garland Publishing.

Walder, D. (1984). *Athol Fugard*. London: Macmillan.

Wertheim, A. (2001). *The Dramatic Art of Athol Fugard.* Indiana: Indiana University Press.

Chapter Four

British Southern Cameroons' Restoration of Statehood and Sovereignty

Internal Affair or Decolonization Conflict?

Michael Achankeng Fonkem I

The former British Southern Cameroons' "restoration of statehood and sovereignty" (Ebong, 1999) struggle in Cameroon Republic (République du Cameroun or former French Cameroon) remains very controversial in conflict terms. The predominant focus rests upon the importance of retaining Cameroon Republic's boundaries and the preservation of the status quo. As a result, ex-British Cameroons' resistance to the hegemony of Cameroon Republic continues to be misunderstood and increasingly distorted in the literature on the conflict. The academic and political discourse on the restoration of statehood quest for ex-British Southern Cameroons can be approached from two perspectives. There is the perspective that views the problem as an "internal affair" of the state of Cameroon. This perspective has continued to characterize the Southern Cameroons restoration of statehood problem as a "terrorist" or "secessionist" attempt directed against the unity and territorial integrity of Cameroon Republic. The perspective views the former British Southern Cameroons' restoration of statehood struggle in terms of a minority in Cameroon Republic clamoring to secede with its oil wealth (Seme, 2009; Dicklitch, 2011). The former British Southern Cameroons' nationalism, as a challenge to the one and indivisible Cameroon framework, was always dismissed as the machination of a small group of individuals advocating secession. This perspective equates Southern Cameroons to Kuwait with a jealous eye on the Bakassi oil reserves fighting only to get their own individual share of the national cake within the plutocratic class in Cameroon, and just using English-speaking, ordinary people as their voting cattle (Seme, 2009).

The second perspective, a colonial thesis, considers ex-British Southern Cameroons as annexed and colonially occupied by Cameroon Republic (Anyangwe, 2014). This thesis views the territory as a colony of the Cameroon state in postcolonial Africa and characterizes the nationalist conflict as an anticolonial struggle (Anyangwe, 2008; Nfor, 2014; Litumbe, 2016). Postcolonial Cameroon and particularly the developments of October 1961, which included ex-British Southern Cameroons in the picture, have not received much attention. Consequently, the image of Cameroon Republic as one of a peaceful African country in which French-speaking and English-speaking kindred peoples live together in harmony sharing many traditions and interacting with one another may not be altogether correct. Proponents of this perspective come from the school of thought that viewed the 1961 federation association as a microcosm of the new Africa, one that combined different colonial heritages, using different languages, and successfully maintaining national unity while other countries remained threatened with disruption and wars. Pope John Paul II, in visiting the country, went as far as describing Cameroon as an island of peace in a troubled continent. How do we understand the difference in the two perspectives within the context of justice and peace, democracy, and development among the people in particular and in Africa in general?

AN INTERNAL AFFAIR PERSPECTIVE

The first perspective emphasizes the colonial link between the Cameroons. This consideration stems from the 1884 Berlin Conference at which *Kamerun* became a German protectorate until World War I. This view minimizes the development of a distinct British Cameroons identity from 1913 (Fanso, 2009) all through the League of Nations, the inter-war years, the United Nations order and the crystallization of a defiant British Southern Cameroons nationalism in Nigeria in the 1950s (Aka, 2002). The view also minimizes the fact that the German *Kamerun* as colonial anchor argument ceased to exist in history and international law since parts of German *Kamerun* are today in Nigeria, Chad, Central African Republic, and Congo. This perspective equally fails to recognize and consider the colonial boundaries of the state of Cameroun Republic as inherited at her independence on January 1, 1960. And if the boundaries of Cameroun Republic at her independence did not include ex-British Cameroons, how then did the hegemonic claim come about? However, the claim is alive with the central assumption that ex-British Cameroons constitutes an integral part of postcolonial Cameroon Republic leading to the portrayal of the struggle to restore the statehood of ex-British Southern Cameroons as "secessionist" in character.

This internal affairs perspective, which invokes some remote idea of a German *Kamerun* to explain the centralized unity or, better expressed, the obfuscation of ex-British Southern Cameroons in postcolonial Cameroon Republic, has been at the core of the academic debate about the ex-British Southern Cameroons' restoration of statehood conflict (Seme, 2009; Konde, 2005). Ex-British Southern Cameroons' opposition to centralized control of the Cameroon Republic or the annexation and colonial occupation thesis is marginalized in this perspective. Writers, including Konde (2005), Ngoh (2017), Forje (1981), and Ondoua Magloire (2013) who have espoused a "one and indivisible Cameroon" framework characterize the relationship between the two Cameroons as "merely an issue of an elder brother opening his hands to admit a younger brother" (Ondoua, 2013), that is, for those of them who even admit that one brother only came!

The literature on the conflict in Cameroon, resting on the acceptance of the "one and indivisible" thesis, has been highly influenced by this outlook. It constrained any analysis of opposition movements which, like the British Southern Cameroons' nationalists, had as their basis the rejection of the imposed unity of the one and indivisible Cameroon. From this perspective, historic opposition to Cameroon Republic's coercive unity was, for over half a century, not openly discussed or denied, but marginalized as a phenomenon of the internal politics of Cameroon Republic. The first time a discussion was openly organized on the two Cameroons came in the form of a panel discussion in April 2013 in the wake of an impending controversial celebration of "reunification." At the behest of the presidency of Cameroon under the director of the civil cabinet at the presidency, Martin Belinga Eboutou, Ondoua Magloire (2013), one of the constitutionalists of Cameroon Republic's origin refuted the idea of "reunification" long taught in Cameroon schools. As he recommended that we should not celebrate fifty years of reunification; rather we should celebrate fifty years of the birth of a state. This idea of "the birth of a state" was a calculated attempt to obfuscate history, and particularly, the history of ex-British Cameroons. With particular regard to ex-British Cameroons, the one and indivisible Cameroon thesis led to the dichotomy between the "unitarists" epitomized by the Pan-Camerounese state and the fragmented nature of the ex-British Southern Cameroons' nationalists.

Studies by Stanley Nzefeh (1994) and Nantang Jua and Piet Koning (2004) on the Cameroon Republic typified this focus. Nicodemus Awasom (2000) also examined the sociopolitical factors that contributed to Cameroon Republic's capability to preserve its identity and unity in comparison to other similar situations in Africa. Many of the authors who focused on the Cameroon federal arrangement in 1961, such as Williard Johnson (2015) and Victor Le Vine (1971), have for a central focus the notion of one Cameroon.

This vision is framed probably from the statist school which sidelines the flawed decolonization process; one that hijacked the independence of British Southern Cameroons planned for October 1, 1961, following the United Nations General Assembly vote on April 21, 1961 (64 yes, 23 no, and 10 abstentions). Opposition to annexation, military occupation and forced assimilation to the *Camerounese* fold was neglected and ignored except insofar as it contrasted with Cameroon Republic nationalism, which itself resulted from the country's independence on January 1, 1960 (without ex-British Southern Cameroons).

Drawing on this tradition, Ewumbue-Monono (2005), a writer on Cameroon's political history, portrayed the former British Southern Cameroons' restoration of statehood struggle as a result of core-periphery tension and one that may even be a perception problem. Ewumbue-Monono argued that ex-British Southern Cameroons attempting to secede from the state of Cameroon Republic is due to the marginalization of the Anglophone minority in Cameroon Republic. Referring to the conflict as the "emerging Anglophone sub-nationalism" in Cameroon Republic as Ewumbue-Monono (2005) put it, this so-called "Anglophone Problem" in Cameroon (Nzefeh, 1994; Kubuo, 2000) continued to be viewed from this perspective as the outright structural marginalization and deliberate inferiorization of the inherited culture of "Anglophones." It is also perceived as the infernal assimilation imposed on "Anglophone Cameroon" by Cameroon Republic with the active complicity of the French. Ewumbue-Monono (2005), for example, also considered the problem as constituting the most conspicuous form of internal sociopolitical contradiction in Cameroon Republic and characterized the problem as a perception problem. In Ewumbue-Monono's words,

> The Anglophone problem in Cameroon simply put is a perception of marginalization by the indigenous English-speaking people of the former Southern Cameroons, which is translated in their exclusion from participating in managing the country's sovereignty, or the inclusion of their Anglo-Saxon values in the process of nation-building. It is further a perception of neglect in the socioeconomic and infrastructural development of Anglophone Cameroon (Roads, railway, airports, seaports, etc.) as well as a systematic destruction of the region's pattern of development and its own development institutions like the West Cameroon Development Agency, the West Cameroon owned Cameroon Bank, the West Cameroon Marketing Board, the POWERCAM, and even the CDC. It is finally the perception by most Anglophones that they do not have equal opportunities in Cameroon for personal and professional development like their Francophone compatriots with similar profiles. (2005, 116–117)

Although Ewumbue-Monono's analysis persisted in the view of the "Anglophone Problem" in Cameroon Republic as a perception problem, he nevertheless recognized it as a national problem and one requiring a national solution through Government and Parliament. He even added that marginalization in the management of national sovereignty included the absence of Anglophones in leadership and policymaking positions in the country's national defense and security, intelligence, diplomacy, territorial administration, finance, and economic departments. From Ewumbue-Monono's standpoint, the appointment of prime ministers like Achidi Achu, Peter Mafany Musonge, Ephraim Inoni, and Philemon Yang may be the solution to the perceived problem of marginalization. The analyst considered the appointment of these prime ministers as a way of resolving the perceived problem.

Appointing Anglophone Cameroonians as prime ministers beginning in 1992 was therefore one of the pillars of the "goodwill" of the government of Cameroun to resolve the Anglophone problem. Ewumbue-Monono (2005) has suggested that the decision to appoint an Anglophone prime minister translated the president's desire to make Anglophones participate effectively in power-sharing in the country and not remain as political spectators or gladiators seeking self-determination. Characterized as the Anglophonization strategy, this policy of the government of *République du Cameroun* to appoint citizens of Southern Cameroons' origin to government posts aimed to stem the "Anglophone problem." Ewumbue-Monono (2005) also affirmed that Simon Achidi Achu was appointed prime minister in the heat of an emerging Anglophone sub-nationalism which was translated by the proliferation of Anglophone activist groups such as the All Anglophone Conference (AAC), Southern Cameroons National Council (SCNC), Southern Cameroons Peoples Council (SCPC), Southern Cameroons Peoples Organization (SCAPO), Free West Cameroon Movement, and so forth.

Since ex-British Southern Cameroons' nationalism increased in intensity from October 2016 beginning with the strike of Common Law Lawyers and Teachers Trade Unions, the government of Cameroon Republic appointed individuals of British Cameroons' origin for the first time to the position of minister of territorial administration and minister of education. After Simon Achidi Achu and Peter Mafany Musonge came Ephraim Inoni and Philemon Yang as prime ministers. Although these appointments are used to counter the independence movement in several ways it is difficult to argue, as Ewumbue-Monono did that the "Anglophonization strategy" as a policy of the government of Cameroon was/is the solution to the problem perceived from the first perspective.

The service to Cameroon Republic of these individuals of ex-British Southern Cameroons' origin is considered among the people ex-British Cameroons as not different from the service of the Israeli foremen in Pharaoh's Egypt. These men and women were all chosen by the president of Cameroon Republic to represent his interest of sustaining the annexation and colonial occupation (Anyangwe, 2014) of ex-British Southern Cameroons.

The prime ministers, said to be representing ex-British Southern Cameroons people, were never elected by the people of that territory to represent them in Cameroon Republic. With the emergence and increasing polarization of Southern Cameroons' nationalism in Cameroon Republic, the leadership of the country saw the need to groom its own leadership of Southern Cameroons and to use such leaders in government to impress upon the world community that the people of ex-British Southern Cameroons were or are part of the country's governance. Whenever many of these Prime Ministers and other senior officials co-opted by the Cameroon government were dropped from the government, they would return to Southern Cameroons, their home of birth, and live a kind of invisible existence. Ex-British Southern Cameroons nationalists consider such imposed leaders like Governor Oben Ashu and Prime Ministers Achidi Achu, Mafany Musonge, Ephraim Inoni, Philemon Yang, Atanga Nji, and others as going into hiding once the Yaounde regime threw them out. When that happens, no one sees them in public anymore.

Many, like Ewumbue-Monono, may doubt the maturation of Southern Cameroons' nationalism and the capability of the nationalist movements to transcend their differences or effectively challenge the authority of the state of Cameroun. It may be difficult to suppose that despite the claims of the nationalist movements, ex-British Southern Cameroons can have entirely displaced a deeply entrenched political culture, nurtured in the factionalism, conflict, poverty, underdevelopment, and corruption that have marked life in British Southern Cameroons and Cameroon Republic in general over five decades.

Some other scholars have viewed the development of the ex-British Southern Cameroons' resistance as a sectarian movement emerging out of tensions between not just center and periphery, also benefitting from the support of the nearby Nigeria, a fellow English-speaking country with historical and cultural ties to Southern Cameroons. During the All Anglophone Conference (AAC) II in Bamenda, the name of Nigeria was cited in the official government owned-and-run media for supporting the Anglophones just as Nigeria was alleged to be behind the launching in Bamenda of an Anglophone political party in 1990.

Similarly, this perspective must have provided the background for excluding the four "Anglophone" members of the thirteen-member Owona Constitution Reform Committee in 1992/1993 when the "Anglophone" members proposed a draft federalist constitution to the committee suggesting a return to the 1961 two-state federation. As one of the four, Carlson Anyangwe (2014) in summary, could be said to have maintained that others will probably recall that my colleagues and I were part of a Constitutional Drafting Committee set up by the Yaoundé Tripartite Meeting to write a constitution. His representation was along the following lines (extrapolated from the records): All Southern Cameroons leaders at the Meeting wanted to correct past ills in the political association of the two Cameroons and to put that political association on a mutually acceptable foundation. From the onset, therefore, we tabled this question for determination. We were alive to the fact that citizens of Cameroun Republic constituted the majority on our committee and that whatever contribution we made would run the gauntlet of cultural and hegemonic prejudice. But since we were all lawyers we thought we could have a full debate on this particular issue and arrive at some acceptable accommodation. Our "friends" were nonplussed by the fact that we should even have raised that question. We told them that that was not our understanding of our remit, especially in the light of the various statements made by all Southern Cameroons leaders at the meeting and the complete unacceptability by the people of the Southern Cameroons of the 1972 gigantic fraud and historical swindle that passed for a "referendum." We reminded them that in 1984 Cameroon Republic reasserted its separate identity as a distinct political expression. We also reminded them that there are two Cameroons: the Southern Cameroons and Republic of Cameroun. Each of these countries was a former Class B Trust Territory of the United Nations under a distinct and separate administering authority. Each country followed its own distinct pathway and Cameroun Republic achieved its independence on January 1, 1960. We argued that if there was still a desire for political association between the two countries that political association had to be put on clear and sound foundations. We stated that it was important to do away with the horse and rider relationship existing between the two countries since October 1961. The committee's chairman, a citizen of Cameroun Republic, brushed aside our submission and ruled that we had to proceed with drafting a constitution for Republic of Cameroun. We replied that while we were willing to assist them as consultants draft a constitution for Republic of Cameroun we were opposed to the Southern Cameroons being considered part of Republic of Cameroun. We told him that in our view it was critical to go back to the federalism that was agreed upon by the two countries as the *condition sine qua non* of political association. His reply was that federalism was tantamount to secession. At that moment, we knew we were dealing with persons who were impervious to reason. We then served notice of our intention to discontinue our participation in the commission. But before we left we told them they had better accept the federalism we were offering. We said we were making the offer at our own risk because, given the long and bitter suffering of our people at the hands of Cameroun Republic, we were not sure they would even accept a federal arrangement with Republic of Cameroun. We then left and later tendered our resignation from the committee giving reasons for our action.

Despite the assertion of all ex-British Southern Cameroons' leaders at the 1992 Yaounde Tripartite Meeting regarding the unacceptability by the people of the former British Southern Cameroons of the 1972 gigantic fraud and historical swindle that passed for a "referendum," and the reminder by the four English-speaking members of the Constitution Committee of the dual heritage of the two Cameroons as stated above, authorities of Cameroon Republic persisted in the idea of a coercive unity. As a consequence of the thinking that Cameroon Republic was one, and indivisible, as often repeated in a hackneyed manner by government officials, the Constitution that was drafted by the Committee and promulgated into Law in 1996 did not as much as mention the ex-British Southern Cameroons nor the dual colonial heritages of the postcolonial African country. Instead, the government of Cameroon Republic insisted on her vision that federalism was tantamount to secession.

DECOLONIZATION PERSPECTIVE

The second school of thought moves out of the shadow cast by the "one-and-indivisible Cameroon Republic" perspective to examine the structure and function of the state of Cameroon and its exercise of colonial domination over occupied ex-British Southern Cameroons as contended by nationalist movements. The nationalist movements included the Southern Cameroons' National Council (SCNC), the Southern Cameroons' Peoples Organization (SCAPO), Southern Cameroons' Restoration Movement (SCARM), Ambazonia Movement, and Free Southern Cameroons' Movement. Constitutional law professor, Carlson Anyangwe (2008), is among those authors, including Nfor Ngala Nfor (2017), Nantang Jua and Piet Konings (2004), and Njoh Litumbe (2017), who have identified the Southern Cameroons' restoration of statehood conflict in postcolonial Cameroon Republic as essentially an anti-colonial movement. Anyangwe argued that Southern Cameroons was "a case of annexation and colonial occupation." As he explained, at the plebiscite the people of the Southern Cameroons voted first and foremost to achieve independence (the effective date of which was set by the UN to be October 1, 1961) and, as a secondary matter, to form a political association with République du Cameroun under certain terms and conditions. At the plebiscite there was therefore no such thing as a so-called "vote for reunification." There could have been no such vote because there was no such alternative. Nor was there any so-called "reunification" on October 1, 1961. That date was billed as the date on which UN trusteeship over the Southern Cameroons was to end, resulting in independence for the territory; it was also the date on which there was to come into existence an agreed federal form of political association between the Southern Cameroons state and République du Cameroun, duly underpinned by an Act of Union subscribed to by both parties. But before that date République du Cameroun had illegally assumed jurisdiction over the Southern Cameroons by performing acts of sovereignty in the territory, while the British conspiratorially looked the other way. On 1 September 1961 République du Cameroun passed in its parliament an annexation law (in the form of a constitutional amendment law deceptively denoted as a "federal constitution") by which it formally claimed the Southern Cameroons as part of its territory and asserted jurisdiction over it. In that same month République du Cameroun's French-led troops marched into the Southern Cameroons and immediately announced their presence and demonstrated their trigger-happy nature by murdering six citizens in cold blood, again while the British looked the other way.

As an illegal occupationist colonial regime, the duty of the United Kingdom and the United Nations as trustee and trustor of the trust was to sanction the illegal acts and apply the principles of self-determination even after the imposition of "independence by joining" concept. The anticolonial perspective is based on the fact that former British Southern Cameroons was a self-governing territory under the United Nations trusteeship from 1954. The logical next step was independence and sovereignty per UNGA Resolution 1514 of 1960. That is why the ex-British Southern Cameroons' question is a colonial question, and not one of secession.

Anyangwe's legal analysis countered the "one-and-indivisible" thesis by characterizing the state of Cameroon as a colonizer and ex-British Southern Cameroons' nationalist resistance as a *bona fide* anticolonial struggle to "restore independence and sovereignty." Echoing Anyangwe's legal argument for ex-British Southern Cameroons independence and sovereignty, Njoh Litumbe (2017) asserted that the République du Cameroun and Southern Cameroons de facto association was an imposition on Southern Cameroons. Fanso (1999) dismissed the notion of an organic unity of Southern Cameroons and Cameroon Republic as one of strange bedfellows arguing that although the two Cameroons had been together for decades they were not one and indivisible. Fonkem (2010) characterized République du Cameroun as a colonial occupying power similar to European colonial powers. Fanso's work traced the former Southern Cameroons' identity struggle as far back in the historic past to 1913 following the defeat of Germany in World War I and the Anglo-French partition of German *Kamerun* known as the Milner-Simon demarcation.

Anyangwe (2014) also argued that Cameroon Republic contrived to make its annexation and colonial occupation of the British Southern Cameroons somehow palatable to swallow in the following suggestion that Cameroon Republic uses reunification as a polysemous expression to camouflage annexation. It has been aided in this cheap language ploy by the polysemous name "Cameroon." There cannot be reunification of two political entities resulting in the existence of only one of the two reuniting entities. In other words, to say that the Southern Cameroons + Cameroun Republic = Cameroun Republic is a mathematical nonsense and is possible only if the Southern Cameroons = zero, which is not and cannot be the case. The equation: the Southern Cameroons + Cameroun Republic = Cameroun Republic signifies in political terms that the Southern Cameroons has been absorbed, annexed, colonized by Cameroun Republic.

Anyangwe (2014) supported his assertion with studies of other jurists and social scientists. According to him, the overwhelming view of even authors who are not citizens of the Southern Cameroons and who have examined the evidence is that the Southern Cameroons was indeed annexed by Cameroun Republic. Aboya Endong Manasse (2002) wrote that "A federal constitution adopted on September 1, 1961 . . . established a very centralized system in which the Southern Cameroons saw its autonomy gradually whittled away up to the point of total annexation. . . . The exploitation of . . . oil marked the beginning of the acceleration of the process of enforced franconisation" (12). Luc Sindjoun (2002), another citizen of Cameroun Republic, also wrote that the "federation" was a mere make-belief strategy by Cameroun Republic designed to hoodwink the United Nations and the Southern Cameroons. It was "a federalism of absorption of the Southern Cameroons by Cameroun Republic . . . a phagocytosis strategy" and it "was used to procure the enlargement of Cameroun Republic." He went further to state that on the 30 September 1961 at Buea the Government of the United Kingdom solemnly transferred sovereignty over the Southern Cameroons to Ahidjo. Exactly the same conclusion was arrived at by other citizens of Cameroun Republic (Donfack and Mbome, 1992, 20).

Pierre Messmer (1998), the last colonial governor of French Cameroun, stated that on 1 October 1961 Ahidjo effected the annexation of the Southern Cameroons to Cameroun Republic. He pointed out that the so-called federal constitution provided merely for a sham federation, which was, except in appearance, an annexation of the Southern Cameroons. In his view, President Ahidjo only came up with a draft deceptive federal constitution, carefully written for him by his French lawyers. Ngu Foncha accepted without discussions what was, except in appearance, an annexation. It was, therefore, sad that Philippe Gaillard (1994) stated similarly that there was no union on October 1, 1961 and that what took place was a mere border adjustment. Frank Stark (1976) argued that a federation in the sense of a voluntary relationship between political units did not exist. He pointed out that there was no true and genuine federation and that in reality the Southern Cameroons was incorporated into Cameroon Republic.

Similarly, J. Vanderlinden concluded that the federation was merely a smoke screen meant to enable the Southern Cameroons to swallow the bitter pill of its annexation by Cameroun Republic, as in the case of Eritrea annexed by Ethiopia. J. Crawford cited the Southern Cameroons as one of a number of former colonial territories "integrated in a state." Jacques Benjamin says there was a creeping annexation of the Southern Cameroons by Cameroun Republic. Deltombe and colleagues indicated,

> Ahidjo effected the political asphyxiation of the Anglophone newcomers. He did so . . . at the Foumban "constitutional conference" where his French advisers devised a water-tight plan which, under the pretext of an egalitarian federation, consisted in reality in the annexation of the Southern Cameroons to the centralized and authoritarian system already in force in Yaoundé since the previous year. . . . In the purest of French traditions Ahidjo annexed the Southern Cameroons . . . thanks to the help of his clever French advisers. He then quickly embarked on a policy of forcible cultural assimilation with the help of "*la Coopération Française*" as always. . . . Noting the effects of this enforced political and cultural assimilation, Bernard Fonlon, a native of the annexed country, quickly sounded the following alarm: "In two or three generations, we shall be French." (2011, 483–485)

Arguing for the legitimation of Southern Cameroons' independence and sovereignty, Anyangwe (2014, 6) contended that the "plebiscite vote was first and foremost a vote for independence," that there first had to be independence as "no 'joining' was feasible without independence having been achieved." According to this constitutional law expert, it is mischievous for anyone not to see the words in the plebiscite question, "achieve independence by joining."

A nationalist leader, Denis Atemnkeng (2018) also observed that British Southern Cameroons may be a small former UN Trust Territory, but it is not insignificant by the standards of the size and population of the smaller member states of the African Union and the United Nations. On the eve of "Independence by joining" in October 1961, the former UN trust territory had an area of 43,000 square kilometers, that is, larger in land area than 63-member nations of the United Nations. Today the territory has a population of about 8 million people which is larger than 94-member nations of the UN.

RELATIONS OF DOMINANCE AND RESISTANCE

It is noteworthy to state that at no point in the over half a century of association did the leadership of Cameroon Republic initiate or even tolerate any policy discussion on the relationship of the two Cameroons. Every effort was made to ignore or marginalize any claims of separate identity, separate colonial heritage, and history. Worse still, the name "British Southern Cameroons," that was said to have joined Republique du Cameroun in October 1961, became taboo and replaced by "Anglophone Cameroon," hence the view of a language conflict in Cameroon common in media accounts on the conflict (Fanso, 2017; Awokoya, 2017; Kindzeka, 2017). There was neither also any effort to underscore the cultural and economic interdependence between ex-British Southern Cameroons and Cameroon Republic as an important legacy of postcolonial Cameroon. From a globalist interpretation of the ex-British Southern Cameroons' restoration of statehood struggle, one can invoke the economic viability of ex-British Southern Cameroons from the existence of a deep-sea port in Victoria and extensive plantation agriculture and other economic crops to oil production in the Gulf of Guinea. Without any wish to regress to economic determinism, one can utilize the economic argument to demystify the 'one and indivisible Cameroon' thesis by incorporating the language of modernization theory, Cold War ideological references, and neoclassical economics.

In the twenty-first-century environment of global terrorism, there has been an attempt to cast Southern Cameroons' nationalist movements, albeit erroneously, as terrorist organizations for reasons of power and state-centered politics. In other words, what may pass for desires of "secession" could sometimes be understood as a manifestation of the interest politics of nation-state actors within a global environment hostile to the making of new states with local and regional implications. Already, the nationalist struggle becoming increasingly intensified has resulted in Cameroon becoming the major source of asylum seekers in the United States (Marquart, 2007) and elsewhere (Pineteh, 2005).

The analyses of several scholars, including those who have firsthand experience of Cameroon life, have suffered to varying degrees from the inability of the various scholars to transcend the myth-cum-reality of one-and-indivisible Cameroon Republic. Johnson, though wondering how "Englishmen" and "Frenchmen" who are black, could live together, nonetheless dwelled on the mechanisms of integration and the types of political actions to achieve integration. Like earlier writers, it is evident from Ngoh and others, including Konde, have reproduced and propagated notions of "Cameroon reunification" as selective facts without historical justification for their claims.

Although some of this scholarship was undertaken at a time when nation-building was the recommended approach to newly independent African states, there is room to question the thinking of other scholars who persist in the "internal affairs" perspective espoused by analysts within the context of the twenty-first century concerned with democratization, liberty, and freedoms, and democratic rights both for individuals, groups, and nations. That is, with the creation of more democratic societies in which all citizens have full standing and enjoy democratic rights and individual freedoms, why would a century favorable to freedoms, democratization and human and people's rights not form the basis for analyzing the desires of colonized societies to desire to be masters of their own destinies? Like earlier scholars, Germain-Gros' (2003) *Cameroon: Politics and Society in Critical Perspectives* continues, within the state-centric perspective, to couch his analysis in the vernacular of a pan-Cameroon framework as in his discussion of the delicate balance between Anglophone and Francophone regions. A similar vernacular of the "internal affairs" perspective is present in this scholar's idea that there is even a nascent, pro-secession movement.

Subscribing to the doctrine of the "internal affairs" perspective while decrying the delicate balance between "Anglophones and Francophones" some of these scholars have not questioned the putting together of two colonies of different colonial masters and traditions in the first place irrespective of the incompatibility theory of plural states (Furnival, 1986; Smith, 1986; Wilson, 1919; Walzer, 1982; Claude, 1969). Both former French Cameroon and former British Cameroons were former Class B Trust Territories of the United Nations under distinct and separate administering authorities. Each followed its own distinct colonial pathway since World War I. In the case of ex-British Cameroons, both the United Kingdom and the United Nations as Trustee and Trustor of the trust disregarded international law in 1961 just as Cameroon Republic blatantly disregarded international law by forcibly annexing and occupying ex-British Southern Cameroons contrary to Article 4 of the AU Constitutive Act. Rather than place the onus on the United Kingdom and the United Nations first for disregarding the UN Charter in Art. 76 (b) and UNGA Resolution 1514 (XV) of 1960; and also on Cameroon Republic, Germain-Gros and others have conveniently redirected their critique to "nascent pro-secession movements."

The work of these scholars who continue to view the ex-British Southern Cameroons restoration of statehood conflict mainly within the boundaries of internal core-periphery tensions do not permit a detailed analysis of the crucial dynamics fermenting in the periphery. In the ex-British Southern Cameroons' independence and sovereignty case, the fact that there were two Cameroons; that each was a former Class B Trust Territory of the United Nations under a distinct and separate administering authority, is enough reason to initiate a scholarly discussion on the conflict. That each of the territories followed its own distinct pathway from World War I such that French Cameroun achieved its independence as Republique du Cameroun (Cameroun Republic) on January 1, 1960 without British Southern Cameroons does not seem to be important to the perspective that promotes a one postcolonial Cameroon vision. Ex-British Cameroons' nationalists argue that British Cameroons had a different date for her own independence, namely October 1, 1961, and that if there was still a desire for political association between the two Cameroons that political association had to be put on clear and sound foundations and that it was important to do away with the horse and rider relationship existing between the two Cameroons since October 1961.

THE ONE CAMEROON REPUBLIC
CONCEPTUALIZATION IN THEORETICAL TERMS

Some who argue for a one-and-indivisible "reunified" Cameroon although without substantiating the "reunification" claim, base such a claim of the Republic of Cameroon hegemony on the foundation of a historic German *Kamerun* of 1884–1913. Scholars use the term hegemony to encompass three different but interrelated and dominant conceptualizations of power relations: realism, world systems, and Gramscian hegemony. From the perspective of Hedley Bull (1977), on superpower hegemonic relationships between the United States and the Soviet Union, hegemony is defined as a relationship in which there is resort to force and the use of force. The relationship between the Soviet Union and the Eastern Europe and the relationship between the United States and the states of Central America were analyzed as hegemonic because each superpower was ready to violate the rights of sovereignty, equality, and independence enjoyed by lesser states, but it does not disregard them; it recognizes that these rights might exist and justifies violations of them by appeals to some specific overriding principles.

British Cameroons' nationalists refute this hegemonic view by recognizing that the onset of foreign control over the Southern Cameroons was British from 1858 with the naming of Victoria by Alfred Saker. They also argue that German *Kamerun* became extinct both as a German colony and as a single entity in WWI. In its place there emerged two separate and distinct legal and political entities: British Cameroons and French Cameroon. Each of the two political entities was placed under a mandate system, the goal being ultimate independence of each mandated territory following the Milner-Simon Declaration. As Anyangwe (2014, 3) put it, "[T]he juridical basis of the two countries are the mandate system, transmuted into the trusteeship system after World War Two" and that "both British Cameroons and French Cameroon were different Category B Trust Territories under a Trusteeship Agreement approved by the United Nations General Assembly on December 13, 1946.

The second school of thought, represented by world-systems theorists such as Immanuel Wallerstein (1984, 38), links hegemony to economic expansion. Viewed through the analytic lens of the world-systems theorists, hegemonic status focuses on the idea that one state can largely impose its rules and wishes in the economic, political, military, diplomatic, and even cultural arenas is typically limited to the most industrialized states. The focus on relations of dominance and subordination are glossed over due to the focus on economic superiority which at times manifests itself in military hegemony.

The third analysis, represented by Antonio Gramsci's articulation of cultural hegemony, encompasses relations of dominance and resistance in cultural, economic, and political spheres. Gramsci focused mainly on state-society relations, the acquisition of power, and the construction of a political discourse by elites and intellectuals which undergirds the exercise of power. In examining the relations of dominance, Gramsci differentiates between the coercive power of the state and the response of various elements within civil society. Gramsci's concept of hegemony takes into consideration the role of intellectuals and the dissemination of knowledge in the mobilization and organization of the people. Gramsci links the production of knowledge and the legitimation of certain versions of history over others to the struggle for power. The application of this thinking to this analysis is based on two central assumptions. First, the legitimation of domination and de-legitimation of any opposition to the terms of order envisioned by the hegemon is a crucial component of a hegemonic power base. Second, opposition to hegemonic domination that threatens the hegemonic status quo is militarily contained or diplomatically isolated from regional and international institutions which are authorized to address violations or redress grievances. Cameroon Republic has worked very hard at the regional and international levels to achieve these goals. Internally ex-British Southern Cameroons' nationalist movements are militarily suppressed with many leaders fleeing abroad and diplomatically the government works hard to isolate and ignore the Southern Cameroons' independence question. Examples here include the Greentree Accord on the Bakassi Peninsula dispute and the follow up or lack thereof to the decision of African Commission on Human and People's Rights in respect of Communication 266/2003 (AU, 2009).

THE REPUBLIC OF CAMEROON'S "REGIME OF TRUTH"

The ability of Cameroon Republic to establish and maintain its diplomatic capability and legitimacy over ex-British Cameroons emanates from its successful development of a hegemonic "regime of truth." The concept of a regime of truth derives from the focus on the relationship between power and knowledge found in the works of Michel Foucault. Foucault's major premise is that every society has its regime of truth, its general politics of truth and the role it plays in the socioeconomic and political order of things, which is central to the structure and functioning of society. This socio-political approach can shed light on the broader analysis of the function of norms and values in the study of conflicts like the British Cameroons' restoration of independence conflict that challenges hegemonic powers and their versions of the regime of truth. The contribution of this approach is in the examination of the international and regional consensus within which institutions legitimate certain views while de-legitimating others. The realist, world systems, and Gramscian theories of hegemonic relationships are based on the exercise of military, economic, political, and organizational capabilities of nation-states.

Within a regime of truth, the decoding of history and the encoding of contemporary "reality" are linked by invoking a superficially "logical" (if ultimately specious) continuum from what is to what was (Iyob, 1997, 26). The driving "logic" is derived from the prevailing regime, that is, from the prevailing norms, values and the sustaining apparatus of those norms and values. Indeed, the only definite and consistent purpose of such "logic" is, in all cases, the maintenance of the regime. In Cameroon Republic's case, by 1970, the country had become sufficiently strong within the OAU and later the AU. Cameroon Republic's role in providing successive Secretary Generals and the emphasis on non-intervention in the internal affairs of member states legitimated its hegemonic claims over ex-British Southern Cameroons. At the same time, Cameroon Republic continued to function as a major member such that its position was used to de-legitimate any claims by the later regarding existing boundaries of member states at independence in accordance with Article 4 of the organization's Constitutive Act.

As an analytical device, the regime of truth is an organization of knowledge in justification of a given distribution of power, defining what is and what is not legitimate discourse. The very pervasiveness of the Cameroon Republic's regime of truth appears to be the foundation of its hegemonic dominance in the political and diplomatic consensus that sustained its interest in occupying ex-British Southern Cameroons from October 1961.

In the case of Cameroon Republic, the regime of truth is conditioned by a number of prevailing norms, values, institutions, and processes with Cameroon Republic, throughout the postcolonial African order, and at the level of the international arena. The mythic image of Cameroon as a quintessential bilingual state as an African example is skillfully woven into a complex fabric of African territorial integrity and international sovereignty. References to Cameroon Republic as a sovereign state have endowed it with a unique status and exposure. The political imperatives of maintaining its extended boundaries, which now include ex-British Southern Cameroons from October 1961, were articulated in terms consonant with the prevailing African consensus of "unity" and the "restoration" of areas divided up by European colonizers.

The idea of pan-Africanism and the increasing discourse on a united African framework on the example of the European Union reinforced Cameroon Republic's claims over other territories such as ex-British Southern Cameroons. Scholarly publications extolling Cameroon as an example for a united Africa, in terms of bringing together peoples of different nationalities, cultures, and languages contributed to the academic legitimation of Cameroon Republic's hegemonic aspirations over ex-British Southern Cameroons, especially as this hegemony brought Cameroon Republic great prestige in the Central African sub-region.

By the year 2000, when ex-British Cameroons' nationalist movements were gaining increasing impetus, Cameroon Republic's sloganeering of "peace," "national unity," "nation integration," and "one and indivisible Cameroon" served as the overriding principles that de-legitimated ex-British Southern Cameroons' struggle to restore her independence and sovereignty. In this connection, the Cameroon Republic's regime of truth was accepted (especially with the help of repression) as the "true" version in the struggle of ex-British Southern Cameroons' nationalists in postcolonial Cameroons.

CONCLUSION

This chapter examined the different portrayals of the Southern Cameroons' restoration of statehood conflict in scholarly works and showed how these different perspectives reflect the ideological and philosophical underpinnings which served to legitimize Republique du Cameroun's claims over ex-British Southern Cameroons' restoration of statehood struggle spanning over half a century. It introduced the concepts of hegemony and the successor to colonial domination, which operate through the dissemination of "national sovereignty and national integration." This situation enables a state with military, diplomatic, economic and/or geostrategic capabilities to annex, occupy, and subjugate another territory and its inhabitants in violation of the international and regional legal instruments of the postcolonial era.

Couching the restoration of statehood conflict as a "pro-secessionist movement" in the "internal affairs" perspective negates the fundamental nature of the British Southern Cameroons' demand for statehood restoration as a people's right and as a fundamental human need. In this regard, there is no room for redress or significant reconfiguration of the status quo other than repression and violence. The practice of conceptualizing the ex-British Southern Cameroons' restoration of independence and sovereignty question in postcolonial Africa mainly in the "internal affairs" perspective further marginalizes and altogether ignores the political and social basis of the conflict. In conflict theory, marginalizing the basis of conflict does not make the conflict go away. Such a perspective also ignores the crucial exercise of the state of Cameroon's diplomatic capability in the African Union and the United Nations and the larger notion of Cameroon Republic's prestige in the international diplomatic circles of nation-states politics.

By the end of the first decade of the twenty-first century, the struggle continued to wax and wane mainly in the shadows (Fonkem, 2013) as the hegemonic "truth" of Cameroon Republic did not face any crucial test. The policy of one-and-indivisible Cameroon was not successfully challenged by any ex-British Southern Cameroons' cohesive resistance except through the African Commission on Human & People's Rights (Communications 266/ 2003 and 377/2007). Until the uprising of the Common Law Lawyers and Teachers' Trade Unions in October 2016, these court cases and the opposition to the celebration of the 50th anniversary of a mythical "reunification of the two Cameroons" were among the only attempts to expose the fallacy of "one and indivisible Cameroon" or the country's mythical national unity and integration.

With reference to Gramscian cultural hegemony, I argued that as a phenomenon of the postcolonial era, postcolonial relations of domination and the legitimation of hegemonic violations of rules is institutionalized. I also argued that the postcolonial African consensus on the principles of "national unity" and "balkanization" has been used effectively by Cameroon Republic to efface ex-British Southern Cameroons' identity by stripping the territory's demands of any regional (African Union) and international (UN, Commonwealth, UNPO) legitimation and support. In his approach to hegemony, Gramsci makes the link between power, language, and the socialization of peoples, classes, and states to a specific interpretation of history and ideas. In this regard, Gramsci agrees with Michel Foucault's emphasis on the political significance of discourses in the legitimation of ideologies of domination.

The free world can help Cameroun Republic and ex-British Southern Cameroons to get free enterprise and a market economy operating well in both formal trust territories and lay the ground work for creation of open democratic societies. The casting of the relations of dominance and resistance in the meeting point of former British West Africa and former French Equatorial Africa in the Gulf of Guinea integrates what may be considered an orphaned problem into the wider realm of global *realpolitik*. From my perspective, this chapter will have served its purpose if it provokes us to think more openly about the questions of freedom, liberty and justice for all countries and peoples on the basis of human dignity and the absence of humiliation for other human beings and nations.

BIBLIOGRAPHY

African Union (2009). Communication no. 266/2003. *Kevin Mwanga Gumne et al. v. Cameroon. African Commission on Human and Peoples' Rights*, 45th ordinary Session, May 27.

Aka, Emmanuel A. (2002). *The British Southern Cameroons, 1922–1961: A Study in Colonialism and Underdevelopment.* Platteville, WI: Nkemnji Global Tech.

Anyangwe, Carlson (2014). "A Country Decolonized Becomes Colonizer," in *British Southern Cameroons: Nationalism and Conflict in Postcolonial Africa.* Ed. Fonkem, A. I. BC, Canada: Friesen Press.

———. (2014). "Dimensions of Postcolonial Annexation and Domination," in *British Southern Cameroons: Nationalism and Conflict in Postcolonial Africa.* Ed. Fonkem, A. I. BC, Canada: Friesen Press.

Atemnkeng, Denis (2017). Why We Must Never Talk about Federation Again. *Ambazonia Independence*, July 5.

Awokoya, Ayo (2017). Cameroon's Colonial Language Crisis: Cameroon's minority anglophone community is protesting francophone domination in their country—a conflict which has roots in the colonial era. *Raddington Report*, Nov. 3.

Benjamin Jacques (1972). *Les Camerounais Occidentaux—La Minorité dans un Etat Bi-communautaire*, Montreal.

Claude, Inis, L. (1969). *National Minorities: An International Problem*. Greenwood, Westport.

Crawford, J. (1997). "State Practice and International Law in Relation to Unilateral Secession," Report 1997, para. 21.

Deltombe, Thomas, Manuel Domergue and Jacob Tatsitsa (2016). La guerre du Cameroun: L'invention de la Françafrique (1948–1971). *Cahiers Libres*.

Donfack, Lekene, and Mbome François (1992). "Les expériences de la révision constitutionnelle au Cameroun," *Pénant*, 808(Janvier–Avril): 20.

Ebong, Frederick A. (1999). "The Actualization of the Independence and Sovereignty of Southern Cameroons Independence." https://www.bareta.news/actualization-independence-sovereignty-southern-cameroons-independence/. Retrieved October 2, 2018.

Ewumbue-Monono, Churchill (2005). *Men of Courage*. Buea: CEREDDA.

———. (2009). *Youth and Nation-Building in Cameroon*. Langaa: RPCIG.

———. (2013). *Peter Motomby-Woleta and Cameroon's Reunification Constitution*. Buea: CEREDDA.

Fanso, V. G. (2017). "Anglophone-Francophone: History Explains Why Cameroon Is at War with Itself over Language and Culture," *The Conversation*, October 15.

Fanso, Verkijika G. (2014). "British Southern Cameroons' 'Independence by Joining,'" in *British Southern Cameroons: Nationalism and Conflict in Postcolonial Africa*. Ed. Fonkem, A. BC, Canada: Friesen Press.

Fanso, V. G. (1999). "Anglophone and Francophone Nationalisms in Cameroon," *The Round Table: The Commonwealth Journal of International Affairs*. London.

Forje, J. W. (1981). *The One and Indivisible Cameroon: Political Integration and Socioeconomic Development in a Fragmented Society*. Lund Political Studies.

Fonkem, A. (2013). "De facto Association, Forced Assimilation and a Nationalist Conflict in the Cameroons: Perspectives from the Incompatibility Theory," *Journal of International Studies and Development*, 3: 142–168.

Furnival, John S. (1986). *Netherlands India: A Study of Plural Economy*. B. M. Israel: Amsterdam.

Gaillard, Philippe (1994). *Ahmadou Ahidjo: Patriote et Despote, Batisseur de l'Etat Camerounais*, Paris. 123.

Germain-Gros, Jean (2003). *Cameroon: Politics and Society in Critical Perspectives*

Iyob, Ruth (1997). *The Eritrean Struggle for Independence: Domination, Resistance, Nationalism, 1941–1993*. Cambridge: Cambridge University Press.

Johnson, Willard. (2015). *The Cameroon Federation Political Integration in a Fragmentary Society*. Princeton, NJ: Princeton University Press.

Jua, Nantang, and Koning, Piet (2004). "Occupation of Public Space. Anglophone Nationalism in Cameroon," *Cahiers d'Études africaines*, XLIV(3): 609–633.

Kindzeka, Edwin M. (2017). "Cameroon City Shuts Down Over Language Issue," *Voice of America*. January 9.

Konde, Emmanuel (2005). *Cameroon: Traumas of the Body Politic*. Xlibris.

Le Vine, Victor T. (1971). *CameroonFederal Republic*. Ithaca, NY: Cornell University Press.

Litumbe, Njoh (2017). "I Am For Outright Independence of Southern Cameroons," *Cameroon Post*, November 3.

Marquart, Niels (2007). "US Embassy "Crucifies" Cameroonian US Asylum Seekers," *L'Effort Camerounais*, June.

Manasse, Aboya Endong (2002). "Ménaces sécessionistes sur l'Etat camerounais," *Le Monde Diplomatique*, Décembre (585): 12.

Mesmer, Pierre (1998). *Les blancs s'en vont—Recit de Decolonisation*. Paris. 134–135.

Nfor Ngala Nfor (2017). "Repression Has Reinvigorated the Demand for Liberation of Southern Cameroons. *The Guardian*, October 22.

Ngoh, J. (2017). "The Anglophone Dilemma in Cameroon," *CRTV Web.*

Nzefeh, Stanley (1994). "The Anglophone Problem in Cameroon: Real and disturbing Dimensions," *Cameroon Review* (June): 4–7.

Ondoua, Magloire (2017). "The Significance of October 1, 1961 in Cameroon," *CRTV Web.*

Pineteh, Ernest (2005). "Memories of Home and Exile: Narratives of Cameroonian Asylum Seekers in Johannesburg," *Journal of Intercultural Studies*, 26(4): 379–399.

Seme, Ndzana (2009). "Cameroon-Neocolonial State: SCNC Claims Met with Denial, Contempt and Terror," in *The African independent*, February.

Sindjoun, Luc (2002). *L'Etat Ailleur. Entre noyau dur et case vide*, Paris. 127–129.

Smith, Michael G. (1986). "Pluralism, Violence and the Modern State," in *The State in Global Perspective*. Ed. Kazancigil, A. Paris: Gower/UNESCO.

Stark, Frank (1976). "Federalism in Cameroon: The Shadow and the Reality," *Canadian Journal of African Studies*, x(3): 441.

Vanderlinden, J. (1985). "L'Etat Federal, Etat Africain de l'An 2000?" in *L'Etat Moderne Horizon 2000*. Paris: LGDJ. 307.

Walzer, Michael, Kantowics, Edward T., and John Higham (1982). *The Politics of Ethnicity*. Cambridge, MA: Belknap Press.

Wilson, Woodrow (1919). "The Papers of Woodrow Wilson," *Journal of Southern History* 57(2): 5–22.

Chapter Five

Eurocentrism and the Place of Ancient Egypt in African Art Scholarship

Michael Olusegun Fajuyigbe

Africa's contact with the West began with series of voyages by European explorers and traders to the continent. It was followed by missionaries, soldiers of fortune, and colonial administrators who recurrently visited and later sojourned in Africa. Their reports, travelogues, commentaries, and documentaries constituted the bulk of information (or initial data) on the arts and cultures of Africa. The publications that came out of this data are generally referred to as "African art." Early writers on Africa discussed and assessed its arts and other material culture using the same yardsticks and aesthetic judgement applicable to "Western art." They used terms like *primitive, pagan, tribal, ethnic, votive*, and so forth, while engaging "African art" pieces; and often, they cited "magico-religious cultures" as sources of these objects (Willett, 2003, 26; Trowell, 1970, 15). These presumptions were erroneous, oblivious, and egotistic in conception, and clearly showcased the ignorance of the writers. As Brain (1980, xii) points out, many writers and art historians lack the requisite knowledge and understanding of the cultural milieu and the "world of ideas that Africans reflect through their arts." In affirmation, Margaret Trowell disagrees vehemently with the Western ethnocentric views of non-European art. Hence, she advocates that "African art," like European art, should be approached, studied, analysed and appreciated "in the same unprejudiced manner," with emphasis on its inherent qualities and values (Trowell, 1970, 15).

Previously, two distinct approaches—anthropological (ethnological) and art historical (aesthetic)—were employed by early European scholars and art historians towards an understanding and appreciation of "African art" (Adepegba, 2000; Trowell, 1970). The anthropological approach focuses on the ethnological aspects of an art object and emphasizes that knowledge of the cultural significance of the art object is crucial to understanding its cultural context. Art historical approach, on the other hand, focuses on the "immanent and formal attributes or qualities of art objects." In addition, Adepegba (2000, 6–9) notes that because of the obvious disparity and limitations of these approaches, researchers often "oscillate" between the two theoretical poles as they try to understand the nature of African art. A distinct approach, favourable to both anthropologists and art historians, emerged and was christened as "multidisciplinary" or "interdisciplinary" approach. In the opinion of Adepegba (2000, 2) scholars who explore the new approach (by combining the previous approaches) would have been able to "undo" the injustices of the past.

"African art" is a coinage of early European writers and it is used for describing and appreciating the material and visual culture of the peoples of black Africa, who inhabit the imaginary and artificial region in the south of Sahara desert. However, modern scholars have deployed the term to describe the visual culture, artistic creativity and aesthetic consciousness of peoples and societies of Africa. Examples of their artworks include sculptures, paintings, crafts and decorative arts, etc. African art has a multidimensional purpose and is more utilitarian in nature than serving purely aesthetic functions. Bewaji (2003, 41) extols the multifarious role of art, and asserts that irrespective of cultural background "all art, at the time of their production have a multi-dimensionality of intention, purpose and utility intrinsic to them." Brain's (1980, xii) observation is apt here. He points out that art in Africa fulfils a multitude of functions, such as status and prestige identifier, means of attaining and maintaining political power, of entertainment, and economic empowerment.

However, the multidimensionality of "African art" has often been cloaked by the partiality of appreciation and rash judgement on the part of Western intellectuals. It would not be imprudent therefore to assert that "African art" is in its own class culturally, socially, and intellectually distinct from Euro-American   art   or   any   art   tradition   for   that   matter. Prior to the twentieth century, anthropologists (ethnologists and ethnographers in particular) and others who were interested in African cultures, viewed the "art objects" from black Africa as interesting cultural artifacts but did not consider them as art. An ethnologist is a cultural anthropologist who engages in the "scientific" study of human culture or the culture of specific societies, including social structure, language, religion, art, and technology. Ethnography, the observational branch of ethnology, describes each culture, including its language, the physical characteristics of its people, its material products, and its social customs. The ethnographers gather information about the location and geographical environment of a particular tribe, its religious ideas vis-à-vis magic, supernatural beings, and the universe; and its artistic, mythological, and ceremonial interpretations of its natural and social environment. The terms "ethnologist" and "ethnographer" are used interchangeably in our discussion.

The ethnologists often took art objects with them to Europe for display in their homes, as personal collection, or for exhibition in collective spaces called museums, for public viewing as tokens of the material cultures of other climes. These art pieces later comprised the bulk of collections in early ethnographic museums in Europe upon which judgments were passed regarding the intellectual capacities of the cultures of origins of these pieces. It is sufficient to say then that art objects from Africa were preserved like fossils to be admired and to serve as reminder of a long lost age. This trend continued until early twentieth century, when European avant-garde artists began to embrace and adapt in their works the conceptual framework and formal properties of African sculptures; hence, it affirmed the concept of modern in the art of Europe. Toward the middle of twentieth century, there emerged some Western Africanist scholars who consciously engaged in the academic study of Africa—its cultures, societies, and history, "using a critical lens that inserts African ways of knowing and references" (Willett, 2003, 34; Gerbrands, 1990, 2).

The Western art historians who came later also focused on the formal properties (qualities) of African art, using the stylistic ideology and critical lens of Western art, aesthetics, and art criticism. This is often, and generally, the hallmark of Western intellectual discourses with respect to African art scholarship. This is unfortunate, as most Western intellectuals failed to understand the uniqueness and multidimensionality of intention in African art. Thelma Newman's attempt at appreciating the immanent qualities of pan-African art is holistic and appropriate here. She submits that "African art explains the past, describes values and a way of life, helps man relate to supernatural forces, mediates his social relations, expresses emotions and enhances man's present life as an embellishment denoting pride or status as well as providing entertainment (dance, music)" (Newman, 1974, 5). However, with a whiff of intellectual suicide, she asserts that "To the African, there is no art" (xii). How can the most sincere Western scholar do justice to the critical art history of "classical" and modern/contemporary African arts if such contradictory assertions continue to surface in Western intellectual art discourses?

Art, as creative and cultural expression, is intricately connected to the philosophy and values of the society that produces it. It is unfair, therefore, that Africa, as rightly observed by Conner (1996, 10), is not accorded any credit in the development of human civilizations despite its long list of great empires, kingdoms and chiefdoms, and contributions to human intellectual and scientific heritage in all aspects of human existence. This intellectual oversight, on the part of western intellectuals, is deliberate and prejudicial to the African essence and personality. It is unfortunate and noxious to "style" Africa—its intellectual, scientific, cultural, and artistic heritage—as inferior to any other regional traditions of humanity around the world. The failure of some Western scholars to accord Africa a significant place in human development is an indication of deplorable Eurocentric educational background.

Eurocentrism is a deliberate and conscious effort aimed at promoting Euro-American agenda of racial supremacy and cultural hegemony, which simultaneously downplay or dismiss any undeniable worth or inherent cultural values that emanate outside Europe and North America, but negatively targeting the continent of Africa in particular. There is a strong tie between art, culture (identity), and place (cultural environment). Every culture contains such elements like dressing, language, songs, and visual expression that distinguish it from other cultures, and allows it communicates deep cultural values and celebrates its heritages. The artists (carvers, blacksmiths, shrine painters, bronze casters and designers/decorators) of precolonial Africa usually make art to assist the public to understand life and communicate values and passions among peoples. It is, therefore, presumptuous to assume that a particular culture (including its arts) is superior in its essential and ethereal qualities when placed alongside other cultures.

No culture, however "sophisticated," is superior to other cultures; and no culture, though "unrefined," is less significant in the comity of other cultures. Generally, culture is simply an established pattern of living and values that are shared among a people; hence, it is that inherent qualities (values) within a culture that distinguishes it from the others. This is cultural identity and should be respected by the "others." To do otherwise is to be Eurocentric, Americentric, Sinocentric, Afrocentric, or chauvinistic, clannish, and generally ethnocentric, depending on which culture is the object of discussion/ study. The universality of art, its conception, creation and appreciation makes it a unique cultural occurrence, and requires that intellectual fairness is deployed in its appreciation.

STATEMENT OF THE PROBLEM

There abound a lot of literature on European ethnocentric attitudes toward the intellectual property and material culture of non-European peoples, black Africans in particular. Likewise, many Africanist art historians and scholars (Willett, 2003; Visona et al., 2001; Adepegba, 2000; Bewaji, 2003 and 2013; Sieber and Walker, 1988; Vansina, 1984; Brain, 1980; Leuzinger, 1976; and Trowell, 1970) have written copiously on African art and the prejudices of earlier art scholars towards the study African artistic culture. They all posited that works of art produced in African societies should be judged on their own merits, independent of Western artistic canons or parameters.

Simultaneously, the scholars rejected the cliché "African art" used in describing the visual culture of sub-Saharan Africa as discriminatory and condescending, since it excluded the Arab-dominated North Africa. Though, the phrase "Art in Africa" (Visona et al., 2001), a more encompassing phrase coined by the Africanist art scholars in place of "African art" has come to stay; nevertheless, the Eurocentric ideals towards Africa still persist. Of these scholars, Adepegba (2000, 1–9) invalidates in totality the Eurocentrism and "otherness syndrome" employed by Western writers and curators which place African art on a lower social pedestal in comparison to Western art.

The imbalance of African art scholarship as presented by Western intellectuals is extensively queried by Bewaji in *Beauty and Culture* (2003) and *Black Aesthetics* (2013). He deploys philosophical and critical lenses in examining the methodology, ideology and analysis of the writings of selected Western Africanist art historians like Frank Willett, Cyril Aldred, Ortega y Gasset, and R. G. Collingwood, respectively. He avers that "most of the philosophies of art in the West have floundered on account of the unidimensionality and partiality of their focus" (Bewaji, 2003, 41). Unfortunately, the "unidimensionality and partiality of focus" observed persists today in Western discourses of modern and contemporary African and African diaspora arts.

In view of the above, the present study reexamines African art scholarship, Western ethnocentrism and prejudices that pervade African art and its contemporary reflections. It draws attention to the subtle domination and outright relegation of African and African diaspora arts and artists despite the fuss about equality and globalization. As rightly pointed out by Ogbechie (2005) and affirmed by Odiboh (2009), the trends in African art marketing, patronage and promotion is still dictated by the West. Odiboh in particular denounces the patently noxious and preconceived neocolonial and xenophobic attitudes of some Western curators, art historians, art collectors, and scholars toward modern and contemporary African art. This chapter, therefore, seeks to inspire contemporary African artists toward having pride in the uniqueness of African visual art culture. It is this distinctiveness that marks the Africanity of contemporary Africans, at home on the continent of Africa and in the diaspora. This chapter asserts (from literature) that art in Africa then and now is a stamp of the peoples' Africanity and consciousness. Hence, it derides erroneous interpretations of African culture—traditional and modern—and discourages misdirected art scholarship influenced by Eurocentric considerations.

EGYPT IN AFRICAN ART AND CULTURE

Art is distinctly a human creative product that validates a people's culture, cultural practices and expression. The glories of ancient civilizations are evident in their visual culture: language, dressing, dance, and art objects. Culture is a determinant of the kinds of art produced by a people; hence, the interrelatedness (symbiosis) of art and culture over time and space has resulted in the formation of both personal and group identity. This identity is often shaped by studying technical, visual, or ethereal qualities of artworks; that is, seeking to understand and compare intelligently works of art which are stylistically related or similar for the purpose of making critical judgement. Stylistic evolution and differences in visual art remain; and as asserted by Henri Focillion (Balogun, 1979, 36), "differences in cultural and sociological orientation of artists often make for enormous differences in modes of artistic expression even within a society." Thus, using geographical context and based on the position of the diffusionist theorists like A. C. Frans Olbrechts, Adrian Gerbrands, among others (Gerbrands, 1990), this study posits that visual culture of ancient Egypt has a lot in common with the historical culture of the rest of black Africa.

Art is the product of creative human activity in which materials are shaped or selected to convey an idea, emotion, or visually interesting form. The word "art" as used in this chapter refers to human ability to process materials into products that are culturally enriching and visually satisfying to the senses. This perception seeks to corroborate Lazarri and Schleisier (2008) view of art, because a work of art is a creative and cultural expression of the people that produced it.

In ancient Egypt and indigenous African society, the relevance of art continues as long as it serves cultural and religious purposes. The various aspects of arts were created for a purpose beyond aesthetic appeal—to satisfy a people's individual and collective yearnings for expressions and facilitate their cordial relationship with the supernatural (Brain, 1980). Unlike Western arts, which in the view of some biased scholars who have weak understanding of their own cultural background and claim that European art are produced as "art for art's sake," works of art from all over the world, especially ancient Egypt and Africa are visual and non-visual objectification of the ideals, values and belief systems of the people.

Lawal (1996, xiii) adds credence to the functional value of art in Africa, as one of the factors which contribute to the meanings of African art. He avers that the interplay of the social, religious and aesthetic is copiously and conspicuously projected in African visual culture in which an object or performance embodies so much value for the people who created it. This is the multidimensionality of the intention of the African art at the time of production.

Until recently, the term "African" was commonly used to designate the arts, cultures, and peoples living in Africa south of the Sahara (Leuzinger, 1976; Brain, 1980; Vansina, 1984; Hackett, 1996); hence, the art of the Maghreb of North Africa, the blacks of the Horn of Africa, as well as the art of ancient Egypt were not included under the heading "African art." However, Africanist art historians and scholars, who are mindful of this deliberate exclusion advocated for the inclusion of the visual culture of these areas, since all the cultures that produced them are located within the same geographical expressions "African continent." The implication is that by including all African cultures and their visual culture in African art, laypersons and art students will gain a better and wider understanding of the continent's cultural diversity. With the confluence of indigenous African, Islamic and Mediterranean cultures, scholars have found that drawing distinct divisions between these nations, including ancient Egypt, makes little or no sense (Vansina, 1984; Visona et al., 2001). Finally, the arts of Africans in diaspora, prevalent in Brazil, the Caribbean, and the southeastern United States, have also begun to be included in the study of African art.

Early studies on "African art" show a deliberate exclusion of Egyptian art (and those of the Maghreb) because of evidences of Euro-Asiatic and Islamic ideals. "Egypt" is a hybrid of civilizations, the melting pot of nations; nevertheless, ancient Egyptian art shared similar values with those of black Africa, geographically and culturally. Jan Vansina, an Africanist art historian opines that the exclusion of Northern Africa (Egypt in particular) from "African art" is conceptually motivated by very strong "influences from traditions centred on Mediterranean and the world of Islam and Christianity" (1984, 2). These traditions are *oikoumenical* because they encompass and transcend local and regional cultures; thus, their "influences" have had a grinding and crippling effect on modern Egyptians art and culture.

To an extent, ancient Egypt, as part of African indigenous tradition and culture, almost lost its identity and artistic heritage to Europe and Asia, but for the massive pyramids which serve as conservatory for the remains of the ancient civilizations of these Africans. Today, the peoples inhabiting modern Egypt and the Maghreb are mostly Arabs with pockets of Berbers and other indigenous people. This is due to the long occupation of Egypt by the Arabs since the latter conquest in the seventh century AD. After centuries of domination by the Arabs and the integration of Islamic values into Egyptian visual culture; it is less surprising that early European scholars excised northern Africa, almost half of the continent's size, from the rest of Africa.

Why did the early Western writers exclude North Africa from the rest of Africa? Why did they use retrogressive and decadent terms like "primitive," "tribal," and "grotesque," among others to qualify the creative and cultural expressions of Africans? How come that Eurocentric ideal still permeates anything related to African art in international art market? Are African arts and culture free from the colonial negative evaluation? The answer may not be far from what Chukwokolo (2009, 29) describes as "colonial legacies." He avers that "colonial experience left two broad legacies: Denial of African identity and the foisting of Western thought and cultural realities and perspectives on Africans."

If Egypt is a hybrid of civilizations—a blend of Euro-Asiatic and African ideals—there is the possibility of its African origin. Therefore, the removal of Egypt and the Maghreb from the "cultural Africa" by Western scholars and the classification of Egypt among the Mediterranean world are unjustifiable, exclusionist, and aimed at satisfying Eurocentric interests. This action or inaction was hinged on the fact that modern inhabitants of North Africa are not black and their present political ideology is pro-Arab. Davidson (1972, 29) questions this hypothesis and notes that "the vast majority of pre-dynastic Egyptians were of continental Africans," though "the early populations included the descendants of incoming migrants from the Near East." In support of this proposition, Martin Bernal, in *Black Athena* (Conner, 1986, 17), avers that "Egyptian civilization is clearly based on the rich pre-dynastic cultures of Upper Egypt and Nubia, whose African origin is uncontested." To imagine otherwise, as many Western intellectuals would want us to believe, is to disprove the nativity of the Berbers and Ethiopians who inhabit the same region. As the melting pot of nations, it implies that there are possibilities of having black-Egyptians, Arab-Egyptians, and European-Egyptians in pre-dynastic Egypt.

The location of Egypt was significant to the evolution and sustenance of subsequent civilizations in the Mediterranean region. No wonder, the Western world had to trace its own origin to ancient Egyptian civilization, and christened it the "cradle of civilization." Most books on Western art history began with the study of ancient Egyptian art, after pre-historic art (Gardener, 1990; Fichner-Rathus, 2001). This does not make Egypt a part of Europe, much less cut off its "Africanness" culturally and geographically. There is no doubt that ancient Egyptian art shares affinity with Western art through the massive structures, pyramids, writing symbols: hieroglyphics, and other innovations. These are also prominent in ancient Mesopotamian and Greco-Roman art and architecture. These indicators of development are not exclusive to Egypt, Mesopotamia or Europe; other earliest civilizations in other parts of the world also have their share in human development. This does not mean that the cultural affinity between ancient Egypt and black Africa has to be generalized since Egypt (Africa) is the origin of human civilization. Based on this distinctiveness, Ademuleya (2005, 3) states that Egypt (as a geographical and cultural expression) cannot be part of Africa without some kind of historical and cultural link with its neighbors, in spite of differences in color and language.

European prejudice is not only perceived in African art scholarship but also extended to African historiography. Davidson (1972, 29) submits that Western scholarship deliberately excluded Egypt from Africa because "the Egyptian records already provide a host of dates that are useful to early African history." This intellectual error is discountenanced by William Pickens (1884–1954), a US educator. His observation is that the white story teller will not do justice to the humanity of black race, simply because he cannot. The publishers of history were white and they have controlled the writings of the history of Africa for so long; hence, they cannot be fair. In this connection, Thomas Hodgkin asserts that

> Most of the available material on African affairs is presented from a European standpoint—either by imperial historians (who are interested in the record of European penetration into Africa), or by colonial administrators (who are interested in the pattern of institutions imposed by European governments upon African society), or by the anthropologists (who are often though not always, mainly interested in the forms of social organisations surviving in the simplest African communities, considered in isolation from the political development in the world around them). (qtd. in Walker, 2008, 15)

The above is, perhaps, the reason why Western intellectuals falter; thus, early European writers were nobody but puns in the socio-political chess game of the time, as they were concerned with fulfilling an agenda that was centred on Europe. This intellectual rascality is denounced by Malcolm X's in his historic speech, *By Any Means Necessary* (Conner, 1996, 2). He links the Eurocentric attitudes of the West toward Africans, African Americans, and diaspora Africans to "a racist ideology of the slave-owners society." It included a devious scheme that "black Africans really had no history, at least no history worth studying or discussing" and that "black Africa did not participate in the major civilization that occurred in other parts of the world." Such thinking, in the words of Thomas Hodgkin, is "a theory that lacks historical foundation" (qtd. in Walker, 2008, 10).

Does it mean that black Africans made no contributions to the development of human civilization or they were uncivilized until the whites introduced civilization from the outside? It is either ignorance or deliberate racism that makes European scholars unable to accept the fact that good things can (did) come out of Africa's "Nazareth" that made European scholars to erase or downplay the possibility of the ancient Egyptians having a common link to the rest of Africa. Was it intentional malice or in error that Newman (1974, 5) avers that "to the African, there is no art; what they fashion and express is just a part of their lives, whether it is fine art or craft"? Does that mean the blacks were not capable of fashioning great works of art or displaying mastery in naturalistic/realistic expressions, and even more significantly, were they incapable or appreciating art before they were alerted to such aesthetic capacity by Europeans? It is appropriate to assert here that in spite of centuries of Greco-Roman art and its legacy of "scientific naturalism," it took just a mask or collection of masks displayed at the ethnographic section of Palaise du Trucadero in Paris to revolutionize Western artistic expression? (Fajuyigbe, 2011b).

The statement by Read (1989, 14) that "African art has little to do with the illusions of the objective reality but its formal and emotional content were the result of intuition rather than intellect" is an insult on the purposeful and impeccable creative skills and intelligence of the blacks. Herbert Read assumes erroneously that the African artist is not intelligent. In spite of this derogatory analysis, Western avant-garde artists such as Pablo Picasso, Georges Braque, Henry Matisse, Max Jacob, Juan Gris, and the rest of the cubist painters were inspired, stylistically, by African art forms in their search for new ways of expression. As pointed out by Fajuyigbe (2011b), this historic incidence simultaneously signalled the beginning of modern art in Europe and the end of an era: the abandoning of representational art. The statements of the Western art intellectuals noted above were obviously underlined by the European "racist ideology."

The racist ideology is hinged on the need to justify Western invasion, subjugation, partition and occupation of the African continent; and today it is sustained through technological, political, social, and economic dominance. Thomas Hodgkin is more emphatic. He points out, "the West pretends to be good to Africans by bringing them civilization and Christianity . . . and they wanted Africans to believe they had no worthwhile history *or visual art culture* as a means of demoralising them so as to keep them enslaved" (Conner, 1996, 14; emphasis added). The black Africans did indeed have a fascinating history; they played a significant role in the earliest development of civilization on this planet. A critical examination of development in various fields of human knowledge like architecture, art, medicine, music, medicine, engineering, and agriculture among others attests to this fact. Both Conner (1996) and Walker's (2008) opinions that black Africa is not accorded any credit in the development of human civilization despite its long list of great empires/kingdom, is not an indication of lack of importance in world history but a function of Western, Eurocentric educational background. To borrow from Bewaji (2003, 41), it might also be due to the "unidimensionality and partiality of focus of Western intellectuals" in the study of African history and visual culture.

Ancient Egypt occupies the present-day southern Egypt and northern Sudan, sometimes called the Lower and Upper Egypt respectively. The land lies on the bank of the great Nile River, which flows north from its source in Lake Victoria, Uganda to the Mediterranean. The Nile was a force to reckon with. The seasonal overflow of its bank brought back fertility and prosperity to the people. Robins (2005) observes that the constant patterns of nature, the annual flooding, the cycle of the season, and the advancement of the sun that brought day and night were all considered as the gifts of the gods to the people of Egypt. Ruffle (1977, 12) points out that "the Nile is the basis of Egypt's wealth" and as affirmed by Fichner-Rathus (2001, 294), "the Nile is an indispensable part of Egyptian life" and without the river, there could have been no life. As a country, her history was described by the art historian, Lois Fichner-Rathus as that which had "the longest unified history of any civilization in the ancient Mediterranean, extending with few interruptions from about 3000 BC through the fourth century AD" (295).

There are ethnographical and ethnological evidences that ancient Egyptians have features that were of Negroid stock, similar to the Nubians and black race in general. History had it that ancient Nubian kingdom was ruled by Egypt for some 1,800 years, but in the eighth century BC the Nubians achieved independence and subjugated Egypt. Specifically, Leuzinger (1976, 7) notes that "as early as the first millennium BC, Cush (Nubia) was a powerful kingdom, and had even ruled Egypt as the twenty-fifth dynasty (751–656 BC)." The Nubians maintained some degree of independence for more than 2,000 years until the Arab conquest in the fourteenth century (Robins, 2005), which implies that the Nubians actually ruled Egypt not only when Egyptian civilization was in decline, but also during the pre-dynastic era. In other words, Egypt had at one time or the other produced black pharaohs, which points to the fact that ancient Egypt was first and foremost an African civilization, culturally and geographically.

The theory of diffusion explored by Adrian Gerbrands is crucial to understanding the place of Egypt in African art and cultures. The theory is derived from Frans Olbrechts' "Stylistic Analysis" (Crowley, 1976, 43) and is based on the principle of stylistic criteria which posits that contact between cultures impact on the form, style, content and meaning of art object. It is used "to prove contact between cultures, demonstrate the diffusion elements and determine the cultural background/origin of museum collections" (Gerbrands, 1990, 19).

People often migrate or relocate to an environment with stable polity and vibrant economy. The postulations of the diffusion theorists, with respect to Egypt, might have been affirmed by the natural environment around the Nile. The Nile river has a magnetic touch that attracted people of all races, color, and languages to the richness of its habitat. Prior to this migration, people had lived along the Nile stretch and began to settle down into village structure. Kingdoms along the Egyptian Nile merged until there were only two: Upper Egypt and Lower Egypt, one in the Nile delta, the other in the valley. In about 3100 BC the two kingdoms were united by Narmer, king of Upper Egypt; hence, it marked the beginning of the earliest dynasty of ancient Egypt (Fichner-Rathus, 2001). As asserted by Ademuleya (2005, 4), religion was the key concept used to cement the unification of the two kingdoms, and art was its tool of commemorating this union.

In view of this, it is clear that Egypt belong to black Africa, geographically and culturally. There may have been some relationships, historically, with the Mediterranean civilizations due to centuries of conquests and occupation by the Greeks, the Romans, and the Arabs respectively; nevertheless, Egypt's affinity, then and now, lies more with Africa than with the Arab world. The following shared values and similarities between the visual culture of ancient Egypt and Africa attest to this fact.

SIMILARITIES IN ANCIENT EGYPTIAN AND BLACK AFRICAN ART AND CULTURE

Ancient Egyptians and black Africans produced art objects with the aim of living peaceably within the natural and spiritual habitats. The similarities are apparent in their belief systems and visual arts. The belief systems include religious pluralism (polytheism), divine kingship, ancestral worship, deification of heroes, life after death, and organized communities; while their visual arts are similar in terms of multidimensionality of intention, purpose, utility (context), materials and symbolism. The art objects, including the embedded motifs, patterns and symbols are produced primarily to project and sustained the aforementioned values.

Belief systems in ancient Egypt and black Africa are all-encompassing, because they affect human existence in all its ramifications. The Egyptians and Africans believe in cosmic powers as guardians of all; hence, their religious activities and practices help in establishing cordial relationship between the gods (deities), the dead (ancestors) and the living (humans). The deities are regarded as agents of the Supreme Being and carriers of supernatural powers. The need for a representation of these deities informs the varieties of sculptures, paintings, architecture and decorative arts created and used by the ancient Egyptian and Africans in connection with religion and human activities generally. Specifically, the ancient Egyptians venerate a number of deities, which importance revolves around the sun and the Nile. The belief in the transitory nature of life and human existence might have been the reason why ancient Egyptians accorded so much importance to the Nile. As opined by Fichner-Rathus (2001, 295) the Egyptians believed that the rising and setting of the sun is an evidence of the endlessness of life. Similarly, in many African philosophical traditions, it is often theorized that living continues in the hereafter.

The concept of life after death is reinforced through the use of art forms. Ancient Egyptians were concerned about their final resting place; so, elaborate preparations were made in anticipation of the "afterlife." Personal materials like cloths, jewelry, food, and other essentials that would make living comfortable in the afterlife are buried with the dead. In the case of their rulers, slaves were buried with them for continued service in the underworld. The ancient Egyptians preserved their dead bodies by drying them and, placing them within a protective covering. Ruffle (1977) points out that burial ritual were of great concern to the people; therefore, the pyramids were conceived to protect the corpse and its materials. The belief in "life after death" also permeates the conception, creation, and use of art objects in African traditional life and thoughts. Africans make use of ancestral figures/objects in various materials in the worship of ancestors (Brain 1980, Sieber and Walker 1988).

Polytheism is the belief in and worship of several deities (gods/goddesses); though Idowu (1991, 140) notes that the concept refers specifically to "an element in the structure of religion . . . or pantheons of the divinities." Nonetheless, both ancient Egyptians and indigenous Africans believed that nearly everything. including the elements and nature, has its own life force which can be tapped for the good of man. Hence, nature and things generally are venerated, to curry their favours. Robin (2005) records that the proclamation of Aton (sun) as the only god of Egypt by Pharaoh Amenhotep IV (Akhenaton) was denounced by the people after the death of Akhenaton, because the belief system of Egypt naturally favors the worship of many gods. Similarly, in traditional Africa, belief in many divinities, spirits and ancestors still persist as the pathway to the Supreme Being. It is necessary to point out here that despite the overwhelming effects of the triumvirate of colonialism, Christianity and Islam in Africa, people still seek the help of these divinities in times of problems.

The institution of divine kingship, its elevated status and the honour bestows on it was of great significance to the Egyptians and Africans. In Africa, kings and ordinary people who had performed heroic deeds are deified as special beings. The Egyptians also believed that the Pharaoh is not an ordinary being, but the son of the gods and direct descendant of the sun (Robins 2005). Referring to the god-like personality of Pharaoh, Flemming (1979, 13) is emphatic noting that "the pharaoh ruled with absolute authority and was responsible only to his gods and ancestors" because he was considered more than human. In black Africa, the king is a divine person. For instance, among the Yoruba (West Africa), the kings are revered as "Igbakeji Orisa" (the second-in-command of the gods); invested with the highest authority in the land. In this connection, Fajuyigbe (2003, 3) points out, in hierarchical order, that the African king is perceived "as the second-in-command of the Supreme Being, the highest representative of the gods (deities), the unequivocal voice of the ancestors and the arch-priest of his people and of all religions in his domain."

In African and Egyptian mythologies, the king represented the soul and vitality of the nation, and gold is used to reinforce this concept.

All forms of art were meant for the services of the pharaoh, the state, and the religion. In African society, elaborate art works are also employed to confer power and prerogative on the kingship. The roles and ranks of the myriads of chiefs, title-holders, priests, court officials, and attendants, are also defined by art pieces. The god-like handling and presentation of kings in both African and Egyptian arts and thoughts are one of the supreme products and examples of the general human tendency to immortalize man's accomplishments (Fajuyigbe, 2003).

Context is very important in the creation and use of art objects in ancient Egyptian and black African civilizations. The form of any given artwork indicates the ideas current in time and place of production. Specific art forms, with symbolic motifs patterns and coded messages are created by the ancients to represent the office and ethereal qualities of the gods/deities. The primary intention of the ancient Egyptian and African artists was aimed at creating images or things to represent the essence of a person or object for eternal relevance. In this connection, the art historian Erwin Panofsky's statement (Fichner-Rathus, 2001, 295) is germane: "the artist's intention in ancient Egypt was directed not towards the variable, but toward the constant, not toward the symbolization of this vital present, but towards the realization of a timeless eternity." Abiodun (1990, 3) echoes Panofsky's submission and asserts that "the traditional African (Yoruba) artist, blessed with esoteric knowledge of things around him is able to see and represent spiritual truths, using symbols to convey ideas that are pregnant with meaning."

The African artist encodes meaning in his work, and it takes a perceptive mind to decode the meaning for proper appreciation of the artist's attention. Therefore, an analysis of the art traditions of Egypt and Africa calls for a sound knowledge of the people's belief system, which reinforces the art.

In view of the shared values highlighted above, it is evident that religion and strong cultural values are the basis for visual expressions in ancient Egypt and traditional Africa. The obvious similarities are noted in form, content, style, and materials used in their arts. These art forms, which depict both history and mythology, are intricately linked with the belief system of the people; while the materials used include ivory, stone, wood, gold, bronze, metals, and clay. The emphasis of Egyptian art and architecture is on religion, death, and continuity, while traditional African art also focuses on religion, ancestral worship, and spirit beings. The two art traditions are in essence the representation of the essence of a person or object. In this way, one can see continuity and permanence.

The most striking examples of ancient Egyptian architecture were the pyramids, *mastabas*, and temples built in honor of the gods. The pyramid is an Egyptian tomb and it has remained the biggest and most famous in recorded history. The largest and most renowned of the pyramids was built by King Khafre at Giza.

Today, it is one of the Seven Wonders of the World and the only survivor. Thomas Hodgkin observes that these feats are not exclusive to Egypt, but are found in other great cultures like the Nubian kingdom of southern Egypt and northern Sudan, Ethiopia, and Southern Africa. In Ethiopia there are monuments of great antiquity in Axum, Roha, and Lalibela, while Southern Africa could boast of at least 600 stones built ruins in the regions of Mozambique, Zimbabwe, and South Africa (Walker, 2008). In addition, Conner (1996, 4–5) mentions Kumbi Saleh, Gao, Jenne, and Timbuktu as some of the great cities with outstanding architectural edifices ever to emerge from black Africa.

The sculptures of ancient Egypt and Africa included rock engraving, stone carving, wood carving, metal casting, and ivory carving in two and three dimensions. Both art traditions use masks, statues, statuettes, figures, and headdresses in rituals and ceremonies to validate the connectedness of art, myths, faith, life and human existence. Egyptian sculptures, like those of black Africa, are conceptual and representational. The forms show similarities in anatomy, structure (proportion); hierarchy and combine frontal and profile views of the same figure, and are arranged orderly to indicate importance. Thus, a pharaoh is shown taller than his nobles, wives, or courtiers (plate 5). This hierarchical representation also features prominently in African art.

Flemming's (1980, 4) opinion that "art begins in myth and magic, in imagery and image making, in tombs and temples" supports sameness in two dimensional art forms of ancient Egyptian and African arts. The two dimensional arts, like drawings and murals (or wall paintings), were specifically intended to create an aura of spirituality, to punctuate the immanent presence of the gods, and to facilitate communion between the deities and their adherents or worshippers. Statues of gods and kings were housed within the temple areas. In African culture, sculptures (and sometimes masks), irrespective of the material, are made in honor of the gods, souls of the departed and for the glorification of kings. Indeed, they are indispensable to festivals and ceremonies that sustain the cultural fabrics of the people.

A lot of the art objects in ancient Egypt and black Africa possess certain stiffness, with figures poised upright and rigid in a most regal fashion.

In Egyptian art, proportions were derived based on mathematical accuracy, purposely used to reinforce the godliness of the ruling caste. Figures are either represented in profile or frontally in hierarchy of importance and according to personality of the user. Thus, the pharaohs, and their counterparts in Black Africa are depicted bigger or larger than life, while others are arranged accordingly. Proportion in African art was also based on the concept of the head *ori* as the seat of wisdom and in this connection, Fajuyigbe

(2011a, 257) avers that "*ori* is the very essence of being and the personality of the soul." Best and precious materials are used for the royalty while ephemeral materials are used for the peasants. Another trait common to both art traditions was the symbolic representation of the gods, the kings and nobles (chiefs). Leuzinger (1976) attests that animals such as lion and elephant are used to depict the kings while birds are used for the chiefs. The intention of this is to allow for easy identification in the hierarchical traditional structures. As containers and visual records of history and culture of the people, the arts of Black Africa were aimed at the unification of both physical and spiritual realms, towards the making of the total man; the Egyptian art however emphasised the need for continuity in life and the hereafter.

EUROCENTRIC ATTITUDES TOWARD MODERN AND CONTEMPORARY AFRICAN ART

Despite the multidisciplinary and interdisciplinary approaches employed in the study and appreciation of African art, trends in African art scholarship still show some traits of ethnocentrism, racism, and prejudice. The perception and appreciation of modern and contemporary African arts outside the continent are not favourable. This bias is more pronounced in Western art discourses, curatorial services, art exhibitions, and marketing, patronage, and promotion of contemporary African art/artists.

An example of the uncomplimentary, noxious and Eurocentric comments on contemporary African art is Brian Sewell's (2005) review, "Out of Africa." He simply denounced the "contemporaneity" of modern African art and summarised it as "vain scramble by African artists to be seen as part of a Western world," because that seems a cheap gateway to prominence and prosperity. He was more emphatic here:

> but my first impression of the exhibition remained after a second and third perambulation—that not much of it qualifies as art in any contemporary European sense, and that what little does is so European in its sad inadequacy that it hardly qualifies as African. This wretched assembly of post tribal artefacts, exhausted materials re-used, and what would easily pass for the apprentice rubbish of the European art school, has about it the air of a state-run trade fair. . . . The contemporary art in this exhibition is so little rooted in any native tradition; it adopts western forms, techniques and devices because it has no models of its own and western models are so readily available; and it is exhibited in the West because it would be politically incorrect not to play with it the silly Western game of recognising as art everything that is made by man, no matter where. As in the West, success and exposure are not controlled by quality; there, as here, it is the patchy business of being noticed by a curator able to exercise patronage . . . in following the West they mimic it in witless

parody, or ape in modern materials and terms what little they know of a genuine African past. (*Evening Standard*, February 18, 2005)

The above diatribe is no doubt very harmful to the future of contemporary African art. Thus, Ogbechie (2005), in response to Brian Sewell and his type, queries such misdirected art scholarship. He observes that many Western curators of contemporary African art have mistaken their role to the "shaping of a lopsided narrative of contemporary cultural practices related to Africa. More so, they often showcase artists who meet very narrowly defined Western criteria of what contemporary African art should look like." How can the West dictate the tune, when it is the so-called "primitivism" of "African art" that sets the stage for modern European art? Odiboh (2009) in agreement with Ogbechie derides western narrative of contemporary art practice in Africa which often is based on an irrational perception that for art to be legitimate, it must conform to Western prescriptions.

The fact is the contemporary African artist does not have to struggle to be noticed, because like his Western counterparts, he has the right to express his intellect using the best visual apparatus and materials that appeal to his aesthetic sensibility. Why are contemporary African and diaspora African artists deprived of adequate attention from Western art intellectuals. Perhaps, it is because the contemporary African artists dare to be different by refusing to fit into the stylistic and ideological molds designed by Western curators and art critics. They dare to, through their art, undo the injustice of the past, to correct the intellectual slip in Western art discourses of African art. In this connection, parochial remarks from some irritable Western critics/curators may be understood.

As pointed out by Steiner (2006) (Odiboh, 2009, 455), contemporary African art is denied relevance in Western art spaces because it often "challenges existing myths of authenticity and otherness that Western commissioners so zealously protect." Perhaps, the "authenticity" expected from contemporary African art is not obvious since it does not fit into the formal configuration of classical African art; neither does it embrace the stylistic modes of Western art. The "disinterest" in contemporary African art may be due to what Ogbechie (2005) describes as "initial preoccupation with the so-called classical African art . . . and Western scholars' assumption that the belief system that inspired the best of African creativity are no longer influential due to the negative impact of colonialism, Western education, urbanization and mass conversion to Islam and Christianity." Contemporary African artists however create works of art straight from their mind, just like their creative ancestors. This is the "Africanity" in contemporary African art.

Most viable art markets exist outside Africa and are domiciled in Europe and the Americas. It is a fact that in contemporary African art, the creation of art cannot be detached from the desire for profit; what Kasfir (1999, 65) describes as "a deeply rooted postcolonial economic dependency." Therefore many artists produce works that fit into the creative moulds designed and financed by Western art dealers/connoisseurs, galleries, and art museums. If such work is not "primitive" or does not align with the ancient forms and configuration of art in traditional Africa, then it is not African. If the work does not embrace modernist or postmodernist tendencies in Western art, then, it is not contemporary or valuable by international standard. Whose standard and who controlled the art market? No doubt, some contemporary artists tend to "Africanize" or "Europeanize" their works for financial gains or contemporary relevance. Perhaps, Kasfir's (1999, 65) assertion that "frequent lack of indigenous art market and the resultant constant flow of 'cultural capital' to foreign patrons," may be responsible for western curators/art dealers' power to controlling and shaping African art discourses. How true is the saying then that "he who pays the piper dictates the tune"?

Do the Western patrons pay the same value for contemporary African art, as modern and contemporary Western art? No! Albert la Vergne, an African American artist noted that works of contemporary African artists attract a different kind of value (usually less) when compared to the price offered African American artists or European artists for their works. This is often reflected in the art exhibition, art auction, pricing, and marketing (la Vergne, 2013). Similarity to ancient African art or modern European art is what actually determines the value of contemporary African art in western art spaces. In this regard, Odiboh (2009, 455) notes that only "authentic" African arts are showcased for sale. By "authentic" he means contemporary arts in Africa must share the same stylistic and ideological nomenclatures with precolonial African art objects erroneously tagged "primitive art."

CONCLUSION

Ancient Egyptian art and culture are a phenomenon that has always dazzled scholars, writers, explorers, and tourists for thousands of years. This can be adduced to the practice of documenting virtually everything that happened in its history. The empire structures, the massive pyramids, awesome temples, the scientific innovations, artistic/cultural development, and cross-cultural influences are some of the legacies of ancient Egypt. The awesomeness and multiculturalism of ancient Egypt, no doubt, may be misleading to imperceptive mind, and they may conclude hastily that Egypt is not part of the cultural Africa. However, ancient Egyptian art and culture before contact with the West through trade and successive conquests by the Greeks, Romans, and Arabs were, by and large, part of the cultural Africa because it has a lot in common with the rest of Africa. The shared values as enumerated previously emphasize this fact.

Modern Egypt (and the rest of the North African nations may claim) to be distinct from the rest of Africa for obvious reason—the need for religious, political, historical, economic, and scientific relevance in a changing world. Nevertheless, the study has shown that black Africa and ancient Egypt share some artistic and cultural similarities. Hence, ancient Egypt is indigenous to Africa, culturally and geographically. This study showed the interdependence of religion, death, and continuity, the ancestors and spirit beings in the two cultures. Specifically, their visual art traditions reflect the continuity and permanence of humanity and their dependence on the supernatural.

In addition, it is observed that Eurocentric attitudes still persist toward the creative and cultural productions of Africa, particularly contemporary African art, despite the efforts of Africanist art historians who have committed so much intellectual energy and discourse to addressing the issue. Western art audience, influenced by noxious reviews by some western curators and scholars, is to an extent sceptical about the authenticity, creativity, and uniqueness of contemporary African art. Even Western exhibition spaces are open to few contemporary African artists who have, through their arts, severed the chain of racism and neocolonialism.

The study also revealed that some contemporary African artists "struggle" to fit into the molds designed by some Western curators for financial gains and social relevance in Western art spaces. Hence, they tend to "Africanize" or "Europeanize" their works to attract prospective buyers. This practice has impacted gravely on contemporary African art.

The world has become a global village; nevertheless, the cultural traits and values that distinguish one culture from the others should be respected. Likewise, race and place should not be the basis of concealing undeniable facts about the worth of other peoples (nations) just because they are perceived differently. The concepts of multiculturalism and globalisation should not blur cultural affinity or erase the shared values among humans, but be strengthened accordingly.

The black African, irrespective of his location, has been the object rather than the subject of documentation. Contemporary African creative and cultural productions should embrace a multidimensionality and multiculturalism that will ensure contemporary relevance, and yet sustain our Africaness. The essence of traditional or modern/contemporary African art is its Africanity. Hence, Abiodun (2001, 33) counsels that "we must try to understand an art work in its cultural depth, as the expression of the local thoughts or belief system, lest we unwittingly remove the 'African' in African art." There is therefore the need to study Africanity of ancient Egyptian art within the scope of African art scholarship, both geographically and culturally. The inclusion of modern Egypt (despite its claim to Arabic ancestry) will definitely signal a better understanding of contemporary arts and artists in northern Africa.

Finally, scholars must look beyond the Western parameters of judging excellence in the arts, if we are to understand the distinctive nature of cultures across the globe. In agreement with Odiboh (2009), there is the need for African intellectuals to devise an empirical approach to "Africanizing" African art history. It is hoped that the rigorous intellectualisation of African art scholarship and its application in African educational establishments and art schools across the continent will advance the fortune of contemporary African art.

BIBLIOGRAPHY

Abiodun, Rowland (2001). "African Aesthetics," *Journal of Aesthetic Education,* 35(4): 15–23.
———. 1990. "The Future of African Art Studies: An African Perspective," in *African Art Studies: The States of the Discipline.* Washington, DC: National Museum of African Art, Smithsonian Institution University Press. 30–63.
Ademuleya, Babasehinde A. (2005). "Egypt and the Rest of the African People: The Relatedness of Belief System and Art Forms." Paper presented at the Institute of Cultural Studies, Obafemi Awolowo University, Ile-Ife, Nigeria, August 18, 2005.
Adepegba, Cornelius O. (2000). "The 'Otherness' Syndrome and the Study of African Visual Art," in *Rethinking African Arts and Culture,* Ed. Layiwola, Dele. Cape Town: Centre for Advanced Studies of African Society (CASAS). 1–9.
Balogun, Ola (1979). "Form and Expression in African Art," in *Introduction to African Culture: General Aspects.* Paris: United Nations Educational, Scientific, and Cultural Organization (UNESCO). 33–81.
Bewaji, J. A. I. (2003). *Beauty and Culture—Perspectives in Black Aesthetics.* Ibadan, Nigeria: Hope Publications.
———. (2013). *Black Aesthetics.* Trenton, NJ: Africa World Press.
Brain, Roberts (1980). *Art and Society in Africa.* London: Longman Group Limited
Chukwuokolo, Chidozie (2009). "Afrocentrism or Eurocentrism: The Dilemma of African Development," *OGIRISI: a New Journal of African Studies,* 6: 24–39. www.ajol.info/index.php/og/article/view/52333/40958.
Conner, Cliff (1996). *Afrocentrism vs. Eurocentrism in Ancient History.* https://archive.org/details/AfrocentrismVs.EurocentrismInAncientHistory.
Crowley, Daniel (1976). "Stylistic Analysis of African Art: A Reassessment of Olbrechts"Belgian Method,'" *African Arts,* 9(2): 43–49. http//www.jstor/stable/3335017.
Davidson, Basil (1972). *Africa: History of a Continent.* London: George Weidenfeld & Nicholson.
Fajuyigbe, Michael O. (2011a). "Ori in African Art and Philosophy: A Review of African Aesthetics and Adornment," *IFE: Journal of the Institute of Cultural Studies.* 253274. Ile-Ife: Institute of Cultural Studies, Obafemi Awolowo University.
_____. (2011b). "Emergence of Art Movements in Modern Art of the 20th Century: Lessons for Nigerian Art and Artists. *Nigerian Art Reflections: Journal of the Society of Nigerian Artists,* Oyo State Chapter, 9, 35–50. Ibadan: SNA Publications & RECACD Publishers.
_____. (2003). "African Royal Court Art: An Appraisal", *Journal of Arts and Ideas,* Ile-Ife: Department of Fine Arts, Obafemi Awolowo University.
Fichner-Rathus, Lois (2001). *Understanding Art.* USA: Wadsworth/Thomas learning
Flemming, William. (1980). *Arts and Ideas.* New York: Holt, Rinehart and Winston.
Gardner, Louise (1986). *Gardner's Art Through the Ages,* edited by Horst de la Croix and Richard G. Tansey. USA: Harcourt Brace Jovanovich Publishers.
Gerbrands, Adrian (1990). "The History of African Art Studies," in *African Art Studies: States of the Discipline.* 11–28. Washington, DC: National Museum of African Art, Smithsonian Institution.

Hackett, Rosalind I. J. (1999). *Art and Religion in Africa*. London: Cassell, Wellington House.

Idowu, Bolaji, E. (1991). *African Traditional Religion: A Definition*. Ibadan: Fountain Publications.

Kasfer, Sidney L. (1999). *Contemporary African Art*. London: Thames and Hudson Ltd.

Lawal, Babatunde (1996). *The Gelede Spectacle: Art, Gender and Social Harmony in an African Culture.* Seattle and London: University of Washington Press.

Lazarri, Margaret, and Schlesier, Dona (2008). *Exploring Art: A Global Thematic Approach.* Belmont, CA: Thomson and Wadsworth.

Leuzinger, Elsy (1976). *The Art of Black Africa*. London: Cassell & Collier Macmillan Publishers.

Microsoft Encarta (2006). *African Art and Culture*.

Newman, Thelma R. (1974). *Contemporary African Arts and Crafts*. London: George Allen and Unwin.

Odiboh, Freeborn, O. (2009). "Africanism a Modern African Art History Curriculum from the Perspectives of an Insider," *African Research Reviews*, 3(1): 451–407.

Ogbechie, Sylvester (2005). "POV: Contemporary African Art in Western Spaces," *H-NET List for African Expressive Culture*, March 8. http://h-net.msu.edu/cgi-bin/logbrowse@H-AfrArts.

Read, Herbert (1989). *The Book of Art*. New York: Grolier Incorporated.

Robins, G. (2005). *Egyptian Art and Architecture*. Redmond, WA: *Microsoft Encarta.*

Ruffle, John (1977). *The Egyptians: An Introduction to Egyptian Archaeology*. New York: Cornwell.

Sewell, Brian (2005). "Out of Africa." https://lists.h-net.org/cgi-bin/logbrowse.pl?trx=vx&list=H-AfrArts&month=0503&week=b&msg=2ONEudvVgtTxzoFQMLfaOg&user=&pw.

Sieber, Roy, and Walker, Roselyn A. (1988). *African Art in the Cycle of Life*. Washington, DC: National Museum of African Art, Smithsonian Institution.

Trowell, Margaret (1970). *Classical African Sculpture*. New York: Praeger Publishers.

Vansina, Jan (1984). *Art History in Africa: An Introduction to Method*. London: Longman Group.

Visona, Monica B., Poynor, Robin, Cole, Herbert M., and Harris, Michael D. (2001). *A History of Art in Africa*. New York: Harry N. Abrams, Inc., Publishers.

Walker, Robert (2008). "When We Ruled," *New African,* June 2008, issue 474. London: IC Publications. Exactedition.com/read/new-african/june-2008.

Willett, Frank (2003). *African Art: New Edition*. New York: Thames and Hudson World of Art. Interview. Albert La Vergne: 60 years, African American artist and Fulbright scholar at the department of Fine and Applied Arts, Obafemi Awolowo University, Ile-Ife. May 15, 2013.

Chapter Six

Aesthetics of Indigenous Faith Tourism

Elo Ibagere and Bifatife Olufemi Adeseye

Tourism has fast become one of the relevant areas in the discussion of national development. The attention generated by tourism is rooted in the culture, artefacts and unique places in a particular country. It is the uniqueness of such cultural practices and places that imbues them with tourism potentials, as bearers of intrinsic and endogenous aesthetic values.

The most significant elements of tourism are places, as well as events, which are mostly of historical or archaeological significance. These are often valued as bearers of notions of aesthetic ideas of communities, epochs and civilizations, given the manner in which they document and codify the intellectual cultures of such communities in the form of material and nonmaterial representations. In the context of Nigeria and Africa, it is however sad to note that many of these festivals and places of cultural significance have been rendered irrelevant as a result of Westernization, which has supplanted many practices having religious or cultural significance. In many instances, there has been deliberate destruction of the historical and cultural elements of the traditions of many African societies. Thus, despite many years of independence, the effects of sociocultural and religious colonialization of Nigeria and Africa continue to reverberate all over the cultural fabric of virtually every African traditional society.

Many cultural traditions, events and practices that possess tourism potentials given their rich aesthetics have become denigrated and relegated to a state of insignificance. Such practices have continued to be regarded only in frivolous terms. This is what Bewaji has aptly described as epistemicide; it is a condition in which the intellectual traditions of colonized peoples are deliberately destroyed, denied or subjugated, to the point of non-existence (Bewaji, 2012). Such, for example, is the state of the Igue festival in Benin City (Edo State), during which the traditional ruler (the Oba) is not expected to receive visitors. During the festival, the Oba goes into spiritual retreat and prays for progress in the kingdom in the coming year. He was, thus, not expected to receive visitors in order to be in a perfect state needed to enable him convey the problems of the kingdom to the ancestors for solution.

It was the refusal of the British emissary to respect this traditional convention that led to the invasion of the Benin kingdom in 1897, culminating in the banishment of the then Oba (Ovonramwen) to Calabar. Though the festival continues to hold annually, it does not attract enough tourists despite its historical and cultural significance, simply because the values which imbue the festival with authenticity and meaning have been negated by the powers of colonization. Such an event should be of academic interest to scholars of Benin and British history, who should be guests of the city during the festival, usually celebrated in December.

The dwindling significance of places and events having tourism potentials can be noted in indigenous faiths, with the consequences for the indigenous identity strictures of the domestic populations. The African continent is replete with different religious beliefs, which give meaning to the lives of the peoples of the various communities in which these religions are practiced. The way the people practice these different religions has significant tourism potentials that can be exploited for national benefit, not just as curiosities but as the avenues for the presentation of the values of the communities. Unfortunately, because even the indigenous peoples whose ways of appreciating themselves and their practices have been denigrated have abandoned these beliefs and practices, this is an area of the Nigerian indigenous religious aesthetics that has not really attracted tourism, compared to other tourist attractions such as ecological sites, monuments and (now) carnivals, which are merely for entertainment purposes. Except for the instances of Osun Oshogbo and a few others, which were brought into global consciousness because of the agency of the curators of the grove, there is very little in the indigenous religious values and practices which attract the kinds of attention which is devoted to the invading religious traditions of Christianity and Islam, which often receive state funding for believers to observe religious tourism in Israel and Saudi Arabia.

It is in the light of the above scenario that this chapter dwells on the need first, to underscore the neglect of the material and immaterial cultures of African peoples as inscribed in their religious traditions, and then emphasize the need to enhance indigenous faith tourism in Nigeria as one of the areas of national development, which has the potential to be an important foreign exchange earner and as a way of understanding and propagating the values of Nigerian communities. In pursuance of this quest, the paper first presents a brief concept of tourism, then it discusses faith tourism as an integral part in the appreciation of the aesthetics of communities where these traditions are embraced. The role of the mass media and the challenges facing the media are equally focused upon. The chapter concludes by addressing the challenges which epistemicide has foisted on indigenous cultures and how to consciously transcend same, before finally recommending ways for better media representation of these ideas and enriching their own performance in this regard.

TOURISM

Tourism relates to movement of a person or group of people to a particular place of interest. The Northern Arizona University Parks and Management regards tourism as a collection of activities, services, and industries that deliver a travel experience including transportation, accommodation, eating, and drinking establishments, retail shops, entertainment business, activity facilities, and other hospitality services provided for individuals or groups traveling away from home (Banakan, 2015).

This definition seems to cover the entire gamut of tourism. Specifically, however, the World Tourism Organization (WTO) conceives of a tourist as,

> any person residing within a country irrespective of nationality, traveling to a place within his country other than his usual place of residence for a period of not less than 24 hours or one night for a purpose other than the exercise of a remunerated activity in the place visited. The motives for such travel may be leisure (recreation, holidays, health, studies, religion, sports) business, family, mission, meeting. (1981, 89)

Obviously, WTO sees tourism in terms of the period one who goes on tourism has to stay at the place visited. It also emphasizes that the place must not be the place the person resides. According to Gumel, "the basic feature of tourism is leisure activity, which includes among other things, merry making, festivals, cultural visitations and exchange, traveling for commerce and health" (1988, 6).

These concepts have common grounds relating to the purpose of such travels. But the period a tourist may stay at the tourist site is irrelevant. A tourist may conclude his tour in less than twenty-four hours, depending on interest. However, there should be a maximum period. This is six months, because to stay beyond six months may make such a tourist a resident.

Flowing from the foregoing, tourism can thus be defined as travelling to places of interest for leisure, business, research, and other purposes for a period not exceeding six months. The motives for such travels may be intellectual enrichment, cultural understanding, aesthetic participation in the traditions of the places visited as well as a means of comprehending the identities of the cultures visited. Ashiegbu and Achinike (2014, 130) have given different classifications of tourism. They opine that tourism can be classified based on geography or on objective. Based on geography, they have identified domestic, regional and international tourism. Under objective, which they refer to as purpose, they mention and discuss five types. These are cultural tourism, nature tourism, sport tourism, business/conference tourism and religious tourism (Okpoko, 2008, 14–19).

Nigeria, like other African countries, has a lot of tourism potentials, which are still undeveloped. Gumel (1988, 6) claims that religious tourism activities were, until colonial period almost an exclusive African tradition. Tourist sites abound in Nigeria. So too are events, because of the many ethnic groups that make up the country with each having its own festivals. These sites and events could be exploited for national benefit. This becomes crucial as the country's economy continues to dwindle, due to its dependence on oil. With the global fall in the price of crude oil, the country now needs other alternatives for its foreign exchange and tourism could be one of such alternatives.

Indeed, one of the areas that potentials have not been fully explored is indigenous faith tourism, otherwise referred to as religious tourism. It is one of the categories of tourism that can be exploited for national development, not just as a means of earning tourism income, but more fundamentally in preserving, propagating and assisting future generations to appreciate the aesthetics of intellectual cultures of these communities. Even more significantly, clear identity preservations and governance values are made possible through the exploration and propagation of the ideas imbued in these religious traditions.

INDIGENOUS FAITH TOURISM

Indigenous faith tourism falls within religious tourism. Religious tourism, (also known as faith tourism) can be defined as a type of tourism where people travel individually or in a group for pilgrimage, missionary or leisure (fellowship) purposes. From the definition, it becomes necessary that a particular religion must be widely accepted or must command a large followership, and equally must have significant sites and events to attract tourists. Such sites and events must have some spiritual significance to the adherents of such religions.

Rojo (2007) gives an example of three religions with such large followerships. According to him, "the three major religions in the world (are) Christianity, Islam, and Hinduism with a 33 percent, 21 percent, and 14 percent worldwide followers (and) have received the highest proportion of religious tourists in their headquarters" (Gedecho, 2014, 42). Two of the religions mentioned are responsible for the colonization of the African continent, and for the hiatus that the African aesthetics identity is slipping into. For this reason, it is important that deliberate effort be made to ensure the resuscitation of these religious traditions and the diverse ways in which they, through aesthetics of being, impact societal well-being.

Nigeria has had her little share of religious tourism, but this has not been commensurate with the richness of religious traditions of the country or the tropes of aesthetics such tourism can disclose to the world at large. Umejei has noted that the growth of religious tourism in Nigeria has been pivoted by Christians, Islam, and traditional believers, through various programs that have become tourism attractions for many, both within and outside Nigeria. It must however be noted that it is mostly Christian revivalist and televangelist activities that attract tourists more than indigenous faiths. Such activities as conducted by Shiloh of the Living Faith Church, as well as crusades by the Synagogue Church of All Nations, led by T. B. Joshua, have continued to attract dignitaries from abroad. When a building of the synagogue church, housing pilgrims collapsed in August 2014, the causalities of that tragedy included 116 South Africans. This shows that foreign tourist constitute a sizeable number of visitors to these church programs.

In some cases, however, faith tourism, where it recognizes indigenous traditions at all, has become a celebration of mixed faiths, with adherents of different faiths celebrating together. Such is the Ojude Oba festival, celebrated by the Ijebu people in Ogun State. Umejei notes that the festival, with roots in Islam takes place on the third day of the Id-el-Kabir, but it is celebrated by all the natives both Christians and Muslims. Umejei traces the commencement of this festival to when the first converted Muslims in the kingdom thought it fit to pay homage and thank the Ijebu traditional ruler (Awujale of Ijebuland) for his tolerance in allowing them to practice their religion peacefully.

The subtext that is not emphasized in the above is clear. Indigenous African religions are tolerant of other faiths, and therefore are not exceptionalist or exclusionist in their understanding of followership of either the deity or the representative of the deity. Clearly such a narrative as the above, being a component of the aesthetics of identity of indigenous Yoruba people, deserve to be recognized and celebrated. The yearly observance of this tradition of homage payment will definitely work to show that religions can coexist and that the spaces within which they co-exist does not have to lead to violence or destruction.

There is also the monastery located at Amangwe village in Awhun town, Udi Local Government Area of Enugu State. According to Ezeani, the monastery is the first in Nigeria and it attracts various religious pilgrims from various parts of the country. Ezeani claims that the monastery has a waterfall known as the Awhun waterfall, which heals various types of diseases as far as you have faith in God; of course with such healing powers of the waterfall, the site may not attract only Christians as those afflicted with different ailments who would certainly go there for healing.

Apart from these examples of tourist attractions involving people of different faiths, there are other purely indigenous faiths that should attract foreign and local tourists. But, as has been noted, the events of these indigenous faiths have been reduced to ordinary cultural festivals, deriving their essence mainly from the entertainment they provide. Thus, many tourists visit religious sites or participate in festivals for mere leisure. But the real essence of faith tourism must include spiritual rejuvenation which the aesthetics of the shrines discloses, as could be seen in such activities as Muslim pilgrims' visit to Mecca during hajj and Christian pilgrims' trip to Jerusalem. The annual hajj by Muslims to Mecca, for instance, is one of the five pillars of Islam which every Muslim is expected to partake in.

Nigeria has a plethora of indigenous religious sites and different calendars of the different faiths, with important events having profound religious significance. Yet these do not attract the number of tourists commensurate with the importance of such faiths. For example, Umejei cites the Udju Iwhurie festival, which is popularly known as Agbassa juju is a colourful display of heritage celebrated by the Agbarha people of Warri in Delta State. According to him the festival has roots in Iwhurie the god of war, reputed for its war prowess. Most of the contemporary persons who attend this annual festival, like other festivals nationwide, do not attach any religious or spiritual significance to it. They attend for leisure or curiosity.

However, a popular festival with religious significance is the Osun Oshogbo. Part of the festival is associated with the worship of the Osun goddess. But, again, many people who attend the festival regard it as a cultural festival, thereby deemphasizing its religious significance. It is an annual festival that has cultural and spiritual significance to the Yoruba people. The 2015 edition lasted one week and climaxed on Friday, August 21, 2015. The Osun Grove, which is managed by the priestess (Olorisa), has been designated by the United Nations Educational, Scientific and Cultural Organization (UNESCO) as a World Heritage Monument. This development was celebrated by the traditional ruler of Oshogbo city, Ataoja of Oshogbo, Oba Jimoh Olanipekun, during the 2015 edition of the festival. Thus, this famous festival now assumes more of cultural significance, connoting leisure, rather than the spiritual status it ought to have, like the annual Christian and Muslim pilgrimage to Israel and Saudi Arabia respectively.

Also Ifá religion has an annual festival which serves as an avenue for spiritual rejuvenation for its adherents. This festival holds at Oke Tase in Ile-Ife (Osun State). A temple which, according to Agboola (2014, 18), had been in existence since1930 stands at Oke Tase. A national council for the religion was constituted in 2002. It is this national council that was responsible for the modernization of the temple in 2014, to celebrate the festival. The 2014 edition held in June and it featured a conference, during which papers were presented on culture and religion. The festival ended with recitations and revelations of the future as well as special prayers. It is therefore a festival with a high spiritual significance, attracting pilgrims from the United States of America and the Caribbean. It is instructive to note that Ifá has adherents in Europe and the Americas (including Brazil, Mexico, Venezuela, and Puerto Rico). Its tourism potentials can therefore not be over emphasized, especially when properly managed.

Despite these tourism potentials, indigenous faiths have not assumed their rightful positions regarding tourism in the country. The number of tourists in this regard cannot, in any sense, be compared with the number of people who visit Saudi Arabia and Israel. For instance, every year, about 2 million Muslims converge at Mecca, the holiest place in Islam for the Hajj. Okonkwo and Nzeh (2009, 291) claim that in 2007, the "two holy sites of Makkah and Madinah hosted about 2.4 million pilgrims, while about 95,000 pilgrims from Nigeria participated in the 2008 edition." But the 2014 Ifá Oke Tase festival did not host up to 30,000 people.

There is, therefore, the need for indigenous faiths in Nigeria to harness their tourism potentials in order to attract tourists. Such a step would be of benefit to both the faithful in particular, and the nation in general.

RELIGIOUS TOURISM, AESTHETICS AND NATIONAL DEVELOPMENT

Faith tourism has some implications for national development. Although this is not the main focus of this paper, it is, perhaps important to mention a few implications of religious tourism, necessary for national development. It has already been stated that religious tourism is a means of foreign exchange earnings for the nation, as pilgrims would come in with foreign currency which would enhance the country's economy.

Again religious tourism can serve to create job opportunities for those near the sites of pilgrimage, who may then be employed in various capacities. They may be guides who explain the aesthetic motifs and values to tourists, as well as they may serve as assistants to some pilgrims. By so doing, international understanding, respect and friendship are established, as citizens of other nations come and go with favourable impressions about the country. With this, friendly relations and cultural understanding can be enhanced between peoples and countries.

One of the implications of religious tourism in national development is the actual aim of such tourism. Here, the aim could be spiritual rebirth and satisfaction. In fact, Okpoko and Okpoko (2002, 23) have affirmed that the main aim of religious tourism is spiritual satisfaction (Ashiegbu and Achinike, 2014, 132). Such satisfaction places the pilgrims in such a state of mind needed to contribute to the development of mankind in general and their country in particular.

More importantly, religious tourism can lead to the development of infrastructure needed to accommodate the tourists on a regular basis and for the use and benefit of locals on a continuous basis. This leads to the generation of local investment in religious and historic capacities and building of resources. This may result in the pride of local communities in their heritage. This will lead ultimately to the improvement of the local economy particularly, and that of the nation, in general. It is thus clear that the development of indigenous faith tourism in Nigeria would contribute in no small measure to the country's development.

This last point is significant, because when a society values its spiritual and cultural heritage, this provides an affirmative psychological boost for identity as well as impetus to the ability of the members of society to take pride in their heritage. More importantly, such a venture ensures that acceptance of foreign religions is not at the expense of indigenous traditions, contrary to the current situation in which African traditional religions are denigrated from all sides as primitive and unworthy of embrace.

THE MASS MEDIA AND FAITH TOURISM IN NIGERIA

For the full potentials of indigenous faith tourism to be realized, there must be a conscious effort to ensure its development. Such effort should not be confined to mere evangelism, which may turn out to be mere propaganda that may produce negative results. Many people do not have adequate information about indigenous faiths in Nigeria. And since the two major foreign religions of Christianity and Islam have gained so much space, traditional religions become relegated to the back seat and scorned. One can then see the role of mass media in the propagation and dissemination of information about indigenous religions of Africa, so that members of the wider society can understand the foundations upon which they are built, and their potential benefit to contemporary society.

The mass media must, therefore, be utilized for the development of the potentials of indigenous faith tourism in Nigeria. And the first task for the media, in this regard, is the provision of information on the relevant indigenous faiths. It should be noted that our mass media space has been colonized by the foreign religions, especially, Christianity, which has several television stations and programs in the major networks as well as on radio. Also, the major national newspapers devote weekly columns for the propagation of Islam and Christianity. But there is no such space available for any of the traditional religions. The mass media should, therefore, seek and disseminate relevant information about traditional religions in the country. This is for the purpose of making some of them that are nationally spread in practice to have national status and acceptability.

The media must thus expand their space to accommodate traditional religions. The information about such indigenous faiths should be conveyed in a way that should serve the interest of improving their tourism potentials. This is because, as Ibagere (2002, 62) notes, "it is the way a message is communicated that determines, to a great extent, the degree of appropriateness and, by implication, the success of the communication activity." A good packaging of the information would serve to establish a proper media space allocation and management which would result in a system acceptable to all. This point is corroborated by Hoggart (1970, 150), who notes that "in a society of clearly marked lines of class distinctions, mass communications style . . . is the creation of an imaginary, yet real world acceptable to all."

There should, thus, be a kind of democratization of the media space. This point is well noted by Nwanne, who examines such democratization from the perspective of conflict. According to him, the mass media "must make their space and airtime available to all those involved in a conflict to ventilate their news" (2009, 23). It is therefore imperative for indigenous faiths to seek out their spaces and utilize same effectively to realize their tourism potentials. When there is this synergy between the media and these indigenous faiths, the adherents of these faiths would know how to utilize the media to their own spiritual benefit. But as it appears currently, this synergy is lacking. Thus, it seems the media are hostile to indigenous faiths. Yet it is only when the media relate to these faiths that the adherents would "see the media as being friendly and sympathetic to their plight" (Ibagere, 2011, 211).

It is clear then that it is virtually impossible to learn and understand any indigenous faith in Nigeria through the mass media, because there is no space for them in the media. But converts continue to be won to Christianity and Islam through the media. Converts are won to indigenous faiths mostly through very tortuous routes. This can only result after economic and social problems have been spiritually solved for such people or when they get cured of some life-threatening ailments. Such converts would then be made to go through tasking initiation processes which can be tourist attractions, but they are never seen in the media.

In disseminating information about indigenous faiths, the focus should be on those aspects that should attract non-adherents to see the events—public initiation ceremonies, rituals for various stages in life such as marriage, naming ceremonies, funeral ceremonies, etc. The essence of this is that the mass media must act as advertising and marketing agents for these faiths. Publicity should, therefore, be the aim of such synergy between the media and indigenous faiths.

CHALLENGES OF USING MEDIA
TO FOSTER INDIGENOUS FAITH TOURISM

As has been noted, the utilization of the mass media to foster indigenous faith tourism is not being explored. This is due to certain factors which militate against such a move. Gedecho (2014) has enumerated the challenges of religious tourism in Ethiopia. Some of these challenges can be seen in Nigeria. These include poor performance in marketing, low level of government involvement, safety and security issues, and others. These are quite prominent in Nigeria.

It was stated earlier that the mass media should help market indigenous faiths for the purpose of tourism. But because of lack of media involvement in the sector there is no adequate marketing. This continues to be a hindrance to the development of the sector. One could imagine if the followers of the various African religions around the Atlantic world were encouraged to visit the original homelands of their faiths. It would not only generate better mutual understanding, it will also have potential for economic cooperation spinoffs.

The low level of government involvement constitutes a hindrance to media involvement because there is no existing policy that compels the mass media to be part of the development of the sector. Therefore, the media confine their focus to mere presentation of their activities from the perspective of entertainment. Thus, festivals like the Osun Oshogbo feature in the media only from the creative perspective without the accompanying religious significance. Even more significantly, the level of ignorance of many government officials about indigenous religions does not bode well for the development of these religions. When government officials are scared, for example, of taking oaths using local indigenous religious symbols, one can see that this is indirectly celebrating the death knell of such faiths.

Another fundamental challenge is the secrecy in which indigenous faiths activities are shrouded. Most indigenous faith activities are not done before public glare like it is in Christianity. Some do not even have written guides like the Holy Bible and the Quran, which have been translated into different languages. So, there is an acute lack of awareness as regards indigenous faiths in Nigeria. Lack of awareness is a problem that militates against tourism development generally, as noted by Obioma (2013, 35).

Again, it is easy adopting foreign religions (especially Christianity and Islam). But adoption of most indigenous faiths is very difficult, because one would have to go through a rigorous initiation process that some people may not complete in a lifetime. It may, therefore, be impossible for the media to purvey the information needed to fully understand indigenous faiths for the purpose of relating to them.

Even then, in some cases, one has to be initiated before being allowed into some inner recesses that have vital information about such faiths. This may be why most of what the media expose to the public can only be contemplated in entertainment terms. In some cases, cameras are not allowed, so activities cannot be recorded. It is therefore difficult to fully understand indigenous faiths fully.

This is more so when the language of expression is localized to the area of origin of such faith. This acts as a clog, in the sense that what the media would purvey as information may not be enough to generate the appropriate interest needed to develop the tourism potentials of such faiths to the level of attracting tourists who would seek spiritual rebirth or satisfaction through participation in the activities of such faiths.

Another challenge in the use of mass media to foster indigenous faith tourism is the lack of a central authority among the various faiths. Most of these faiths often have different temples that are authorities unto themselves, with no allegiance to any other authority. This is why it is difficult to forge a synergy with the media for the purpose of marketing such faiths.

In some cases, internal squabbles regarding leadership result in disintegration of some faiths or dissipation of energy on unnecessary bickering. The National Council for Ifá religion, for instance, is enmeshed in a leadership tussle in the last two years. So, there cannot be any articulated plan to forge a synergy with any corporate media body for the purpose of marketing their activities in such a situation. The Igbe religion, mostly found in the Niger Delta of Nigeria, is made up of different little shrines and temples, each with its own authority and not subject to any other leadership. Thus, there are several versions and variations of the same religion with all laying claim to its authenticity. In such a situation of fragmentation there can hardly be anything the media can do for the purpose of tourism beyond the presentation of their activities in purely cultural, creative, and entertainment terms.

To tackle these challenges, the mass media must make a conscious effort to reverse the trend of encrypting indigenous faiths in a web of secrecy. They should be opened up by the media, which must reveal what the faiths are all about. The media must go beyond mere presentation of artistic or cultural activities that are associated with such faiths. The significance of such activities and other secret ones must be exposed to the public or interested persons for better understanding. This would enable intending converts relate to the spiritual essence of such beliefs and related activities. The media must not restrict themselves to focusing on mere entertainment, but it must serve to educate the people on the essence of such faiths' activities.

The media should, thus, design their messages with the aim of marketing such faiths to those who lack information about them, to attract their attention and elicit their interest in them. The media should assist these faiths to evolve a central leadership, through constant exposure of the issues arising within these religious organizations so that they can embrace best practices found in other aspects of life, and by so doing making them understand the advantages of a central authority which would liaise with the media for the development of their faith.

CONCLUSION

It is clear from the foregoing that the indigenous faith tourism sector is an area that should be explored and utilized for local, regional and national development. The sector has, all the while, not been considered as worthy of developing, largely because of the vilification it has suffered from the imported religions of the Arabian Desert. This is partly because indigenous religions have not received proper valorisation, compared to Christianity and Islam, and even more critically its economic value has not been appreciated because the Nigerian and African economies have focused only on petroleum and other natural minerals as the sole sources of income for the different governments. But with the drastic fall in the price of oil and other commodities from 2015 to early 2016, the federal government of Nigeria and other African governments have started to consider other areas to generate the funds needed for infrastructural development, as well as improvement of their national economies. The indigenous faith sector is one such area hereby suggested for exploitation in this regard. However, this will take a relatively long time to actualize, since packaging and marketing has to be done to attract tourists to both sites and activities of such faiths. This invariably depends on the emphasis by the governments as well as adherents of such faiths who must be prepared to encourage the exposition of such faiths, rather than making them more obscure and esoteric.

It is clear too that the mass media have not done much toward promoting indigenous faith tourism, due to some challenges which have conspired to scuttle any effort towards synergizing with indigenous faiths for the purpose of developing their tourism potentials. This suggested synergy may be long in coming, because of the enormity of these challenges, but if no effort is made to begin the process of rejuvenating the religious traditions, then the synergy may never arrive. It is therefore suggested that these challenges should be first addressed in order for the media to play their role in the development of indigenous faith tourism.

BIBLIOGRAPHY

Agboola, Abiodun (2014). "The World Ifa Temple Project," *Elerii Ipin: A Magazine of the International Council for Ifá Religion,* vol. 6.

Ashiegbu, Paul O., and Achinike, Hilary C. (2014). "Religion and Tourism in Nigeria." *Research in Humanities and Social Sciences,* 4(15): http//www.iiste.org/org/journal/.

Bewaji, J. A. I. (2013). *Black Aesthetics.* Trenton, NJ: Africa World Press.

———. (2012). *Narratives of Struggle.* Durham, NC: Carolina Academic Press.

Ezeani, John Paule (2015). "Awhun Monastery in View." enugustatetourismboard.com>php>u. Accessed January 12, 2016.

Gedecho, Ermias K. (2014). "Challenges of Religious Tourism: The Case of Gishen Mariam, Ethiopia," *American Journal of Tourism Research,* 3(2): http://www.worldscholars.org.

Gumel, A. (1988). *Archaeological Treasures: Influence on Nigerian Tourism Development.* Smithsonian Libraries: African Art Index Project.

Hoggart, Richard (1970). *Speaking to Each Other,* vol. 1 London: Chatto and Windus.

Ibagere, Elo (2002). "Communication and Rural Development: A Model for Developing Countries," *Humanities Review Journal,* 2(1). Ile-Ife. Humanities Research Forum.

———. (2011). "Human Capital Development in the Niger Delta: The Role of the Mass Media in the Process," in *The Humanities and Human Capital Development.* Ed. Egonwa, Osa. D. Ibadan: Asaba Press.

Nwanne, Ben (2009). "The Media and Conflict Management in the Niger Delta," in *Communication Approaches to Peace Building in Nigeria.* Ed. Wilson, Des. Uyo: African Council for Communication Education Nigerian Chapter.

Obioma, B. K. (2013). "Tourism Potentials and Socio-Economic Development of Nigeria: Challenges and Prospect." Cited in Emmanuel-Thankgod, Omowumi (2015). "Eco-Cultural Tourism as a tool for Environmental, Cultural and Economic Sustainability: A Case Study of Osun-Oshogbo Grove." MA Project for the Department of Theatre Arts, University of Ibadan, Nigeria.

Okonkwo, Emeka, and Nzeh, C. A. (2009). "Faith-Based Activities and their Tourism Potentials in Nigeria," *International Journal of Research in Arts and Social Sciences,* vol. 1.

Okpoko and Okpoko (2002). Cited in Ashiegbu, Paul O., and Achinike, Hilary C. (2014). "Religion and Tourism in Nigeria," *Research in Humanities and Social Sciences,* 4(15): http//www.iiste.org/journal/.

Okpoko, P. U., et al. (2008). *Understanding Tourism.* Nsukka, Nigeria: University of Nigeria Press.

Page, S. J. (2009). *Tourism Management: Managing for Change* ,(third edition) Boston: Elsevier.

Rojo, M. D. (2007). "Religious Tourism: The Way to Santiago" (MA thesis), cited in Gedecho, Ermias K. (2014.) "Challenges of Religious Tourism Development: The Case of Gishen Mariam Ethiopia," *American Journal of Tourism Research* , 3(2): http://www.worldscholars.org.

The Northern Arizona University Parks and Management (2015). Cited in Banakan, Christiana, "Heritage, Tourism and Museum Management." pdf.www.tour.teithe.gr.

Umejei, Emeka (2015). "Religious Tourism Nigeria's Fastest Growing Tourism Sector." https://emekaumujei.wordpress.com>rel. Accessed January 12, 2016.

Vanguard (2015). Friday, August 28.

———. (2015). Friday, September 8.

World Tourism Organization (WTO) (1981). *Tourism Multipliers Explained.* Madrid: WTO and Horwath.

Chapter Seven

Racialized Beauty

*The Case of Skin Bleaching
as an Identity Crisis
for Non-Whites*

Sandra McCalla

The practice of skin bleaching, which involves the lightening of the skin through the use of various chemicals, is not a new phenomenon. Although it is not a new phenomenon, the practice is becoming more widespread across various non-white cultures, as the pressure to embody the "white ideal" of beauty increases among non-white peoples. The prophet Jeremiah, in the Jewish bible (2009) ask in chapter 13 of his book: "Can the Ethiopian change his skin or the leopard his spots?" (Bible, 2009, 446). One can argue that Jeremiah was lamenting here about the difficulty of trying to liberate a person's mind rather than his body. More than two thousand years later, "the question remains relevant; and it is made current by those unwise Jamaicans bleaching in quest of a lighter shade of skin" (*Gleaner*, January 9, 2011).

The above infers that although Africans know that their "blackness" cannot be erased, they continue to use products that aim to lighten their complexions. This they do as a result of a preconceived mental notion that the black skin does not exude beauty. Although this speaks to Africans, it also holds true for other non-whites who are insecure in their skins and believe that bleaching is the answer to their quest for upward social mobility and aesthetic acceptability. Skin bleaching is, for example, also predominant in some Asian cultures, as we will explore later. Within some non-white communities, we see evidence of skin bleaching on almost every street corner. In the Jamaican context, for example, individuals either openly sport bleaching creams on their bodies while wearing stockings, scarves, hoodies, and/or long-sleeve shirts in the blazing sun; this is to achieve the desired results in a short time span. Or, one notices the pale orange or pink undertones upon seeing these individuals at a bus stop, in the market, in university lecture theaters, or in business places. Skin bleachers believe that a lighter complexion will afford them better job/economic opportunities. Although we would like to believe that this is not so predominant, yet in most businesses today, the color of your skin is believed to land you the jobs, for example in the banks, massage parlors, and other organizations. This means that the mental notion that white or brown is the "ideal complexion" is a view that is not accepted by only one or certain groups of individuals, but by a wide cross section of classes and groups. This is striking, especially in the countries that have such vast non-white populations. We argue that, unconsciously and sometimes consciously, this "color complex" is rooted in racist ideas about "good"/light and "bad"/dark skin color.

It is this racist notion that causes the need to embark on this research as it seeks to embody the erasing of one's racial identity. The problem is that dark skinned individuals are viewed as inferior to white skinned individuals, which would make one race dominant over all others. The urge to identify with another race speaks to more than cosmetics and hinges on a racist mind-set, to hate that which is black. This practice is also harmful to the individual, as we will discuss later, as it removes the melanin from the skin. It is for these reasons why we identify skin bleaching as a problem that needs to be addressed in terms of the importance of identifying with the race to which one belongs without prejudice or the need to look like "the other." In other words, acknowledging that there is a serious epidemic of color prejudice in some societies, skin bleachers are psychologically yearning for racial acceptance; and this will continue as long as human beings in such societies are taught that they are inferior.

This research is important as it seeks to highlight a denigration of certain values in terms of the promotion of lighter or white skin as a strong indicator of beauty, social status and power. This serves as necessary and relevant addition to the extant literature, as it seeks to strengthen the view that skin bleaching needs to be taken more seriously in terms of an identity crisis, the health hazards that it poses and the long term suffering that it engenders in terms of irreversible skin damage and not just to be viewed simply as a fashion statement.

It is in light of the above that we view skin bleaching as an identity crisis, a kind of racism, as most individuals involved in the process do this with the intention of altering their racial identities. We argue that skin bleaching is a form of self-hatred, in terms of preference for a particular race other than one's own and hating oneself for being a particular hue and not the preferred lighter hue. This is racism borne of years of colonial domination and is a mental one against the "self," which cannot be fixed as long as African and other non-white races are reminded daily that they are not beautiful or good enough, through different forms of socialization and information media. The ideal of beauty being "whiteness," "lightness," thereby implying anything that is not fitting this ideas is considered black.

We know that one cannot truly erase one's race, but skin bleachers seem to be willing to launch an attempt in the hope of hiding their racial identities. In order to garner an understanding of the skin bleaching problem in the Caribbean and Asia, it is imperative to understand how race, skin color, colonialism, slavery, media, and culture influence the ideology of the people. In light of this, we commence the first section by explaining racism and racial identity, by exploring the view of Charles W. Mills on racism, as well as categories developed by Edward Lynch to segregate slaves. We then discuss ways in which skin bleaching is racism.

Having made the key concepts clear, we move into the second section with a focus on skin bleaching in the Caribbean. Here we outline and review several documented cases of skin bleachers, as well as the possible health issues associated with skin bleaching. We highlight and explain the socio-cultural theory in a quest to garner a deeper understanding of the cultural influences that are associated with skin bleaching. In the third section, we address the problem of skin bleaching in several countries as well as the role that media plays in inculcating what is ideal in terms of skin color. We then discuss certain measures that the Jamaican government has put in place to fight the skin bleaching crisis. We end with findings and conclusions.

RACISM AND RACIAL IDENTITY

In this section we focus on the concepts of racial identity and racism in order to give a clear view of these key concepts. We employ the views of Charles Mills, who explained the concept of white domination as a political system. We then examine skin bleaching as a form of self-racism in terms of preference for a particular skin color other than one's own.

Racial Identity is seen as "complex and holistic, influenced by specific historical and social contexts, and framed by the dynamics of social power and privilege" (Wijeyesinghe and Jackson, 2012, 4). From this we can garner that individuals may tend to identify with a particular race based on factors such as history, socialization, as well as a need to be affiliated with a particular class or privileged group. Since racial identity is influenced by so many factors, this may be subjected to change and not remain static. This change is possible though only in terms of identity and not race in as far as one can alter certain physical features to resemble another or to be associated with a particular social group. There are times when there is a demarcation with racial identity as the lines may not be clearly drawn. An instance, for example, where mixed races are involved, individuals are often not sure which race to identify with. In many instances the preference may be for the identity that attracts the most prestige and power. This choice is often based on culture and socialization, which suggest white or light ideal is preferred.

Charles Mills saw the system of white domination that existed during slavery and which is still in existence as a political system that many do not acknowledge. He therefore calls for a recognition that "racism (or global white supremacy) is itself a political system, a particular power structure of formal or informal rule, socioeconomic privilege and norms for the differential distribution of material wealth and opportunities, benefits and burdens, rights and duties" (1997, 3). We believe that Mills is correct that the system of white domination is a political system. It is a political system, since those who are in control have the power to impose rules, laws, and values that are not necessarily just and right. It is this political system where whites dominate and blacks are placed in a situation where rules are accepted and followed without question. These rules are viewed by humans as norms that should be followed whether good or bad. It is a political system that endorses equality in theory but practices segregation and classism. One can argue that, throughout history, whites have been using the other races as a means of building their wealth and power. They always find ways to manipulate and control the "other," non-white, in such a way that, the work is done by them but the dominant whites reap the benefits. In this system, non-whites are classified as being inferior to whites; non-whites often times resent whites for treating them inhumanely. It is this inferiority complex, along with low self-esteem that persuades the victim, in this case the skin bleacher that he or she is subordinate and inferior, because of a darker skin color.

Racism is the belief that phenotypical or alleged genotypical characteristics are inherently indicative of certain behaviors and abilities, and it leads to invidious distinctions based on a hierarchical order (Alleyne, 2002). Racism is, then, a system of privilege and disadvantage of groups of persons, according to their assigned race. It is a hatred that one develops for others who may be classified as inferior to them or of the opposite race. We believe that racism also exists even across races as individuals may dislike others of similar race, based on their actions and their physical features. It has been argued that

> the notion of human race is a concept that, in general, classifies human beings according to particular physical features or national ancestry. However, race is a socio-cultural concept in that, the racial categories are defined in terms of a particular socio-historical context, given a specific time and place, reinforced and violated by institutional structures. (Yee, 2007, 52–53)

These classifications were later influenced by the powerful, self-centred individuals in society who believe that one race is superior to all others and seek to exploit others.

It may be correct then, that what makes racial classifications wrong or harmful are when these arbitrary classifications are instituted in social structures of power, to justify the adverse treatment and unwarranted moral prescriptions for persons, based on race. What is inferred here is that, when the idea of race becomes the racist ideology, the socio-cultural phenomena of racism is produced. We find, then, that such racist ideology is often embedded in the systems and policies of social institutions. What results from this is, as long as some racial groups consider themselves superior and seek to dominate, is that there are no changes to the ideologies that inform dominant social organizations hence, racism will continue. Although we will be discussing skin bleaching as a form of self-racism, we would like to acknowledge that race is not the only primary indicator of social status in the Caribbean. Social class, deriving from wealth and education, has been one of the main sources of privilege. We see skin bleaching as one form of racism in so far as it is geared towards preference for a particular skin color and hate for the other. It involves a dislike or even hate for one's own black skin tone, as a marker of poverty or low class. The preference is to make that black complexion as light or white as possible.

This color preference has its origin from slavery where the mulatto slaves, persons who are of mixed races, "black and white" etc., were treated better than dark complexion slaves. As a result of preferential treatment afforded to slaves of mixed ancestry, "a stratification based on skin tone developed among the slaves. The light complexion slaves classified themselves superior to the dark complexion slaves. This conflict created intense fields of resentment that kept slaves from uniting" (Culbreth, 2006, 15). It is now so many years after the abolition of slavery, and some, are yet to acknowledge that they are free beings. The system that was implemented to keep families apart during slavery is still persistent today, with color and class prejudice being obvious manifestations.

This system devised to separate and conquer was documented in the Willie Lynch's letter (1712). Written by a white slave owner, this letter instructed slave owners on how to keep the black race in a subservient position. Lynch instructed slave owners to keep the black race separate by identifying the differences among the slaves and making these differences appear larger than they were. Lynch developed a list of categories that were used to segregate the slaves. The list included age, skin tone and shade, physical size, gender, hair texture: "all slave owners to encourage slaves to turn against each other. By turning the young against the old, the tall against the short, women against men, and light skin against dark skin, distrust would be stronger than trust, envy stronger than adulation, respect and admiration" (Lynch, 1712, 15).

One can infer from this that, the goal was to force the slaves to depend on their white owners. This kept slaves from depending too much on each other. Families were already separated, so most of the slaves were already in an environment where they had to create and form new relationships. There then needed to be measures in place during slavery where relationships among slaves were not vast and strong. It is understood from this, that if the slaves were not unified, the masters would have greater control. Not only that, but, if slaves were not united, there would be less support to rebel against the masters. The above categorization, one can argue, was a form of indoctrination. This indoctrination was the foundation of the interracial colorism among persons across the globe.

This interracial colorism also led to class stratification. As stated earlier, in Jamaica for example, we find that groups are formed not so much only in terms of race but in terms of class. Although there are many affluent, wealthy, dark skinned individuals living in Jamaica, "brown" complexion is usually associated with power, wealth, and beauty. Although most Jamaicans may be of the same race, class identity is important and this is one of the reasons, as we will see later, that individuals offer for bleaching their skins. They do this without acknowledging that who they are biologically cannot be altered; their racial identity cannot be erased by harmful chemicals, but they can move up in class.

In the Jamaican society today, mulattoes are still given preferential treatment. Some deem themselves to be superior to other blacks and some prefer to live in communities that are predominantly comprised of others of the similar skin color and of individuals who possess similar power and wealth. One can argue then, that the ideas generated from slavery, in relation to separation based on skin color has been strongly internalized and passed on from one generation to the next.

SKIN BLEACHING IN THE CARIBBEAN

Skin bleaching, we define here as the process through which skin is made lighter through the application of various chemical compounds. Campbell-Chambers (2012) at the beginning of her discussion defines skin bleaching as

> the use of chemical substances to try to lighten skin tone or complexion by reducing the amount of melanin in the skin. Melanin is the main substance that gives the skin its color. It helps to protect the skin from the damaging effects of sunlight, like sunburn, skin aging, and skin cancer. Darker-skinned individuals generally have more melanin and may have slightly different types of

melanin than fairer-skinned people. This gives darker skinned individuals
more protection from sun damage. (August 8)

Jamaicans who practice skin bleaching are therefore reducing their own natural protection from the sun. Persons who bleach themselves are therefore, withdrawing a form of skin protection in order to gain recognition and acceptance. It begs one to question whether or not some individuals value group acceptance over health. Having seen some of the scars derived from bleaching, one may also question if the recognition that some of these bleachers are getting is not negative, as opposed to the desired positive expectation. We believe a response to this may be dependent on the result derived from bleaching, as some persons' skin may react differently to bleaching creams.

Some of these individuals would like to change their complexion so badly, it does not matter to them the quality of the products they use to achieve this. It has been argued, for example that, lightening creams are not effectively regulated in Jamaica. Lightening creams can be obtained from roadside vendors. These vendors sell these creams in tubes and even plastic bags on sidewalks in market districts. Persons really do not know what they are buying in some instances. They are only told it will be effective in removing their "black" skin. As Richard Desnoes, president of the Dermatology Association of Jamaica, argued in the *Jamaica Observer*, many of the tubes are unlabeled and one could not know their actual ingredients. In many instance, the hardcore bleachers use illegal ointments smuggled into the Caribbean country that contain toxins like mercury. We believe that neither the fact that these products are illegally smuggled into the country, nor that the ingredients in the skin bleaching creams are dangerous, are important to the bleachers, as long as they see a change in the color of their skins. This harmful practice of skin bleaching is to achieve the effect of "browning," a term used to describe Jamaican blacks with light or brown complexion.

These "bleachers" allow themselves to be enslaved through bleaching in the aim of attaining that "white ideal," as they have to continue to use skin toning chemicals for the rest of their lives to maintain the light complexion. This is the kind of thing Frantz Fanon implicitly refers to when he stated that, "for the black man, there is only one destiny and it is white" (1967, 10). This statement can be interpreted as an issue of identity, an identity created for the colonized by colonial racism. Although Fanon never referred directly to skin bleaching in his writing, we can apply his work to the inferiority complex that accompanies skin bleaching. It reflects a mind-set of the black man, which is shaped by the Eurocentric world in which he lives and operates. He identifies himself with the "white man" and tries to imitate this ideal. We disagree with Fanon that all blacks fall in this category, but it seems that there is no doubt that his analysis does well to reflect the idea behind the skin bleaching craze.

Despite the known hazards of using skin bleaching creams, "including severe acne, increased risk of skin cancer, stretch marks, and even darkening of the skin, its use has not abated" (Fluehr-Lobban, 2005, 56). The aim, then, is for those individuals to look anything other than the color they were born with. The idea that being a "browning" is better, beautiful, superior, is clear and "bleachers" aim to become all the above, because they believe that being in a black skin will not allow them to possess any of these qualities. Are these beliefs and ideas really culturally based?

One theory that addresses skin bleaching is socio-cultural in nature. According to Christina Gorke, based on this theory, Fallon suggested that "body image will be developed in terms of cultural standards, the extent one thinks he/she conforms to these standards and it also depends on how important other members of the cultural group think it is to match these standards" (2014, 26). What is inferred here is that culture plays an integral role in shaping our knowledge of who were are, as human beings. Body image is important as it is one way in which human beings are identified.

This socio-cultural theory takes into consideration the skin bleaching phenomenon as a learned or observed behaviour that is influenced by social and cultural contexts. These influences occur both formally and informally. Individuals then copy their environment in different ways and through different means. It is not always bad to copy one's environment, but there are instances where it becomes harmful, such as in skin bleaching. Copying skin bleaching is learning to hate oneself.

We believe that if skin bleachers would stop and evaluate themselves, they would realize that they are more than a skin colour. It is sad that some of the individuals even believe that the "blackness" will be so erased that any offspring that they may produce will also be of brown complexion. Although this may be a view held by a small percentage of the "bleachers," this mindset is unscientific. Any who believes this needs to be reeducated as to the effects of bleaching, as well as to the biological makeup of humans.

It is for the reasons mentioned above that health officials, and other persons within the country, are concerned about the bleaching craze and the "real" reason behind this craze. This, along with the fact that, some of these individuals are not only applying these toxic products to themselves, they are also bleaching the skins of their young children as well, constitute grounds for careful study of this destructive phenomenon. Doctors say the skin lightening phenomenon has reached dangerous proportions. The risk of the negative effects of skin bleaching therefore affects those who are also not in the position to choose for themselves. We believe that as long as it can be proven that these practices are occurring and the extent of the harm, it may be necessary for the relevant authorities to find legal means of dealing with the menace.

Based on "bleachers" account of why they participate in this practice, they all tend to deny upfront that bleaching is a form of "self-hate." But we believe that if these individuals did not hate their "blackness" for whatever reason, they would not go through such lengths to even bleaching their own children as well. They may do this because they view their children as reflections of themselves and the reflection that they have of themselves is that of "ugliness." It is this kind of self-hate that we equate to self-racism. Arthur Spears supports our view on self-racism when he argues that "connection to racism and a contradiction—a people struggling against racism but harboring a form of it within themselves. Skin bleaching among people of color is but one example of a behavior reflecting white supremacist racism directed against the self" (1999, 17). It is inferred here that, skin bleaching only gives the "white" more power in the quest of having other races believe that they [whites] are really superior. Bleaching, to derive this "ideal" complexion may be one way of saying "we realize we are inferior because of our skin color and we will not stop until we change this."

While accepting the views that skin bleaching may be a form of racism against the self, we would also like to acknowledge that Jamaicans who bleach their skins are facing a real identity crisis. This is a crisis that sees professionals, persons of lower and upper classes in Jamaica, males and females having the desire for a skin color that is anything but black. A young Jamaican when asked

> why she bleached her skin responded, "when you are lighter, people pay more attention to you. It makes you more important." This Jamaican hopes to transform her dark complexion to a *cafe-au-lait*-colour common among Jamaica's elite and favoured by many men in her neighbourhood. She believes a fairer skin could be her ticket to a better life. So she spends her meagre savings on cheap black-market concoctions that promise to lighten her pigment. (Samuda, 2011, 4)

It is usually the belief that skin bleaching was only prevalent among the lower classes in society and was practiced by mostly adults. However, we see students from the high schools to the university levels participating in this practice, as well as adults from various classes and subclasses with the society. According to one dermatologist, some individuals believe that skin bleaching is only practiced by the poor and lower class citizens, but she explained that it is also predominant amongst lawyers and doctors as these individuals visit her for bleaching cream (Samuda, 2011, 4). From this, one can imply that individuals may claim to bleach their skins for various reasons and depending on circumstances. For example, these doctors and lawyers would not use the excuse of wanting a better life, as they are already highly paid professionals. We believe, however, that no matter what reason is given for bleaching, it leads back to the reality that these individuals are just not comfortable in their black skins.

We share the same sentiments of Cooper who sees a disturbing trend in Jamaica and the Caribbean today, of black women bleaching their faces and necks so as to approximate the "light skinned" ideal and erase their natural "racial" identity. Rodriquez, Boatca, and Costa quoted her as saying, "the mask of lightness becomes a signifier of status in the racist society that still privileges lightness as a sign of beauty" (qtd. in Cooper, 2010, 204). It is a way of advancing a beauty that is not evident in the black skinned individual even if other facial and bodily features are the same. This beauty, therefore mainly surrounds the color of the skin.

It is our view that if more members of the black race seek to rise against this prejudice against their skin color, others may begin to realize that the black race is proud of who they are regardless of the shallow believes of others. Skin bleaching reflects the opposite of being proud of one's racial identity, which leaves room for doubts and questions. Questions arise relating to the real reason persons make the conscious decision to change their skin colours. More significantly is the fact that the real reasons they have for their actions are ones that they may be afraid and embarrassed to admit, because others may perceive them as being self-racists.

We believe that, in order to avoid dealing with issues surrounding self-racism, skin bleachers sell the notion that their practice is a form of fashion. In viewing skin bleaching as a fashion statement, it becomes "not about imitating a white ideal but about presenting the original 'browning' as a construction in a way which is meaningful to the bleacher and which in turn makes her blackness clear. As a superficial form of styling, bleaching is then thought of as another form of adornment, along the same lines of wearing green or pink wigs" (204). Bleaching to make a fashion statement is therefore linked to seasonal bleaching, as it can be seen as forming a part of the dress or costume. We believe however that the practice of skin bleaching is far removed from making a fashion statement. The bleacher develops the fashion construct as a way to cope with the situation, since it is frowned upon by many.

As mentioned earlier, no one wants to be referred to as a self-proclaimed racist. We would like to acknowledge that facial and others scars from bleaching cannot be readily removed in a similar way as wigs, clothing and other forms of fashion accessories. Also, the very idea of linking bleaching to a fashion statement is absurd, since one's complexion is likened to a piece of accessory that can be changed at one's will. This in and of itself, cheapens and degrades how skin color is perceived by many.

SKIN BLEACHING IN SOME ASIAN CULTURES

We would like to acknowledge that the practice of skin bleaching is not unique to the black race. Having white complexion is also considered important in constructing the "ideal" female beauty in Asian cultures. Societies such as India, Hong Kong, Japan, and Korea are all plagued with the skin bleaching epidemic. Skin bleaching in Asia varies from country to country. Rondilla and Spickard (2007) gave an account in their book of how skin bleaching affects other races. A Korean American, Sunny Young, gave her account as follows:

> ever since I could remember, my parents always encouraged my sister and me not to tan. They always said we looked like a black person or a country bumpkin when we got dark. The meaning behind this comment was that we looked like lower class people. In Korea, lighter skin colour was more desirable as marriage material than darker skin colour because it represented the status of the person throughout history. Somehow, as little children, we understood that being lighter was better. No one ever said they wanted to look white. Then again, what community will openly admit to such prejudices...? I think we all just know. (2007, 9)

We can infer from this that persons are socialized into believing that they are inferior to the white race and those with "brown skin" should be careful to keep it as light as possible. This fear of getting darker or of being dark is, therefore, a near universal problem among persons of color. From all the discussions so far, we can agree with Sunny Young that no society will admit to harboring prejudice. This adds to the problem of skin bleaching, since we believe that individuals first have to admit that they are faced with a crisis of prejudice before measures can be taken to correct it.

According to Eric Li, Hyun Min, and Russell Belk (2008, 444), "in India, white skin is considered as a mark of class and caste as well as an asset. While in China, 'milk-white' skin is a symbol of beauty and some Chinese women used to swallow powdered pearls in the hope of becoming whiter." From this we find that even persons of lighter complexion see it necessary to attain an even lighter skin tone. These individuals also seek to lighten their skins in the hope of securing certain jobs, social status and marital prospects. This is due to the cultural focus on the "white ideal" that we have been discussing, with the view in mind that white is beauty, white is power, white is superior, and white is superior especially to black.

Media also plays a role in inculcating what is ideal. Based on the cultivation theory, "the media have the tendency to stereotype and repeat their representations of social reality. If human beings are frequently exposed to media images they are expected to adopt a 'mainstream view of social reality'" (Gorke, 2014, 28). This view holds true today not only in terms of film and television but especially with the vast number of social media formats, such as Facebook, Twitter, Skype, and so on, which help in spreading messages at a rapid rate across geographical, socio-economic and traditional borders. The media plays a major role in how different ethnic and racial groups are perceived. Some individuals easily adopt what is fed to them through these forums, which further complicates the skin bleaching problem.

One cannot fix an issue if the real problem is hidden. We strongly agree with Fluehr-Lobban that "as long as lighter skin is perceived as a passport to upward mobility and improved social relations its use will continue" (2005, 56–57). This is owing to the mind-set that these human beings have, and the unwillingness by some to realize that they are more than their circumstances. The issue will continue, because the bleachers act based on what they observe in their societies.

If workers at a massage parlor, for example, are told that their customers prefer females with light complexion, these workers may feel that the only option they have is to change their skin color. What we are saying here is that bleaching does not only reside with the bleachers, but it is deeper in the wider society; so, in order to curtail its continuation the underlined societal views that brown and or white complexion is the only skin color that is beautiful will have to change. We find, then, that as long as this prejudice exists, the practice will survive.

Ken Jones said it best when he argued that, "we may campaign against bleaching creams and soaps. Those are not the problem. Many people use them legitimately to treat skin conditions such as age spots, melasma, scars, and acne marks. What we need to provide as an alternative is that product that cleanses the mind and opens the eyes of a community denied instructions in self-respect" (2011, n.p.). This holds true for skin bleachers of all races and cultures. One respects the color of another and not theirs, because of what has been implanted in their minds from the very race whose skin color they prefer and try to attain. Cleansing the mind of this prejudice is important in terms of healing and acceptance. As a people, we need to stop blindly accepting the perception that others have of us and respect our skin as a form of beauty in comparison to other skin tones. In other words, all skin tones are beautiful and each person ought to accept and respect the one that their minds are housed in. As human beings, we ought to accept that we are more than physical beings, so we should not define ourselves only by skin color.

FIGHTING THE BLEACHING CRISIS IN JAMAICA

In an attempt to curtail the practice of skin bleaching, which is deemed dangerous to health, countries have responded in various ways to the phenomenon. We will outline the Jamaican response to the crisis in this section in terms of educational campaigns, as well as regulation of the bleaching products.

The Jamaican government, in response to the national outrage of skin bleaching, decided to regulate the distribution of bleaching creams (Higgs, 2002, 45). We believe that regulation of bleaching cream is not enough. It is also difficult to regulate creams that can be obtained from a dermatologist or from just about any street side vendor. Since the issue is perceived to be a larger one than individuals and the government seek to admit, the target should first be changing the perception that "brown and white is better," starting from those in society who hold the most power. Governments should for example, find a way to reduce the request for "light skinned" workers by employers.

The Heart Trust Agency is a government agency that places students with viable employers. If this agency is steadfast in not fulfilling any of those requests where skin tone is a requirement, we believe that this is a start in curtailing skin prejudice. This means that the starting point would be to reduce one of the rewards that some members of society always seem to give to lighter skinned individuals.

For this to be possible there needs to be greater awareness of the extent of the problem of color prejudice. We therefore agree with the view that, if Jamaicans really want to control the spread of the skin-bleaching virus, we first have to admit that there's an epidemic of color prejudice in our society (Jones, 2011). None of the "bleachers" mentioned in this chapter acknowledged that the problem is one of color prejudice. Employers are saying that having a lighter skinned person as customer service agents is good for business, for example, and others argue that they would just like to be accepted by others. We find a case where persons are blaming everyone but themselves for their bleaching practices. These individuals prefer to hold on to the superficial views that they have chosen to accept, rather than face the real dilemma. It will take the combined effort of all stakeholder involved (employers, government, and those involved in the practice) to try and combat this crisis. Regulation of bleaching cream will not stop the problem if the problem is deeper than cosmetics.

Outside of regulating bleaching cream, the Jamaican government, through the Ministry of Health, undertook several programs to target children since this dilemma tremendously affects this group. In 2008, for example, the Ministry of Health launched an educational campaign to discourage the fad, especially among high school students (Campbell, 2012). It is believed that if this group sees bleaching as a dilemma they can help their parents and others to realize that it is a dangerous practice. It is also through the continued awareness of how skin bleaching can damage the skin, that these individuals can begin to make a conscious decision as to whether or not continuing the practice outweighs the possible dangers. With this awareness, it is hoped that children will understand that damaging their skins cannot be a logical fashion statement. They may also begin to understand that bleaching cannot change the fact that they are biologically "black" beings. In order to heighten this awareness, health officials are running warnings on local radio stations, putting up posters in schools, holding talks, and handing out literature about the dangers. These ventures, however, did nothing to reduce the practice.

The Ministry of Health (MOH) declared that, despite a vigorous effort to address the local skin-bleaching phenomenon, the practice is extremely difficult to change. We agree that the climb will be more laborious and less productive unless we make the conscious effort to revise the curriculum to suit the needs. Our noble accomplishments must be recorded in books, as some are; they must also be told continually by radio and television programs. The media must consciously devise ways and means of balancing the present menu that overwhelms us with muck music, noisy speech, and crude utterances (Jones, 2011).

In most high schools in Jamaica, although history is taught, this is mainly American history, which means that some students are only introduced to the teachings of Marcus Garvey and other Jamaicans, only during black history month or National Heroes Day. This is not enough to teach all the lessons on black pride that should be constantly instilled especially in the minds of students who believe that bleaching the skin is the best way to be recognized and accepted. So, along with anti-bleaching campaigns, black history should be more formally incorporated in the school curriculum.

In 2009, the Marcus Garvey Technical High School elaborated on the theme spoken by Mr. Garvey; the black skin is not a badge of shame, but rather a glorious symbol of national greatness (Jones, 2011). That is a lesson that should be taught constantly in Jamaica; but we are bashful about it; embarrassed by the question; chained to thoughts and acts that confuse race pride with race prejudice. The only way persons can be educated and constantly reminded of Marcus Garvey and other teachings on black pride, is through constant reminders not only in schools but also in the family and other social settings. If parents are more aware that "blackness" is beauty and not the opposite as they were socialized to believe, they will be better able to help their children to understand the importance of accepting their skin color. Color prejudice will not disappear overnight, but accepting the skin that one has, will reduce the impact that this may have on the individual. We believe that, bleaching is not a solution but a part of the problem as it will not stop color prejudice as it implies a self-hate for one's complexion.

We agree, then, that, one needs to focus on the deeper problem of skin bleaching which is that illness of the mind that causes the bleachers to resist those who seek to educate them on true beauty. At the root of this form of skin bleaching is a function of lack of self-esteem and an inferiority complex that persuades the victim that he or she is inferior because of a darker color of skin. Failure to snare a mate or land a good job is attributed to shade rather than grade; what Martin Luther King Jr. described as color of skin rather than content of character (Jones, 2011). This feeling of inferiority, one can argue, is not an issue that will disappear overtime.

However, if persons continue to hide that this is an issue and attempt to erase it, some will never experience black pride. Black pride is something that national hero, Marcus Garvey, made his life's work; and yet, nearly 100 years since he began upholding that philosophy, many of his own country-men and women remain wallowing in self-pity, convinced that their God-given pigmentation is a handicap to progress. Individuals need to be more proactive in the quest to maintain the legacy that Marcus Garvey and others have left in spite of all the difficulties that came with slavery. Individuals are no longer in chains as they are able to choose their courses of action, so they should no longer be accepting the inferiority complex derived from slavery, but chart their courses based on the fact that one race cannot be seen as superior to nor more beautiful than the other based on skin color. The prob-lem is that this is something that ought to be taught, thus the importance of re-education.

We believe these perceptions can be changed but the individuals who are wrongly labelled as "ugly" and "inferior" are the only ones who can effec-tively bring about this change. Skin bleaching is not the answer; a mental release of that wrong perception may be the only answer. We however ac-knowledge that this will be difficult to accomplish especially since there are still employers in Jamaica who continue to request "light skinned" workers. According to one local newspaper report, "a hundred and seventy years after slavery was abolished in the British West Indies, Jamaica national training agency—Heart Trust Agency—still has to deal with color prejudiced em-ployers who are requesting that trainees be brown or light skinned as a prerequisite for employment in their firms. The color-specific requests come from proprietors, personnel managers, or the administrative staff who are asked to handle the process of securing trainees for the organizations." If this is the case, persons seeking employment in these agencies may develop the feeling that they are inferior to their "brown" competitors since they are "specially requested." When skin color is presumed to take precedence over experience and education in hiring persons for a job, we have a big problem. These employers are one source that continues to drive the acceptance of color prejudice in Jamaica, a practice that should be stopped immediately. If individuals are constantly reminded by family members, employers and DJ artists that they are inferior to others of their own race, the mental mind-set will be even harder to erase.

FINDINGS

We found that how light or dark skinned an individual is has for centuries been linked to beauty, self-esteem, power, and privilege. The epidemic of skin bleaching is not merely a fashion statement but a self-hate that has been embedded in the minds of some individuals through socialization, culture, media, and other forms. Skin bleaching is dominant in cultures that possess a history of European colonialism and African slavery. These individuals tend to uphold a "white ideal" in order to be accepted in certain social circles. Some believe that they cannot enjoy the privilege of social mobility unless they embody this ideal. So, there is a bias in certain non-white cultures for lighter skin tones and these values are taught from early in life. This would mean bleaching, lightening or whitening their skin tones. We have found that skin bleachers may take different approaches to bleaching but the end result is similar in terms of the need to be accepted socially based on skin color. The practice is of social and public health concerns and has implications for public policy.

CONCLUSION

Some human beings, across different non-white cultures, have allowed standards of beauty to be dictated by the wrong notions that were inculcated by white supremacists and persons of power who believe that they are superior. As a result, some individuals are damaging their skins in order to live up to this white ideal. We can conclude that, there are different reasons for skin bleaching and, there also are different kinds of bleachers. There are some who bleach to remove spots and blemishes but that is the only aim so they stop as soon as these are removed; there are the professionals who can afford to obtain bleaching creams from dermatologists as needed; there are others who buy from street vendors and others who make their own bleaching creams at home from whatever ingredients they can find that will give the desired results. All of these groups claim to bleach for different reasons as their situations are not all the same.

We believe, however, that most of the reasons that are given stem from the false notion that the black skin is not beautiful and should be rejected. This rejection hinges on racism as it informs a dislike for that which is not white This kind of color prejudice is embedded in the minds of individuals and with the constant reminders from all segments of the society, from beauty contest winners having the "ideal almost white look," songs and music videos reinforcing how pretty the brown or white skin is, to companies specifically requesting "brown" or "lighter skin" employees, the fight is not an easy one. We believe, however, that any fight against prejudice will never be easy and one should not accept skin bleaching as a solution as the fact is, some will still not be considered as good enough.

Bleachers need to admit that they have a psychological problem and work on rejecting the existing prejudice while developing an acceptance that beauty comes in all skin colors. We believe however that affected nations need to admit that there is a crisis and work together in unity to solve it. It will take time, but a journey cannot be completed without a start.

BIBLIOGRAPHY

Alleyne, Mervyn C. (2002). *The Construction and Representation of Race and Ethnicity in the Caribbean and the World.* Barbados: University of the West Indies Press, 2002.

Bewaji, J. A. I. (2012). *Narratives of Struggle.* Durham, NC: Carolina Academic Press.

———. (2013). *Black Aesthetics.* Trenton, NJ: Africa World Press

Campbell-Chambers, Arusha (2008). "Skin Bleaching: Who Says Lighter is Better"? *The Gleaner.* http://jamaica-gleaner.com/gleaner/20120808/health/health1.html.

Campbell, Howard (2012). "Bleaching Shop Scores for Exco Levi," *The Jamaica Observer*, Sunday, March 4.

Culbreth, Donna Marie (2006). *Employment Discrimination in the 21st Century: An Empirical Investigation of the Presence of Intraracial Colorism Discrimination Among Black Americans in the Work Place.* Proquest.

Fanon, Frantz (1967). *Black Skin White Masks.* New York: Grove.

Fluehr-Lobban, C. (2006). *Race and Racism: An introduction.* Lanham, MD: Rowman & Littlefield.

Jeremiah. *The Holy Bible* (2009). New King James Version 13: 23. Nashville, TN: Holman Bible Publishers.

Jones, Ken (2011). "Bleaching is More than Skin-Deep," *Gleaner*, Sunday, January 9.

Li, Eric P. H., Hung Jeong Ming, and Russell W. Belk (2008). "Skin Lightening and Beauty in Four Asian Cultures," in *NA-Advances in Consumer Research*, vol. 35. Eds. Angela Y. Lee and Dilip Soman. Duluth, MN: Association of Consumer Research.

Gorke, C. (2014). *The Role of Advertising in Indian Women's Desire to Be Fair.* Hamburg, Germany: Anchor Academic Publishing.

Higgs, C., Barbara A. Moss, and Earline Rae Ferguson (2002). *Stepping Forward: Black Women in Africa and the Americas.* Athens, OH: Ohio University Press.

Mills, Charles W. (1997). *The Racial Contract.* Ithica, NY: Cornell University Press.

Moschella, Marlisa Sen Yee (2007). "A Defence of Institutional Racism in the Face of Individualist Criticism." MA thesis, University of Colorado at Boulder.

Reid, Tyronne (2011). "Browning Please," *The Gleaner*, Sunday, September 11.

Rodriquez, E. G. M. Boatca, and S. Costa (2010). (Eds.) *Decolonizing European Sociology: Transdisciplinary Approaches.* Farnham, UK and Burlington, VA: Ashgate.

Rondilla, J. L., and Paul R. Spickard (2007). *Is Lighter Skin Better?: Skin Tone Discrimination among Asian Americans.* Lanham, MD: Rowman & Littlefield Publishers.

Samuda, J. (2011). "Professionals Bleaching Too," qtd. in Steven Jackson (Reporter) in *The Jamaica Observer*. March 29, Section: News.

Spears, A. K. (1999). *Ideology: Language, Symbolism and Popular Culture.* Detroit, MI: Wayne State University Press.

Stewart, C. (2010). *The Greenwood Encyclopaedia of LGBT Issues Worldwide.* Santa Barbara,CA: Greenwood Press.

The Jamaica Observer (2011). "AP: Skin Bleaching a Growing Problem in Jamaica," Monday, April 11. http://www.jamaicaobserver.com/news/AP--Skin-bleaching-a-growing-problem-in-Jamaica#ixzz2TrvX0QQ6.

Wijeyesinghe, Charmaine, and Bailey W. Jackson (2012). *New Perspectives on Racial Identity Development: Integrating Emerging Frameworks* (2nd edition). New York: New York University Press.

Chapter Eight

Toward Utilizing Social Media to Sustain African Culture and Identity

Babafemi Jacobs and Margaret Solo-Anaeto

Africa is a continent made up of fifty-four nation states comprising different ethnicities and peoples that have their own unique language and cultural patterns. One of the institutions upholding any society is the media that it operates. One of the results of the interaction between the European societies and African societies is the introduction of the Western mass media into African societies. The Western media also known as the mass media is because of development in Western technology and communication skills.

According to Ihebuzor (2013), using the erstwhile and traditional understanding of news dissemination media, the mass media comprises mainly of newspapers, radio, television, and books. A recent addition to the media family is the social media, which came forth as a result of the invention of the Internet. Kietzmann et al. (2011) define the social media as interactive platforms via which individuals and communities create and share user generated content. The mass media is a tool that can help in the growth and sustenance of the society, as it is structured to gather and provide the society information about itself that will inform, educate and entertain its members.

The influence of technology on the media in any society is one of immense value. The speed at which information is gathered and disseminated through a medium has to do with the medium involved. "Technology," derived from the Greek word *Techne* means art, science, or skill. Technology can be defined as the systematic application of scientific or other organized knowledge to practical tasks (Omoniyi, 2005). It involves the systematic and integrated process of managing and sustaining humans, machines, ideas and procedures to achieve the goal of educating, entertaining, informing, and

117

enlightenment members of the society. The history of the mass media is replete with the invention of numerous technological equipment. In relations to the field of mass communication and the process of information gathering, packaging, and dissemination, technology can be said to be the use of equipment by media workers to gather, edit and disseminate information, news, and ideas to as many people as possible in the society.

The commercialization of the Internet in 1992 (Cohen-Almagor, 2011) has made information gathering and dissemination faster. It has also led to the expansion of the mass media to accommodate websites that can be used for various forms of social interactions between individuals, groups, organizations, etc. Onabajo (2012) sees the Internet as the most technologically advanced medium of communication. The social media as a new addition of the mass media also performs the roles and functions of the mass media.

Hence, it is important to look at how the social media can help to promote and sustain the identity of Africans. Concepts like virtual ethnicity, virtual communities, African identity, and the interrelatedness of these concepts in a world that has become a global village, where diverse persons interact at a distance, become important in understanding various elements of social media interactions. The role that the social media can play to sustain and promote ethnic values and cultures in contemporary Africa will be looked at in this chapter, despite the Western imperialism that is taking place.

THE SOCIAL MEDIA

Advances in technology have expanded the mass media and created a new form of media known as social media. The social media is a media form on the Internet in which users create, process, send and consume information on an informal level. It is classified as social media not just because it allows information to be shared, but because it gives people the platform to share as much information as possible, in an informal way at their leisure time, without any form of institutional gatekeeping. For Morah and Uzochukwu (2012), it is due to their inherent access to social participation in creation and usage of information that this technological derivative and application of the Internet for informal mass communication is regarded as a social media.

Some social media forms include Facebook, Twitter, LinkedIn, YouTube, Buzz, MySpace, and Orkut. Edosomwan et al. (2011) explained further that the Social media is a phenomenon that has transformed the interaction and communication of individuals throughout the world. In recent times, social media has impacted many aspects of human life through unrestrained communication and sharing of ideas and information. The social media can thus be said to consist of all equipment and processes that the individual can use to express himself on a daily basis without any form of guidance and censorship. Social media provides power to connect, inform, and mobilize and act as catalyst for facilitating the formation of more intimate content specific communities (Morah and Uzochukwu, 2012).

The social media embodies features like interactivity, adaptability, portability, and convergence. These features have led to their phenomenal growth and usage. A survey conducted on 17 thousand Internet users in 2008, by Universal McCain, as reported by Morah and Uzochukwu (2012), show that social media, particularly blogs, are becoming more important part of media consumption of an Internet user than the traditional media and social media is turning to be a global phenomenon.

The total estimated global active Internet audience in 2013 was 625 million. Mobile Internet usage has now reached nearly a fifth of all active internet users. There are 200 million active users of Facebook with 100 million users logging on at least once every day in 170 countries/territories in 35 different languages. It has been observed that there is an average of 100 friends for every Facebook user. The number of users of Internet and its applications are increasing at an exponential pace.

The use of the social media to influence, educate and entertain people is nonetheless one that gives the pan-Africanist cause to worry about the extinction of his/her culture. Though it is Western oriented, the social media is a platform that can be used to protect and sustain the ethnic and cultural values of individual African societies and ethnic groups.

AFRICAN IDENTITY

The identity of a person or groups of individuals refers to the characteristics and set of behaviors that are common to the group or persons in virtue of their experiences and the social coping mechanisms they have devised. Identity is one word that means different things to different peoples and scholars in different fields of study. The definition of identity is one that has been evolving for years. Identity refers to the ways in which individuals and collectivities are distinguished in their social relations with other individuals and collectivities (Jenkins, 1996). According to Hall (1989), identity is a process, identity is split. Identity is not a fixed point but an ambivalent point. Identity is also the relationship of the other to oneself.

Fearon (1999) explains further that there are two types of identity, which are role and type identities. Role identities refer to labels applied to people who are expected or obligated to perform some set of actions, behaviors, routines, or functions, in particular situations, for example, taxi driver, toll collector, mother, father, president, professor, businessman, students, etc. Type identities refer to labels applied to persons who share or are thought to share some characteristic or characteristics, in appearance, behavioral traits, beliefs, attitudes, values, skills (e.g., language), knowledge, opinions, experience, historical commonalities (like region or place of birth). The label "African" is an example of type identity that sees the people resident and rooted in the African continent as a particular group that have similar feature(s) in common.

Africa encompasses 54 nations, nearly a billion people and more than 800 distinct ethnic groups. From its history, to its cultures, to its politics, to its climatic conditions, and landscape Africa is unique with its distinctive ways of life.

The term African identity is a representation of Africa; one that has deep social and historical meaning. It can be seen as a projection that encompasses the rich cultural diversity, strong respect for moral values, communality, rich food, and clothing of the African people. The African identity embodies everything African.

The concept of an African identity has been a contentious one among scholars, with no straightforward conclusions. Some say there is nothing like an African identity, saying it is a feeling from those out of the continent. Others say that there are diverse sources of African identities. Mudimbe (1988) cited by Chikafa and Mateveke (2012), argues that African society and bodies are heavily invested with Eurocentric representation and that the only way to come up with a true African identity is to discard the Eurocentric way of looking at Africa which tends to stereotype Africans. This is because the geographical structure of the African continent was done by the Europeans who did not understand the ethnic and town structures on ground before merging different ethnic groups with different and distinct culture, language and traditions together as one state.

Appiah (1992), on the other hand, embraces the position that Africa is diverse and African identities are hybrid, due to the contact of Africa with Europe. This African identity may not exist or may not be as clear cut as many scholars have argued, but nevertheless there are peculiarities that make Africans distinct and those are the things we subject to critical analysis in this chapter. It is thus necessary to look into how the social media can be (has been) used to promote the growth and sustenance of the different ethnic groups, societies and nationalities, that fill up the geographical place called Africa.

In examining the role of the social media in sustaining the African identity, this discourse is anchored on the democratic participant media theory articulated by Dennis McQuail (1987). The theory advocates the democratization and decentralization of the communication process. It encourages increased interaction and participation of media audience. The theory supports media pluralism as this will make for a media that is close to the people and serve their needs and interests better.

In this regard, the social media represent a media form that is decentralized with increased participation of the people as stated by the theory. It guarantees easy access to the media for all potential users and consumers. Users are able to express themselves, share, and exchange ideas and information. Social media has this dynamic, engaging, and easy to use platforms and applications thus creating powerful online communities and transforming the way people express opinions and views.

The analytical approach was used for this study drawing largely from books, journals, and online articles. The researcher's observation of the usage of the social media was of immense importance and inferences were drawn from the contributions of scholars and online authors as gleaned from their articles relating to this study.

SOCIAL MEDIA AS AN AGENT OF SOCIALIZATION

Socialization is one of the building blocks of the society. It is the cornerstone on which the values, behaviour and culture of a particular ethnic group from one generation to another is built. For Ihebuzor (2013), socialization is the process whereby a child or an individual comes to adopt the standards and culture of a society.

There are however many agents of socialization of which the mass media is one. The social media as part of the mass media can perform this socialization roles. This is supported by McQuail (2005) in their contention that the media are continually offering pictures of life and models of behaviour in advance of actual experience. This position fits the operations of social media tools that aim to give one the opportunity to express oneself and communicate with one another on a social level. It must be stated the social media has always given an individual a virtual opportunity to create new images and personalities which might contradict what he is in real life. The social media, through the kind of information and statements posted on it by individuals from similar and different ethnic backgrounds, can be used as a means of building good behavior and lifestyles to those who are connected and exposed to it on a consistent basis.

Crouch (2010) posits that a cultural or ethnic group that resides inside a non-indigenous state will use a social media tool that can connect them globally across all cultures and also use tools that connect them just within their cultural or ethnic group. He defined global social media tools as those tools or services that are agnostic to a culture or ethnic group and enable communication in any language (text, audio or image) and have global reach. Group specific social media tools are tools that are language (usually indicating culture or ethnicity) specific or culture/ethnic group specific. This is because language is a tool that is crucial to the survival of any ethnic group within or outside the African continent. Examples include Vkontakte, which is Russia's Facebook, or Sonico.com, which is for Latin Americans and Portuguese speakers, AbairThusa, a Gaelic speaking social network, and Ameba, a microblogging service in Japan that is like Twitter but for those speaking Japanese. We also have search engines like Google Yoruba, Igbo, and Hausa for information gathering purposes.

This is important when considering peoples engagement in social media. We all belong to different cultural, ethnic, and social groups. Immigrant populations inside a country can be very positively engaged in their new home country. We also have research interfaces such as Google having their own localized platforms meant for people from different ethnic groups even within the same country. But the majority of their activity takes place on services that are specific to their culture or ethnic group. This can offer significant opportunities. It is important to look at who an African is and how the social media can be an agent of socialization and thus promote people's cultural virtually

VIRTUAL ETHNICITY

Miller and Slater, according to Martin and Covaci (2000, 55), define virtuality as complexity and diversity of relationships pursued through media and which are embedded in ongoing social lives in cyber space. On and offline worlds penetrate each other deeply and in complex ways when realizing existing concepts of identity and pursuing new modes of sociality.

One of the most interesting "unintended consequences" of the Internet has been the creation of mediated social networks of sociability and collective belonging, populated by an ever-increasing number of individuals of different national origins and backgrounds. A quick tour of the Internet reveals a diverse ecology of virtual neighborhoods, online communities, cybersalons, cyber-commons, community networks, and digital nations, formations that are novel and ambiguous (Diamandaki, 2003).

In any country, people belong to different cultural ethnic and social groups. People identify with ethnicity and race wherever they are. Omu and Ogboh (2008) sees ethnicity as a concept that applies to the consciousness of belonging with and being loyal to a social group distinguished by shared cultural traditions, a common language, in-group sentiment and self-identity. Being on the Internet and social media does not diminish this notion rather it offers tools for a more fluid nature of recreating one's identity (Padilla-Miller, 2008). Commenting on this, Rogers in Chervokas and Waston (1997) sees virtual ethnicity, that it is a reflection of social reality. They would also suggest that there are a growing number of sites that are ethnically based because people identify with ethnicity and race. We have both general social media tools as well as language specific social media tools. For instance, the Japanese *Ameba* and the Russian *Vkontake*are examples of language specific social media. These go on to reinforce virtual ethnicity.

The Internet and the social media play on ethnicity in two ways. On the one hand, it diminishes the ethnic identity of the user because it allows a user to assume any identity they wish at any given time but, on the other hand, it also reinforces existing ethnic links and ties. Social media facilitates greater connectedness among users of the same ethnic group. Poster (2010) in Bainum suggests that the Internet use also has the effect of linking together web users with the same ethnicity, into a tightly knit online community.

Virtual ethnicity on the Internet and social media can be seen in many forms. Although many commentators tend to over emphasize the dissolution of social and national markers on the Internet, national and ethnic identities are present everywhere in the Internet. Part of e-mail and web address is the country suffix that the individual, group, organization, etc., belongs to or identify with, for example, www.lcu.edu.ng or www.ogunstate.gov.ng. In the homepages of many individuals we find symbols, pictures, texts, and images that point to the creator's identity, either inherited or self-defined. In interactive environments such as MOOs and MUDs, a participant may structure her online persona in terms of ethnic characteristics such as names, such as GreekKaterina or Tom.CaliforniaSunshine.

In online dialogue, ethnicities are either consciously projected by individuals or unconsciously "given off" in the process of conversation. Users sometimes make posts and comments on Facebook wall in their local languages. Others use idioms, proverbs, tales and myths that are peculiar to their ethnic group. These are all online expressions of ethnicity. The social media thus serve as a channel to showcase and introduce users to different ethnicity/ culture as well as sustain these ethnic and cultural values and strengthen the ties between users of the same ethnicity.

The projection and sustaining of the African identity can thrive on this ability of the social media to create virtual ethnicity. It would mean users from other parts of the world and Africans not resident in Africa can fully appreciate Africa and its identity.

CONCLUSION

It has been argued in this chapter that social media has come to stay as a channel for expression, idea sharing, interaction and socializing. It has become a daily practice in some users' lives. Its informal nature makes it user friendly, engaging, and dynamic.

The social media in its own ways performs the socialization function helping its users become acquainted and imbibing general and acceptable standards of behaviors in society. In the same way, the social media promotes virtual ethnicity (i.e., keeping the ethnic ties of its users alive in cyberspace). The social media is thus a veritable tool that should be tapped in our bid to project and strengthen the African identity. An identity that promotes everything African in terms of language, dressing, values, food, music, history, politics, beliefs, and so on.

RECOMMENDATIONS

Having looked explicitly at and discuss on the African identity, social media, and virtual ethnicity, it is important to make the following recommendations:

1. Media workers and all other stakeholders involved in the generation and distribution of information on social media platforms should be focused on the positive aspects of the social media and campaign consistently against the negative use of the social media. There should be programs and broadcast contents aimed at reducing the way we Africans imitate the worst and negative aspect of the Western culture, which Westerners themselves don't promote or attach importance to in any way

2. Other agents of socialization like the family, government, and other traditional institutions should look into how they can create social media programs whose contents reflect and promote the traditional beliefs, religion, ways of life, and culture of every ethnic group in Africa.

3. There should be a round table discussion where every stakeholder will sit down and discuss how we can take the best of the Western culture and our indigenous culture to form and socialize a culture that can be used for the overall development of Nigeria.

BIBLIOGRAPHY

Bainum, Brad (2010). *Virtual Ethnicity.* Retrieved June 22, 2013 from http://learn.bowdoin.edu/courses/sociology-022-fall-2010-bbainum/2010/11/virtual- ethnicity/.

Chervokas, J., and Waston, T. (1997). *Afrocentric New Media*: Separate but Equal Hurdles. http://www.partners.nytimes.cm/library/cybe/week/051697afrocentricnewmedia.html.

Chikafa, R., and Mateveke, P. (2012). "The 'Africa' in Big Brother Africa: 'Reality' TV and African Identity," *Journal of Communication and Media Research*, 4(2): 43–58.

Cohen-Almagor, Raphael (2011). "Internet History," *International Journal of Technoethics*, 2(2): 45–64.

Crouch, G. (2013). *Culture & Ethnicity in Social Media.* www.mediabadger.com/2010/06/culture-ethnicity-in-social-media/.

Diamandaki, K. (2003). "Virtual Ethnicity and Digital Diasporas: Identity Construction in Cyberspace," *Global Media Journal*, 2(2).

Edosomwan, S. Prakasan, et al. (2011). "The History of Social Media and Its Impact on Business," *The Journal of Applied Management and Entrepreneurship*, 16(3).

Fearon, J. D. (1999). "What Is Identity?" www.stanford.edu/~jfearon/papers/iden1v2.pdf.

Ihebuzor, Lambert (2013). *Book Publishing in Nigeria: Theories and Issues*. Ibadan: College.

Hall, Stuart (1989). "Ethnicity: Identity and Difference," *Radical America*, 23: 9–20.

Jenkins, Richard (1996). *Social Identity*. London: Routledge.

Kietzmann, J., et al. (2011). "Social Media? Get Serious! Understanding the Functional Building Blocks of Social Media," *Business Horizons* 54(3).

Martin, L., and Covaci, M. (2004). *Virtual Ethnicity: Ethnic Identity Construction in the Internet*. http://www.urmila.de/UDG/Lehre/ws0405/Virtual%20Ethnicity%20071204.pdf.

McQuail, Dennis (2005). *Mass Communication Theory* (5th edition). London: Sage.

Morah, D. N., and Uzochukwu, C. E. (2012). "New Media and Climate Change Communication in Nigeria," *Journal of Communication and Media Research*, 4(2): 119–132.

Omoniyi, T. (2005). *Principles and Applications of Educational Technology*. Ibadan: Bash-Moses.

Omu, Fred, and Ogboh, G. E. (2008) (Eds.). *Mass Media in Nigerian Democracy*. Ibadan, Nigeria: Stirling-Horden.

Onabajo, S. O. (2002). "The New Media and Technology in the Twenty-First Century," *International Journal of Management Science*, 6(1).

Padilla-Miller, Alina (2008). "Virtual Ethnicity in MySpace." http://citation.allacademic.com/meta/p232666_index.html.

"Trends in Social Media." Retrieved from www.matthewningram.com on June 22, 2013.

Chapter Nine

Social Media Transcending Longstanding Stereotypes?

Chimamanda N. Adichie's Americanah *and Belkacem Meghzouchene's* Sophia in the White City *as a Case in Point*

Fouad Mami

Heavy media, often known as corporate or traditional media, according to both Adichie and Meghzouchene, has done a considerable damage to both Africa and its people. Inaccurate and gross generalizations of African realities can be easily qualified as crude stereotyping and downright essentializations. The trouble with stereotypes and essentializations is that they have been the deployed as a rationale for colonial occupation and economic exploitation. Despite the fact that, in most cases, colonial powers have retreated and African flags have been raised, heavy Western media still approach African realities with stereotypical gazes. An example of this category of narrative delineates African individuals as too naïve or too lazy to be ever engaged in nation building. Consequently, they unthinkingly succumb to the lure of extended stays outside the continent; and presumably getting indulged in the material wealth of the global north. Hence, Africans are all potential émigrés, whose hearts and minds are portrayed as insensitive to nationalistic aspirations of social betterment and economic progress. That is why these two authors are keen to decry the nefarious effects of heavy media and meanwhile explore the potential of social media, like Facebook and blogs, hoping it can serve as a counter measure against heavy and traditional media.

   Given this stance, the two texts do not share a number of characteristics and aspects. Adichie's comes as her fourth major publication, while Meghzouchene's is his first. One is authored by a woman and the other by a man. This latter is an Algerian author, and his work has been celebrated as the first Algerian novel in English. As a necessary reminder, Algeria had been a French colony for 132 years, and with more than half a century of independence now, there exists a deeply entrenched tendency in Algeria to write fiction in French, not English. Therefore, the fact that Meghzouchene decides to write in English (and by the way, his text is written in highly refined and polished English) underlines his awareness of the need to reach not only British or American audiences but worldwide readership. This again contributes to the de-stereotyping agenda that Algerians and Algerian realities are often portrayed in either French or Arabic. Such demarcation from traditionally enmeshed linguistic means of expression relates to the author's dissatisfaction with easy and categorical classifications of peoples and their experiences. While Meghzouchene's character never has a metropolitan experience, Adichie's Ifemelu is a returnee from America. This detail highlights the fact that Nigerian migrants account for their fleeing in fiction but rarely account for their return experience.

Having outlined this, the two texts do share nevertheless the vivaciousness of the principal characters. Both Ifemelu and Ramice are two identifiable people. They are economically independent and successful. They do not have recourse to the comfort of either corporate business or the safety often sought in salaried government positions. Both are comfortable with the liberal jobs they have themselves created: one runs a blog; the other, an e-magazine. While Ifemelu works alone, Ramice has a team and domestic charges to pay. Their exemplariness proves that with a certain amount of will and intelligence, entrepreneurial activity can be still a viable option for African youth. The thriving of their individual passions and their talent in making this passion sell, reminds aspiring African migrants that a life opportunity can still be located in the ever closing global economy.

Defying the strictures of their respective local markets, and their ability to expand beyond mere survival, is a mind-set which the present chapter finds worthy of pursuit. For both authors do not seek to simply say that material gains and cutting a margin is still possible. On the contrary, the two novelists seek to banalize the idea of success through their characters' resilience of spirit and insistence on drawing an identifiable narrative. Both have managed to come up with a narrative that builds up and thrives on transcending longstanding devastating stereotypes; stereotypes such as Africa has a serious problem with success. Indeed, nursing and integrating success have been often portrayed as antithetical to Africa. Remarkably, opportunity and cutting a margin happens to be in social media: the sector probably the least expected to render either personal or communal rewards. Probably, both in Nigeria and Algeria social media has not been taken seriously in the sense that ordinary Africans in these countries still approach social media as mainly entertainment. The narrator of *Sophia in the White City* explains that Algerians actually swarm to newly founded cybercafés only to grab whatever opportunities (fake or genuine: they usually do not bother to inquire) in order to flee their country.

As will be shown in what follows below, such counterproductive costs of social media does not downplay the fact that the authors chosen for the scope of this study insist on painting a different picture about life and reality in either Nigeria or Algeria through social media. Aware of the possibility of a relapse, the principal characters gain the wealth and status they subsequently enjoy through hard labour and creative passion. As role models, their careers seek to galvanize other members of their respective communities into constructive actions. Once this is massively considered, Africa can take a deliberate step as an actor in its own fate and start putting an end to the culture of lethargy and self-blame.

THE CRITICAL RECEPTION OF BOTH NOVELS

At this stage, one needs to underline the fact that both novels have received scanty critical attention. Apart from critical appraisals in reviews, the inhibitive impact of the media industry and how it continues to shake Africans' trust in themselves remains largely untouched in full-length studies. The present study proceeds via the means of exploring the following questions: What kind or genre of social media do the two novels deploy? How are they used? Towards which end are they triggered? And, to what extent the authors are confident that the type of social media considered for action never fires back?

Most critical reviewers of *Americanah* (since the novel has not been studied in full length academic articles or book chapters yet) point to the fact that the major preoccupation of the text is racism. More precisely, reviewers point out how America is prejudiced against Africans and how the color line is still a dividing issue in the United States today. However, the niche which the present study claims to have established is that in as much as racism is highlighted in the novel, Adichie's principal foci lie rather in the economy of race. The problem of race, according to the author, is exacerbated due mainly to the ways in which media covers stories pertaining to race. The author offers a satisfying portrayal about the quality of mind that generates racism, and by racism one means that state of being that can be qualified as racist.

Put differently, the portrayal of race as carried on in heavy media impairs not only African Americans but even new arrivals from Africa: Nigerians, Kenyans, Ugandans, Malians, Senegalese, etc. Centuries, of conditioning to racism have the consequences of begetting a stale culture of race, where both whites and blacks become equally its victims, both mutually feeding on this inhibitive culture. Characters and the situations in which these characters are enmeshed in leaves readers with little doubt as to the role which the stereo-typing and prejudice-generating machinery of the media plays. Differently put, the role which the media plays is but one variation of "reified conscious-ness" that keeps connections and relationships always tense and stranded. The successful blog Ifemelu keeps can be better approached as a living manifestation of Adorno's non-identitarian dialectics heralded in *Negative Dialectics*. In this connection Adorno suggests that

> The name of dialectics says no more, to begin with, than that objects do not go into their concepts without leaving a remainder that they come to contradict the traditional norm of adequacy. . . . Dialectics is the consistent sense of non-identity. It does not begin by taking a standpoint. My thought is driven to it by its inevitable insufficiency, by my own guilt of what I am thinking. (1973, 5)

Through her two blogs (both the American and the Nigerian ones), Adichie demonstrates how social media can be mobilized in the task of resisting the inhibitive forces of cultural modernity. When consistently and brilliantly deployed, social media make conscious people realize that consumption, global capitalism and racism cannot be embraced as fate. The totalizing impact of the mass media eventually leads to a reified ideology with equally destructive results on both Africans and non-Africans.

For purposes of exploring how media is deployed in the two selected texts by Adichie and Meghzouchene, one notes that each author refers to social media in his or her own terms. While Ifemelu prefers to replicate her American blogging skills in Nigeria, Ramice, who does not enjoy a life experience in the metropolis, starts as an editor-in-chief of French-language weekly on-line magazine: *Hebdo-Sciences*. Instead of hitting walls in the manner of a hittist, like thousands of Algerian graduates or fixating on the brain-drain syndrome which actually marks Africa, Ramice rents a locale in downtown Algiers, opens his own cybercafé and soon starts a scientific e-magazine that keeps abreast of news of discoveries and innovations in three major sections: archaeology and anthropology together; physics, astronomy and chemistry comprise the second section; the life sciences and medicine the third. "Hittist," in the Algerian colloquial language is adopted in referring to graduates who long after the end of their formal studies remain jobless, aimlessly sitting in public squares or around coffee shops and do not own a fare for a simple beverage.

In spite of the bureaucratic hurdles, Ramice fights teeth and nail to start his own business. The narrator reports, "But the hard truth was that one must have gone through the teeth and fangs of awful bureaucratic meanders to make things struck. Connections mattered too much. A vitality in Algeria. And Ramice was not an exception to eke out his own living. *Damn it*"

(Adichie, 2013, 3). Later in the story, the phrase "*Damn it*" repeatedly peppers the text, suggesting how suffocated Ramice often is with the bureaucracy and the state officials' sabotaging reflexes.

Adichie's Ifemelu, too, takes matters in her own hand, and instead of behaving like other Americanahs, by pretentiously complaining about difficulties of adjustment to life in Nigeria and missing some cherished consumerist amenities, decides to critically account for moral and social degeneration among rank and file Nigerians. She too chooses an aesthetically appealing place to live in and uses its panoramic view as a background picture in her blog named, *The Small Redemptions of Lagos*.

Mark that the word "small" insinuates that besides the massive chaos and ugliness, patches of beauty are still left and redemptions, however small, are nevertheless possible. Such a socially reformist conception of art and society in general and fiction-writing in particular, however lofty and inspiring, does not appeal to the sensibilities of certain critics, one among whom is Ashleigh Harris. This latter observes that as far as literary form is concerned, Adichie's and others' "body of writing is capitulating to a notion of literary form . . . is not in dialogue with African everyday life and as such eliminates Africa as one of the sites upon which form is (globally) contingent" (2014, 5). The author of this piece blames creative writing programs sponsored by US universities of compromising Adichie and others' vision so as to acquiesce to these condescending sponsors' reductive idea of Africa.

Indeed, while this reviewer may or may not have a point in advancing his defense for authentic conceptions of African works of art, an editorial piece like this one risks alienating potential audiences and tax the author as irrelevant, hence studies like the present one are crucial. Far from defending either Adichie or Meghzouchene's fiction, the present study finds it imperative to single out the added value (both moral and cultural) these two writers' perspective result in. Both novelists contribute in terms of a visionary outlook that eventually generates a positive appreciation of self for African youth.

THEORETICAL GROUNDING OF DE-STEREOTYPING

In the scope of the present study, de-stereotyping comes as synonymous with the intellectual work of de-anesthetizing audiences and readerships from the reificatory effects embedded in corporate media largely responsible for despair and self-blame. The logic pursued in this article emphasizes the trajectory that the various manifestations of social media can be considered as are ample mechanisms that can disinfect (in the Adorninan sense) people/readerships from the inhibitive reflexes of culture industry. In his refusal or distrust of metaphors and insistence on the idea of "shudder," Adorno reminds readers with the ideal quality of a given work of art; the quality that promises truly liberating potentials:

> Art holds true to the shudder, but not by regression to it. Rather, art is its legacy. The spirit of artworks produces the shudder by externalizing it in objects. Thus art participates in the actual movement of history in accord with the law of enlightenment: By virtue of the self-reflection of genius, what once seemed to be reality emigrates into imagination, where it survives by becoming conscious of its own reality. The historical trajectory of art as spiritualization is that of the critique of myth as well as that towards its redemption: The imagination confirms the possibilities of what it recollects. This double movement of spirit in art describes its proto-history, which is inscribed in its concept, rather than its empirical history. The uncheckable movement of spirit toward what has eluded it becomes in art the voice that speaks for what was lost in the most distantly archaic. (1997, 157)

By the quality of the work of art, Adorno implies locating those works that push the boundaries and create a potential for positive social transformations via means of desterotyping. For only when armed with rigorous and meticulous attention to reality, despair cannot be overwhelming and a positive narrative will be set in motion. Such a transformation functions more in terms of an awakening to an accurate state of reality, or consciousness. Unlike metaphor which Adorno finds semantically restrictive and socially damaging as they can divert attention from reason resulting in instrumental reason, shudder draws a perfect example of what Adorno means by the reversal of the false condition of the world. In line with Walter Benjamin's idea of "aura," shudder "through the aesthetic shudder that the reading subject is provided with an unmetaphorical and immediate sense of actuality" (Franks, 2006, 197). Hence, literarily speaking, de-anesthetizing takes place most of the time through the author's arduous labor of foreshadowing and immersing in the historical background of his or her central characters.

METAPHORS VERSUS HISTORICAL DEPTH: WHICH COURSE TO EMBRACE?

Trusting in metaphors according to Adorno would be like deceiving readerships; a dishonest choice that sacrifices depth and confuses the minds through the selling of romanticized fantasies as viable alternatives. Metaphors, in this connection, are one certain way of insulting readers' intelligence. Adorno warns that the unstated comparisons implied in metaphors, however emblematic and suggestive, keep imprecise and superficial. Probably one unmistaken observation regarding literary technique in Adichie's *Americanah* and Meghzouchene's *Sophia in the White City* is the consistent evasion of metaphors either in character development or in setting construction. Readers notice that the authors are tacitly not comfortable with and cannot trust the elastic meanings that everyone seems to freely draw when flooding an artwork with parables, fables, symbols and allegories.

And, in order to consistently carry on their distrust of metaphor, they have recourse to lengthy but close historical accounts, all aiming to lift whatever confusion readers might encounter while following the progress of the principal characters toward their successive and appealing careers. Technically considered, the setting of Adichie's novel is quite simple: the major character, Ifemelu, has finally decided to move back to Nigeria after a thirteen-years stay in the United States. Readers meet her first on her way to a hair salon outside Princeton, part of her eventual return chores to Nigeria. As she is braiding her hair, each moment at the salon brings reminiscences and details from her high school years in Lagos, down to flashes from her early stay in the United States, all the way till she becomes an Americanah, a returnee.

The merits of Adichie's technique are better articulated in the following account of Walter Benjamin's technique: "Benjamin's [and by extension, Adichie's] images functioned like switches, arresting the fleeting phenomena and starting thought in motion or, alternately, shocking through a standstill and setting the reified objects in motion by causing them to lose their second nature familiarity" (Buck-Morss, 1977, 102). Readers can acknowledge the seriousness of the plot in *Americanah*, particularly when its inherent content tacitly strives to unsettle docile society. Despite its simplicity, the surprising and disturbing qualities of the plot ensure an exemplary interaction with readers as they fully acknowledge, appreciate and supply erstwhile missing details pertaining to Ifemelu's life before, during and after her experience in America.

Similarly, Meghzouchene leaves readers with no opportunity for guess work about Ramice Taslent, the principal character. The young novelist sets a story in limited time and space frameworks. All the actions of the story take less than a fortnight between late October through mid-November 2006, and almost all are located in Algiers, nicknamed the white city. Sophia's scheduled visit to join her father who represents a German science publisher in Algiers' book fair and subsequent stay in the north African city punctuates the entire drama in the novel. After a brief sketching of Ramice's typical day and brief background before he starts his internet space and hitting on the idea of *Hebdo-Sciences*, the author tactfully evokes the 1990s (famously known as the black decade in Algeria or *la decinée noire*, also as the national tragedy or *la tragedie nationale*). Ramice is portrayed as a former conscripted army soldier who fought terrorists in the mountains of Cheria, and whose brothers in arms fell victims in the blood pool. The reference to the unhappy events of 1990s, at least in each Algerian's *imaginaire*, shows Meghzouchene's infatuation with Yasmina Khadra's fiction, an Algerian novelist using French as his medium of expression, and who too worked in the army during the bloody nineties before he eventually left for a career in fiction writing.

References of this sort do consolidate elements in Ramice as a character like his passion and resilience. Anybody who overcomes odds of such magnitudes and returns alive from what can be fairly considered as the Algerian Vietnam is an exception, not the common. Still exceptional Ramice is, as he declines the glamour in fleeing to France on the pretence of pursuing an academic career like his former classmates, Yacine Ledjeni. The following passage shows that there exists a widely circulating presumption among Algerians that no matter how tough life could be outside their country, that situation is still better than staying home. Such an unchecked presumption massively embraced as a fact of nature, passing among individuals as common sense, presumably frees them for looking into real causes of their supposed misfortune, all for the sake of fleeing their country, no matter what.

This passage shows that eager and frustrated youth use social media not for research or cultural exchange, but instead as a means that apparently guarantees their entry tickets to Europe or the Americas. Though this mindset can be traced to an age considered as the precursor Internet, Internet and the social media, in particular, have fuelled this perception when applications like Skype and Facebook become more and more democratized. Aware of the fact that social media can exacerbate the problems facing Algeria, the author shows that like any other two-edged stick, Internet can be deployed for constructive purposes like galvanizing consciousness to a more active resistance against instrumentalized reason.

Meanwhile, there lies undeniably an ironic twist about the title *Americanah*. To begin with, the wording is drawn from a famous American novel with, more or less, the same title, *Americana*, by Don DeLillo (1971, 1990). The letter "h," which Adichie adds only accentuates Adichie's exploration of DeLillo's theme, which is how the media inflames already festering issues in a given society. The difference between the two works, however, is that while DeLillo satisfies himself with exploring how media does a lot of damage than good, Adichie exceeds in providing an alternative and procures a visionary outlook. Hence the word "Americanah," which is a little-checked metaphor widely circulating in Lagos about Nigerian returnees from England, but mostly from America. The irony about Americanahs is that they are individuals who often cover their personal shortcomings and frustrations with endless nostalgic musings about amenities and services they claim they miss in Lagos. Yet this metaphoric layer of understanding does not apply to Ifemelu as she is not a typical Americanah. Every aspect of her life choices, so exuberantly detailed throughout the novel, contradicts the solid yet pretentious convictions of the rest of Americanahs. She complains both of Lagos and of America, but not in the way typical Lagosian Americanahs do; her complains are not effusive nostalgia, feeding on an abashed ego aspiring for notice and recognition. Hers, though, are critical views that are historically grounded and not easily digested by either Americanahs or fellow Nigerians. The content of blogs she writes does not even attempt to cater with the egos of her respective audiences. Instead, her writing finds the egos of the audiences of CNN or NBA ridiculed; therefore, it assesses such egos as inhibitive and destructive, and through its illuminating insights tries to break free and subvert this destructive drive. Only in this connection the metaphor is distrusted and displaced in favor of in-depth historical accounts.

Now, what makes Ifemelu critical of both Nigeria and America is the intended (never accidental) lack of depth in abundant portrayals of realities and historical experiences of Africa and Africans, and whose cost is the perpetuation of reification. For Ifemelu, the media industry reduces historical experiences and sells targeted audiences a false and shallow notion of self. As a matter of fact, clichés and stereotypes keep people (Nigerians and Americans) unauthentic about themselves and the lives they are confronted with.

The fact that Ifemelu has been a communication major at university and lands a job in the hearts of the media industry, falls into this dynamics that aspires for subverting means of disseminating her storyline. Similarly, her encounters with blogs and websites, like happykindynappy.com (a website that offers useful tips to do African American women's hair), is an early incentive in her subsequent de-anaesthizing campaign. Indeed, most of the cultural commentaries Adichie draws in this novel originate from observations about hair. Hair in *Americanah* stands as an extended metaphor that demarcates two different cultures and mind-sets, but the demarcation is never processed with the purpose of erecting closures. The hustle and bustle inside the hair salon where readers meet the central character for the first time can be considered a reflection of the power of the media industry and its role in shaping sensibilities and tastes. As readers, we are confronted with a number of ups and downs in Ifemelu's life before she is finally reconciled with her Afro hair. "I have natural kinky hair. Worn in cornrows, Afros, braids. No, it's not political. No, I am not an artist or poet or singer. Not an earth mother either. I just don't want relaxers in my hair—there are enough sources of cancers in my life as it is" (Meghzouchene, 2010, 297).

An element that is not to be downplayed is that, in order to be taken seriously for a job interview and thus cast a professional outlook, Ifemelu had to undergo a lot of chemicals in terms of moisturizers. After some months into this denaturalizing situation, Ifemelu decides to call off this pretention, and she literally removes her hair completely. For three days, she called in sick. Finally, she went to work, her hair a very short, overly combed and overly oiled Afro. "You look different," her co-workers said, all of them a little tentative. "Does it mean anything? Like, something political?" (Megh-zouchene, 2010, 211).

Ifemelu's eventual reconciliation with her Afro style is in fact a reconcili-ation with nature, her nature. This is not easily appreciated to media-hypno-tized co-workers. Adichie portrays this shift within Ifemelu as a kind of a leap of faith, probably living up to her name significance *Ifemelunamma* meaning: "made-in-good-times" or "beautifully made" (69). The ingrained allusion to beauty delineates the aesthetic formula, which Adichie highlights and proposes as her cultural model. Afro-hair becomes a culturally charged symbol that betrays Ifemelu's dissatisfaction with the global media as it publicizes Western paradigm of women's beauty as a norm that fits all wom-en, regardless of origin. Of course, such a degenerate state of affairs which excludes African women from the category of beauty (since they are the ones more likely to have kinky hair) could not stay uninterrupted by dictating the fashion industry without years of exposure and conditioning by nefarious media. Indeed, it is media that ushers in a world marred in sick and denatu-ralizing processes.

Other instances of denaturalization caused by media abound, but no major transformation or reconciliation with self on parallel with what takes place with Ifemelu like this one. Early on in the novel Ifemelu observed that, for her secondary school boyfriend, Obinze Maduewesi, for it was weird for a teenager to come up all by himself with an observation like: "'You look like a black American was his ultimate compliment' [the author interjects] Man-hattan was his zenith. He often said, 'It's not as if this is Manhattan,' or 'Go to Manhattan and see how things are'" (Adichie, 2013, 67).

Like many of his Nigerian peers, this young secondary school student has been raised to think that only American fiction is true fiction, speak only American English in earnest, not only for the sake of appearing smart and sophisticated, but presumably as second nature. Emenike, another classmate of Ifemelu and Obinze, and upon yet another classmate's—Kayode—return from a trip to Switzerland "bent down to caress Kayode's shoes, saying 'I want to touch them because they have touched snow'" (Adichie, 2013, 65). Ifemelu prefers her father speaking Igbo because "his mannered English bothered her as she got older, because it was costume, his shield against insecurity" (47).

On one occasion, Ifemelu is astonished at Obinze being familiar with some Igbo proverbs: "Many guys won't even speak Igbo, not to mention knowing proverbs" (62). The early part of the narrative details how the newly Nigerian rich try to beat each other in choosing foreign schools operating in Lagos, because the Nigerian school system, according to media-dissipated and pretentious middle class, cannot be as professional and competitive. Offended and bored with such pretentions, Obinze ridicules Kosi and her patronizing friend at a party when the topic of his daughter's schooling was broached upon: "Didn't we all go to primary school that taught Nigerian curriculum?" The women looked at him; their puzzled expressions implied that he could not possibly be serious. And, "in some ways, he was not" (Adichie, 2013, 29).

Euphemisms of this sort are indicative of how far Nigerians are caught up, not only in egoistic and dead-end pretentions, but far worse in the reification of their collective corrupted consciousness. Exposure to denaturalizing media industry deliberately demeans and ridicules one's sense of being, by systematically endearing ordinary Nigerians to foreign schools, books, tastes, and styles of life. Even Obinze's obsession with America and his presumed need to leave for America is initially nursed, even fuelled, with the amount of Hollywood films he watched, the books he read and the magazines he glossed over. One needs to account for this kind of subconscious damage taking its toll on Obinze, the second major character in the novel, in the following excerpt:

> It had always been America, only America. A longing nurtured and nursed over many years. The advertisement on NTA for *Andrew Checking Out*, which he had watched as a child, had given shape to his longings. "Men, I'm checkin' out," the character Andrew had said, staring cockily at the camera. "No good roads, no light, no water. Men, you can't even get a bottle of soft drink!" While Andrew was checking out, General Buhari's soldiers were flogging adults in the streets, lecturers were striking for better pay, and his mother had decided that he could no longer have Fanta whenever he wanted but only on Sundays, with permission. And so, America become a place where bottles and bottles of Fanta were to be had, without permission. He would stand in front of the mirror and repeat Andrew's words: "Men, I'm checkin' out!" (232)

Not only the narrator draws on the central character's dissatisfaction with classical forms of media films, shows, and women magazines, but goes further to locate the ways in which this media shapes a parallel or hyper reality for ordinary Nigerian youth of whom Obinze is but an example. Ever since childhood, Obinze has been conditioned to exteriorize his disappointments with the cost of staying forever blind from finding out the reasons for the absence of simple pleasures like Fanta, hence his constant but unaware borrowing from the ad's character: "Men, I'm checkin' out." Of course, his mother's pampering has a hand in his not seeing why Nigeria denies him a simple joy like a bottle of Fanta, but the advertisements, the books and the magazines he has been exposed to and consumed throughout his formative years all amount to his acute experience of reification of foreign values.

This reification translates in the deliberate distanciation from one's immediate (Nigerian) historical setting and an awkward identification with an alien and unwelcoming context. The least provocation, in terms of shortage, crisis or any other mundane inconvenience, becomes for young men like him a justified call for "I'm checkin' out": an extended metaphor uncovering how young men deserve a better place and better standards (not because they have worked to deserve these places and standards, but merely as an inherent right) than what already exists, drawing an ahistorical and unfair comparison between two countries: Nigerian and America. With a visa application rejected, Obinze lives a pathetic life until his mother forged a UK visa application. Three years and half later, he is deported, and even with his unscrupulous involvement in the "national game" and the sudden wealth years later, Obinze keeps an apathetic attitude vis-à-vis life because of his childhood misguided and media-induced longings.

Meghzouchene's narrative also provides ample evidence of how media, mainly Algeria's state TV, agitates stymied Algerians to leave their country for good. Half through the novel, readers find Ramice Taslent together with Sophia and his old friend Abd al-Halim attending a press conference by Algeria's renown literary giant Yasmina Khadra, in "the Literary Café," part of the cultural activities of Algiers' book fair that year. The three were all excited and satisfied with Khadra's erudite answers. Later that day, Ramice and Abd al-Halim expect a decent journalistic coverage in the evening news. To their disappointment, the TV airs little images of the writer with no words. Ramice's comment is that this is "sheer ostracism in his [Khadra's] country he so loves," subsequently "he [Ramice] changed channel in distaste of the infinite affront" (71). This zapping of channels occurs repeatedly in the course of the novel. Ramice leaves readers with the insight that with so little interesting or stimulating TV programs, Algerians are stranded between escape to Europe or fall easy prey to drugs, self-abuse and moral derangement. Such unprofessional, intelligence-insulting and even suffocating TV contents oblige Algerians seize the event of the book fair not as an opportunity to boost their knowledge and expand on their culture, but simply as a way to vindicate their frustrations vis-à-vis women. With huge crowds of Algerians visiting the different foreign stands of the fair, Sophia is duped to think that this reflects a population eager for culture and learning. Ramice quickly corrects her: "Don't be astonished, Sophia. Algerians are the world's most curious people vis-à-vis foreigners. Above and beyond, they've got bags of frustrations about women" (27).

Denied of a chance to visit these foreign countries, representatives of international publishers become natural targets for inquisitive and curious Algerians, not necessarily because Algerians admire the content presented in the stands. The day Ramice shows Sophia his cyberspace and editorial office, nearly all clients stood aghast as they could not cover their sick admiration of the German beauty.

The narrator keenly observes that "The Internet surfers present that afternoon unglued their eyes from the monitors to set them on the blond [Sophia] who had walked past them. Curiosity. Always Algerians' killing curiosity"

(Meghzouchene, 2010, 31). One notes that the context in which Ramice refers to Algerians' curiosity is vilification. Denied of visas, a European or American in blood and flesh walking down the streets of Algiers becomes the materialization of all the frustrations amassed from years of watching Hollywood films. Nabil, Ramice's cybercafé manager, is no exception and his reaction is representative of a large section of uncultured and hypnotized Algerian youth, who in the absence of informative and inspirational media shows slip into moral degeneration.

The sexual allusions in Nabil's interest in Sophia cannot be downplayed. Terms like "heart beat," "licking," and "stealthily" are there to indicate the amount of frustrations Nabil suffers. While following Sophia's every move in and out, Nabil feigns himself watching a live pornographic performance. Amazingly, he gets is high because of the scene of the German woman walking around. A pathological response like this one indicates how alienated he is and by extension how degraded the moral standards of large sections of Algerian youth have become. Obviously, this is not the author's a naive indictment on the youth of his country, as much as an indictment of the state media coverage. Indeed, this kind of media keeps Algerians intimidated with shiny facades and too naively yearning for foreign countries as the ultimate dreams of their empty and vilified lives.

The distinction between the two novels is that Meghzouchene's principal character makes his mission the banalization of scientific news (disseminating the state of art in the sciences), while Adichie's finds daring ways of uncovering Nigerians' alienation from themselves. From the outside, both can be seen as working toward different ends, but when considering the inner dynamic of each author's narrative both share a keen interest in carrying out campaigns of inspiring, self-trusting, and impressive intelligence. Both show that the new heroes of Africa do not succumb to the survivalist strategies dictated by either local or global pressures. Both can be leaders, independent in their judgments and course of action, but still humane with no toxicity toward anyone around in their lives.

CAN SOCIAL MEDIA BE TRULY SUBVERSIVE? POTENTIALS VERSUS LIMITATIONS

In *Americanah*, the idea of starting blogs and thus making use of social media is genuine and does not follow an already prescribed pattern or trend as Ifemelu's need for expression is urgent and unpretentious. Her US experience in press editing functions as a necessary background experience and helps her subsequently to locate what is missing in the business of corporate media. When her white boyfriend, Curt, complains of the racist innuendoes which he presumably finds in *Essence* magazine as this last features only black women, Ifemelu insists they go to a bookstore where they "took down copies of the different women's magazines from the display shelf." What follows next is an erudite argument about how unfair and culturally insensitive racist these magazines can be. Ifemelu pushes for the need for a counter and alternative pattern to the approach and the conception of women beauty (Adichie, 2013).

What is rather impressive in the above exchange is Ifemelu's exceptional capacity for synthesis of ideas. Not everybody is able to deconstruct large details with far-reaching hints and allusions, and at the same time remains capable of retaining a personal opinion that is well informed and meticulously articulated. Even the courage to say it loudly and clearly to liberal Americans at the risk of appearing eccentric has not to be undermined. A day after this exchange, Ifemelu sends one of her former Kenyan classmates, Wambui, an email about what she thinks that fuels the problem of race in America. Indeed, it is this former classmate who encourages her to start a blog as her opinions are widely relevant and can make sense to a large and confused audience. It is worth noting that the idea of the blog that is supposed to begin the reversal of the status quo, the one tightly observed by corporate media has been put in motion in response to corporate media misconceived portrayals.

Remarkably, it has all started from this accurate articulation of how women with kinky hair can be left with no clues for beauty. Breaking the monopoly over beauty as strictly defined by white media and locating alternatives of for non-white beauty seems to be Ifemelu's initial step in stipulating a decent outlook for African women. This is already subversive of the capitalist outlook that exercises exclusion of black beauty through its media. As put by Ifemelu, it does not need a lot of intelligence to see that black women are not considered worthy of attention: in short, they apparently do not qualify for inclusion at the level of the concept of beauty. Whether corporate media is aware of it of it or not, its editors basically keep black women ugly and invisible ghosts, with no clues for beauty and savoir fair. Through their careful choice of words—like, *everyone* and curly— their deliberate evasion of tips for kinky hair, these magazines commit primarily an aesthetic violation amounting to racism, however minor or insignificant this may look. Such evasion and violation could not take place without the cultural structure premised on racism and systematic exclusion of non-whites. As explained and detailed in one interesting blog, the first one after having it re-titled to *Raceteenth or Various Observations About American Blacks (Those Formerly Known as Negroes) by a Non-American Black* (Adichie, 2013, 315).

Overall, there is an emphasis on the racist mind-set that vigorously operates a deeply entrenched culture of racism and aggravated in the first place by the media. For apart from having lucid details about the functioning of racism in the United States—having racism as a solidly integrated culture that goes unnoticed, and hence largely unquestioned—there lies the element of sarcasm in suggesting a purely medical treatment. "Radical disorder syndrome" is a suggestion that derides mainstream American tendency for the scientific categorization as cultural. Certainly, racism cannot be seriously approached from the perspective of medical attention. Instead, it is the culture that needs to be revisited and reversed and, in order for this to happen, social media has to be implicated in such dynamic.

Near the end of *Sophia in the White City*, Ramice declares before Sophia what can be considered his "I-have-a-dream" speech: "I have a dream of making science information a treasure endeared for by Algerians" (Meghzouchene, 2010, 138). Of course this testimony echoes Martin Luther King Jr., the African American leader during the civil rights era in the United States. While some readers find these parallel unnecessary effusions of needless romantic sensibilities that downplay the seriousness of the novel, still others can put things in contexts and see why science stories of inventions and achievements of dreams, when largely disseminated, can indeed animate a sense of pride and mission to despaired and suffocated Algerians. It is true that these youths' escape wish is generated from a background that is nefarious and baffling. They are almost justified in seeking new horizons as any income-generating activity they think of turns into a herculean undertaking. The state's bureaucracy is too much on the people's nerves, since it is one of the heaviest and ugliest in the world (Meghzouchene, 2010).

Again, Ramice insists on his dream, in spite of his constant recourse to swearing. While requests for bribes exacerbates Ramice's plans, his determination nevertheless never wanes. As noted earlier, phrases like "*Damn it*" are frequently interjected in the text to indicate how repulsive to state officials' indifference to his magazine Ramice is. Further, the phrase also casts the setting in an unmistakably authentic background that every Algerian experience at one time at least. Algerians with no connections complain of the devices which crooked officials deploy in order to win bribes. "But the hard truth was that one must have gone through the teeth and fangs of awful bureaucratic meanders to make things stuck. Connections mattered too much. A vitality in Algeria. And Ramice was not an exception to eke out his own living. *Damn it*" (3).

These are mounting difficulties of exceptional magnitude which Western media does not help at all in alleviating these youth's burden. Instead of a positive or at least accurate portrayal, Sophia testifies that in school she was taught that; "To Europeans, the Maghreb is all the same; geographically, historically, culturally, and politically. Due perhaps to the fact that they just visit it for a short period of time. If they were to stay longer, differences would emerge clear-cut as to Algeria, Tunisia, Morocco, Mauritania and Libya," as Ramice commented on Sophia's beforehand notion (Meghzouchene, 2010, 18).

The coverage of the Western media according to Meghzouchene is rarely analytical. Fatalist accounts desperately try to sell the idea that acts of butchery are ingrained in the Algerians' genes and chromosomes. The overall impact is often adds insult to injury. Differently put, though sometimes informative, the portrayal cannot be helpful in the task of nation building. It robs Algerians of the right to dream. This last is a necessary incentive to start constructive work. In this sense readers can see how Ramice's scientific magazine can switch Algerians to the beautiful and more intimidating side of their country. While hopes for getting printed are not yet materialized, social media can lessen some of Ramice's burdens and help him massively inspire Algerians in being agents of their own fate, thus obliging media industry in the long run to draw a positive outlook.

With her eventual return to Nigeria, Ifemelu seeks a job first at a women's magazine known as *Zoe*. Beside the fact that this experience offers, more or less, similar conclusions as to the inhibitive costs of corporate media, it nevertheless sheds light on other layers as to why commitment to social media is compulsory for pumping a new blood in a country such as Nigeria. As she soon understands, *Zoe* is caught in a diatribe competition with *Glass*. Each seeks the expansion of readership and maximum advertisements. Ifemelu's approach is that as far as their content is concerned both are vapid and commercially not business savvy at all. There is no creative passion either in conception or in the editing process of each. Both feature interviews with supposedly successful ladies, but under Ifemelu's critical gaze that personal success is simply marred in corruption and fraud. The ladies featured are caricatured as successful simply because their husbands are intricately involved in the national game. They are wives of army generals, general managers of leading national banks; they are over pretentious and Ifemelu is often suffocated with their religious overtones.

By the time she learns that these women actually pay (not give donations to the magazine in which they feature) the editor in order to be featured, Ifemelu decides to leave the magazine for good. She could not stand even the atmosphere in the magazine, which despite the pomp of an office car with a driver that can be intimidating for some, co-workers nevertheless doggedly fight in between to please the editor. In addition, her new reconcilement with Lagos leaves Ifemelu ample time to seriously think of working independently by starting her blog. She starts it under the title: *The Small Redemptions of Lagos*. There are religious overtones of the blog title: "redemptions" cater to the pretentious religious culture shaping life in contemporary Nigeria. The awkward beginnings do not stop her from adjusting to her new setting and subsequently improving afterward. The word "redemptions" also suggests that there is no intention on the part of Ifemelu to seek unwelcome attention of power mad officers.

One blog scorns the phenomenon of young women desperate either for husbands or sugar daddies. Here, one notes how corporate media, through TV channels of whom NBA is a shining example, are designed to keep girls aspiring for a gold-mine relation as the ultimate accomplishment in of their life. These young ladies, similar with young men who look for fleeing their country, both in *Americanah* and *Sophia in the White City*, process their unfortunate destines in terms of a telos: only an outside solution in terms of luck or godly miracle can save God-fearing individuals from the ramshackle economies of their respective nations. As victims, they are short of addressing their misery in historical terms with causes and their logical consequences. Only migration can put an end to the young men and marriage or a relation with a filthy rich man does the same for the young women. Personal value in society is ensured through the wedlock with men who are wickedly active in the national game. Once that is done and in order to make this state of bliss last, the unbelieving wife or mistress has to give birth to a male offspring. She too has to pray desperately in order to have that male offspring. The false and overdone religious drive of some of the characters is probably best summed up in the following: "dauntlessly stating the obvious truth, Nigerians are religious, not because they love God, but because they need a fast and justified way of denouncing poverty. It becomes a survival of the fittest, the Pastors or the faith clenching congregation" (Ewejobi, 2014, 117). Kosi has to guard her new status from supposedly jealous and ill-wishing adversaries hiding as friends and relatives. Obinze's wife, Kosi, stopped talking and inviting her former friend. Right after childbirth, she looked sorry at Obinze and apologized for giving birth to a baby daughter, saying she hoped next time it will be a boy. When Obinze feels unease she—pretending innocence—asked him "aren't you supposed to expect a baby boy?" Her fake and packaged emotions decide the day.

Now if marriage is too far as a target, the girl in question can settle for a sugar daddy. Meanwhile, she keeps her options alert for any marriage prospect. Ranyinudo laughs at Ifemelu, saying who cares for love. Without the murky conditions that sets the stage for the Nigerian economy, young ladies would not be as fatalist as both Kosi and Ranyinudo. In reference to marriage, too, Meghzouchene's principal character, Ramice, on his second day of taking Sophia from the airport and thinking of all Algerian young men who opt for sham marriages with European or American women to escape their country (Meghzouchene, 2010).

This state of affairs is not limited to young men only. Readers of *Sophia in the White City* find that young men, like Ramice, do not find their partners because women too embrace the lure of Europe. Abd Al-Halim concludes that "Nowadays, women look for wealthier men. Love is really nugatory" (122). Upon Sophia's insistence to know his romantic past, Ramice confesses, "I met two other women. They too cast me aside for moneyed men. All my care and love to them wound up on the rocks. Especially the latter one, who plainly genuflected before an emigrant she barely knew on the Internet, and got married with him" (127).

Regarding the conceited religious zeal that is massively sweeping Algeria, Abd al-Halim accounts of his beach experience, "Three yards away from us, five veiled women, seemingly from the same family, stripped off to let just their bikinis. They swam all that day. In the evening, they donned their veils, unscrupulously." And Ramice reiterates; "We're just Muslims by the *clothes* and the names," (157; emphasis in the original). At the end of the novel and to his complete bewilderment and disappointment, Ramice finds out that head-scarfed Nessrine is involved with Nabil in producing porn movies, turning the cybercafé to a porn studio.

ARE ACADEMICS INTELLECTUALS?
MODERN INTELLECTUALS AS CULTURAL WORKERS

If social media can alleviate, however partly, the inhibitive cost of corporate media the authors feel entitled to explain why only a few people are involved in the corrective work of social media. Why academics, for example, cannot seize the potential which this alternative media offers? Towards this end, Adichie distinguished between academics and cultural workers. Some of the comments Ifemelu draws help readers understand Adichie's position regarding US black academics.

It is interesting to note that Blaine, the African American Yale professor of political sciences and Ifemelu's boyfriend does not take Ifemelu's blog very seriously. In his self-righteous zeal for books and films that "push the boundaries," he could not perceive what boundaries *Raceteenth* is breaking. The narrative keeps on reporting the blog's success: commentaries, advertisements and even donations. Ifemelu also gets some remuneration and flight tickets as she gets regular invitations for talks at diversity workshops throughout the United States, and live radio interactions with listeners.

One non-misleading indication of her blog success is that she resigns from her well-paying job at the press editing and supports herself entirely from the blog. Without his self-righteousness, Blaine and his group of literati would have been more receptive and less critical of Ifemelu's efforts. The African American academics' colleagues are but a varied extension of Blaine's personality and state of mind: their misguided sense of righteousness and child-like earnestness are part of the cost of the culture of racism; overall they cannot be part for a catalyst for a major change. To take one example, Nathan, Blaine's literature professor colleague, complacently states that he does not read any fiction published after 1930, because according to him taste simply relapses ever since then. Later that day, Ifemelu announces to Blaine her verdict, "academics were not intellectuals, they were not serious, they built their solid tents of specialized knowledge and stayed securely in them" (Adichie, 2013, 323–324).

Only Boubacar, the newly arrived Senegalese professor at Yale, stands atypical from this category of impractical academics. He insists on Ifemelu to apply for the Princeton fellowship and recognizes the propitious change she tries to establish, suggesting "it is the only way to change conversation [about race]" (340). Because of such openness and readiness to step aside from the ivory tower, Boubacar can be qualified as an organic intellectual in the Gramscian sense. Adichie hints at the fact that probably Boubacar's upbringing, his experiences of Francophone culture and recent arrival in the over densely racist US culture made him a truly cultural worker. He is immune to racism and not entirely consumed by the racist culture in the way African American academics are.

Indeed, the exemplariness of Ramice, when considering the Algerian case, is undoubtedly vital for Meghzouchene's cultural project from the novel. Ramice has been conceived by the author as a fictional variation who comes against a background marred in lethargy, self-blame and violence. "Ramice since he had launched his science publication, aiming at generalizing the cutting-edge scientific breakthroughs and developments to the rank and file" (6).

In line with his "I-have-a-dream" philosophy, Ramice is too preoccupied with the good work for his community. Thus, "While his fellow men strived to go abroad and got arranged marriages in order to settle there legally in Europe or the Americas as 'husbands' of permanently resident wives, Ramice saw the inverse scenario taking stage for him" (12). Indeed, it is Sophia who arrives in Algiers, not him travelling to Berlin, seeking his love and care. Remarkably, Sophia confesses her love for him twice, yet he prefers to take his time and weigh things. Though he has sincere feelings for her, he is never in a hurry. Readers finish the novel, yet Ramice has neither confessed, nor is thinking of Sophia taking a toll on his time or efforts. The magazine remains on the top list of his priorities. This is so, because Ramice's type of intellectual works toward cultural regeneration was to replicate *Scientific American* in Africa (Meghzouchene, 2010, 85–86).

Given the entire pathetic cultural climate, finding the Algerian parallel to major American and European science publications is not a small step at all. Indeed, it is this spirit that compels Sophia to tell her father; "His keen talk about Algeria underscores his love to his homeland. He isn't the sort of guys who would endanger their lives to cross the Mediterranean Sea and live therefore underground in Europe." Gerd Weize replies, "It's nice to see South Hemisphere's people working their countries so complacently. Otherwise these countries would be emptied of their brains" (Meghzouchene, 2010, 23).

While Sophia underlines Ramice's exceptionality as an individual, her father situates that same exceptionality in its exact historical context. Algeria, according to Gerd Weize cannot be constructed with dollars only from the oil and gas industry. Almost every forward-looking community needs before engineers, architects and doctors loving, earnest and dedicated people who generate hope and give people a dream for a better possibility. Indeed, every aspect about Ramice suggests that he as a character is conceived in direct opposition to the prevailing image of Algerian youth in Western, mainly French media. See how aspects of Ramice's intellectuality can cure the damaging consequences of the harrowing experience of 1990s Algeria:

> The new situation that all Algerians had to face after 1992 putsch was the sudden irruption of political violence into their lives. The outbreak of guerrilla activities coupled with the arbitrariness of state policies weakened and destroyed long-standing formal and informal social and political arrangements. People came to believe that political violence was the main engine of change and that they had no choice but to take part in this necessary evil if they wanted to remedy the social, economic and political inequalities that affected them. This 'democratisation' of violence also reinforced the perception of the state as a 'predatory' one and of the guerrillas as organised criminality. (Volpi, 2003, 93)

Indeed, the beauty of Meghzouchene's narrative is that capacity of transcending the violence dissipated in the everyday culture. *Sophia in the White City* re-appropriates that violent culture in the Ramice's non-budging ethical choices. The merit of a text of this quality is the readers' capacity to locate instances of individuality that resist despite all odds the encroaching instrumental forces of reason. Other people in Ramice's shoes would not think twice before moving to France or elsewhere as life in Algeria is indeed troublesome. The violence which many historians refer to is now consumed in the spirits of the people which years after the end of its physical manifestation, its moral side decides how relations are governed and deals concluded. Even after forgiving Nabil and Nassrine for jeopardizing his redemptive efforts and turning his Internet space to a porn studio, Nabil violently retaliates and sets Ramice up for smuggling artefacts. Therefore, resisting the temptation to leave it all at that and escape with Sophia, shows an intellectual of exceptional quality and undying spirit.

CONCLUSION

Through their tactful and masterful use of social media, both authors illustrate that resisting global forces of capitalism is indeed possible. The capacity of the principal characters in both novels in drawing their own synthesis despite the stereotyping reflexes that mark their respective cultures demonstrates that resistance is tenable. Ifemelu's blogs and Ramice's e-magazine, together with their rising audiences are living instantiations of the much needed work characterized as deanesthetization of people's consciousness. The two novels incite the need to bypass prejudiced media portrayals as such portrayals are less constructive and more antagonizing. Narratives, like Adichie and Meghouchene's are needed not only by Africans, but Westerners as well. In suggesting that there is some human activity of interest and value carried on in either Algeria or Nigeria; that here too men and women think, work, laugh, and fail, but ultimately succeed, African youth may have the incentive to stop postponing their legitimate dreams of the life they dream until they settle in either Europe or the United States. Similarly, giving Africans some of their stolen centres back can encourage non-Africans, and mainly Westerners, to respect Africans and cooperate with them more on equal grounds. Everyone can observe that Sophia's relationship with Ramice in Meghouchene's novel is tensionless and easy. It is freed from the complexes of master/slave divide. However sad or far from this ideal Africans' relationship with Europeans and Americans today, such an adverse situation does not impeach the two novelists considered here from the right to dream and envisage a better world.

BIBLIOGRAPHY

Adichie, Chimamanda Ngozi (2013). *Americanah*. London: Fourth Estate.
Adorno, Theodore W. (1970). *Aesthetic Theory*. Trans. Robert Hullot-Kentor. London: Continuum.
———. (1973[1966]). *Negative Dialectics*. Trans. E. B. Ashton. New York: Continuum.
Buck-Morss, Susan(1977). *The Origins of Negative Dialectics: Theodore W. Adorno, Walter Benjamin, and the Frankfurt Institute*. New York: Free Press.
DeLillo, Don (1971). *Americana*. London: Penguin Books.
Ewejobi, Dorcas Iranwo-Oluwa (2014). "Reflections of Religion: Review of Chimamanda Adichie's *Americanah*," *Hirentha: Journal of the Humanities*, 1(1).
Franks, Mary Anne (2006). "An-aesthetic Theory: Adorno, Sexuality and Memory," in *Feminist Interpretations of Theodor Adorno*. Ed. Renée Hebeale. University Park: Pennsylvania State University Press.
Harris, Ashleigh (2014). "Awkward Form and Writing the African Present," *The Johannesburg Salon*, 7: 4. http://jwtc.org.za/resources/docs/salon-volume-7/3_TheSalon_Vol7.pdf.
Meghzouchene, Belkacem (2010). *Sophia in the White City*. ALgier: Editions l'odyssée.
Silverstein, A. Paul (2004). *Algeria in France: Transpolitics, Race, and Nation*. Bloomington: Indiana University Press.
Smith, L. Andrea (2006). *Colonial Memory and Postcolonial Europe: Maltese Settlers in Algeria and France*. Bloomington: Indiana University Press.
Volpi, Frédéric (2003). *Islam and Democracy: The Failure of Dialogue in Algeria*. London: Pluto Press.

Chapter Ten

Adaptability of the Affective Essence of *Ifá* Lore

Examples from Rotimi's The Gods Are Not to Blame

Bifátife Olufemi Adeseye

Literature often has the pleasant effect of jolting the reader into a new aware-ness of hitherto remote similarities in subliminal ideas that may now promote a better understanding of experienced realities. Ordinarily, a lot of changes occur around us daily that we do not seem to notice because, phenomena can become so familiar that we really do not see or notice them at all, as they are taken for granted. In considering the objective of this chapter, the researcher observes that, if we fail to apply and affectively utilize things within our ecosystem, our perception of the world can wither away so completely, leav-ing us with only hazy recognition. The study adopts development communi-cation trope as it attempts to show that *Ifá* literature can be adapted and used to provide some form of supportive healthcare strategies as was done in the past by indigenous Yoruba *Ifá* priests. The affective use of *Ifá* chants for hypnotism in *The Gods Are Not to Blame* by Ola Rotimi provides the needed aesthetic, epistemological and ontological paradigms for the study. The study extends the use of dramatic arts beyond the confines of mere entertainment, as it affirms that *Ifá* lore may be employed as hypnotic tool to help someone to change an unwanted habit.

Affectation is here related to the act of taking on or displaying an attitude or mode of behaviour not natural to oneself or not genuinely felt through the manner of speech or conduct not natural to oneself and induced by exposure to some external influence. To this extent, affectation may result in emotion-al expansive, habitual display, or pretentious mannerism, which enables the agent to accomplish or attain new horizons, either positive or negative.

The challenge of the study is to show that *Ifá* lore is capable of stirring emotional or habitual instincts in its audience. Care delivery is a concept that has been carefully selected to stand in for the supportive healthcare accessible through the indigenous channels of counselling by *Ifá* priests, which may not necessarily be coming from the expert modern healthcare givers.

The research adopts the popular dictum of being your neighbour's keeper, in the sense that health care-giving is both communal and institutional. The concept of *Ifá* is explicitly discussed later in the chapter, using extant literature, to show the socio-communal context of its practice, deriving from the lived realities of the people, which give meaning to the experiences and expectations of members of society. It is clear that this shared ontological perspectives and epistemologies underwrite all medical, social, religious practices in all societies, giving them meaning, importance and acceptance.

A term like "healthcare" naturally attracts some other medical or para-medical terms like "therapy" and its sub-sets. *Thomson's Concise Medical Dictionary* (1973, 325) defines "therapy" as "treatment"; while "supportive therapy" is one that does not treat or improve the underlying condition, but instead increases the patient's comfort. Supportive treatment may, therefore, be used in palliative care. All medical practices and systems globally recognize the value, meaning and importance of palliative care in various circumstances, some of which may be beyond the control of caregivers, patients, their families or the community of persons in society in general. What such practices provide is the kind of resources and capacities to alleviate suffering, pain and stress brought about by conditions beyond the control of professionals and their patients.

THEORETICAL FRAMEWORK

This chapter deals with development communication in an attempt to show that *Ifá* literature can be adapted and used to provide some form of supportive healthcare. The main theory of "catharsis," ascribed to Aristotle, although never clearly stated in his *poetics,* forms a springboard for this discourse. This chapter adopts an observation by Lucas on catharsis, that, "Aristotle had used the term catharsis purely in its medical sense (usually referring to the evacuation of the *katamenia*—the menstrual fluid or other reproductive material). However, he employed it as a medical metaphor" (1967, 440).

Here, we adopt *purgation* and *purification* of emotion as most relevant meanings of catharsis that are useful in our discourse. The chapter is discussing the potential of *Ifá* literature for health-care management; while the notion of therapy within *Ifá* practice is taken as being a term more related to healing process. *Ifá* lore is chosen for this study as a paradigm of other health care literatures indigenous to Africa. The framework for this work is structured on creative adaptation, such that it examines the capability of one field of study being useful in another; specifically, we explore the capacity of *Ifá*, as a system and as a practice to influence health care.

The concept of development communication agrees with the assertion made by Isola that, "of all the weapons used by various cultures to ensure continuity and vitality, literature is undoubtedly the most potent" (1995, 311). Literature is a very salient aspect of every culture, because it is the power house of its language, encapsulating the various perceptual, apperceptual and subliminal relations between the members of society and the world they inhabit. We also observe that culture consists of ideas, customs and arts that are produced and shared by the members of a particular society (Bewaji, 2013). The contents of culture are coded into diverse traditions, a tradition being a custom or belief system that the people in a particular group or society have practiced or held for a long time.

But what is "culture"? For our purpose, following Bewaji (2013, 97) we can understand culture in an elastic way, to involve what can be seen as those evolved aspects of non-biological inheritance of ways of life of members of society. In this regard, it covers the beliefs, customs, skills and other such artificially contrived efforts of members of society for coping, managing, and conditioning their existence, thereby ensuring that they minimize stress, maximize comfort and ensure the continuity of what is regarded as social advancement. So many things come to mind as features of culture here, such as language, religion, the traditions, educational systems, literature, and the arts, and more importantly the various accumulations of experiences and creativities which are inherited from previous generations of members of society, even while selectively discarding or acquiring aspects of these inheritances. One aspect of Yoruba culture that stands out is *Ifá* literary corpus, a lore that has helped to conceptualize the epistemic, axiological and ontological ideas of generations of Yoruba philosophers, theologians and physicians.

The use of literature, in this respect, is to communicate, to transfer what is being depicted in a culture into a "sphere of new perception." Of language and culture, Isola correctly observes that, "The socialization (of children) into particular cultures or societies involves the use of particular languages— the life blood of any culture. The literature of a culture is created and used in its indigenous language. The use of a foreign language can only be a poor second best" (1995, 312).

The discussion, therefore, will be within the context of African literature, in an African language, and the illustrative examples are chosen from *Ifá* lore in Yorùbá literature. Aside from the projected potential for the use of *Ifá* lore for therapy, every literature has some basic functions of entertainment and education. To provide a reasonable background and a comfortable landing pad, a brief discussion of the concept of *Ifá* is needed.

THE CONCEPT OF *IFÁ*

Ifá originated as a religious/cultural practice among the Yoruba of the south western Nigeria; evidence of its proliferation abounds in variations of this religious traditions and cultural practices across the globe. According to Bascom (1991, 1–9), *Ifá* divination system is identified by a series of names among the immediate and remote neighbours of the Yorùbá people. The Fon people of Dahomey (in the current Republic of Benin) call it *Fa*. The Ewe people of Togo refer to the system as *Afa*.

Divination objects, such as peas and tortoise shells, are common among many ethnic groups, notably the Gwari people. The Nupe people, who live north of the Yorùbá, beyond the Niger River, use a string, *Ebba*, of eight pieces of calabash fastened together; corresponding to the Yorùbá *Òpèlè* divining chain.

The Jukun of Nigeria employ a pair of strings or chains (nook), each of which has four pieces of calabash or metal. *Agbigba*, among the Yoruba, appears to be confined to the Yagba-Yoruba in the present Kogi state of Nigeria. Four divination chains of this type are known as *afa, aha,* or *efa* among the Ibo and Ekoi people respectively; as *eba* among the Idoma; as *eva* among the Isoko and Edo.

Divination tools may vary in all the listed ethnic nations, but the concept is the same: to search for a clue to a subject believed to be shrouded in mystery. Researches have shown that *Ifá* oral literature has a poetry bank that is seemingly inexhaustible. *Ifá* narrative is presented in 256 corpuses and each corpus accommodates about 1680 *Ese Ifá* (*Ifá* verses). Adeseye and Ibagere recount Bogunmbe's explanation to buttress this submission:

> *Ifá* poems are best sourced in *Iyere Ifá* (*Ifá* verses) usually chanted during *Ifá*
> divination exercise. *Ifá* poetry bank is seemingly inexhaustible. Each of the
> 256 Odus or corpuses of *Ifá* sacred teaching is identified by between 8 to 16
> strokes; having very scientific (mathematical) combinations of varying strokes
> in 16 square columns to make up to 256 chapters in the ancient *Ifá* records.
> (1999, 10)

The sixteen square columns achieved in a graphic display of *Ifá* combinations have been the subject of many computer and scientific studies. For instance, Longe presented an inaugural lecture at the University of Ibadan on *Ifá and Computer Science* in 1982. We observe that scholars have done tremendous work on the potentials of *Ifá* for literature, language, religion, and indeed, culture, but not enough attention has been paid to the relevance of *Ifá* to this kind of cross-pollination of ideas in the effects of communication in health care delivery. The term therapy belongs in the medical sciences; this study is deploying this concept within literature, an art material for use by paramedics for the facilitation of wellbeing of members of society.

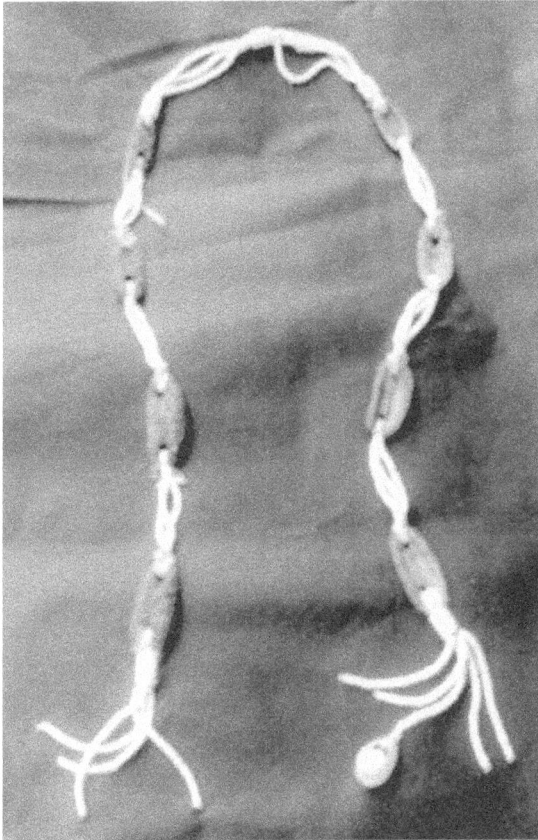

Figure 10.1. *Ifá* **divination equipment.** *Source***: author's personal collection.**

This has been one aspect of health-care which indigenous Yoruba people are accustomed, but which has been on the wane since the invasion and supplanting of indigenous traditions by western religio-cultural practices.

THE POWER OF THE SPOKEN WORD

One of the myths of the creation of the world, as contained in the Christian *Bible*, and also found in its twin Arabian desert religion, the Holy *Quran*, asserts that the Almighty God commanded or decreed creation through spoken words. Exalting the power of the spoken word, the President of International Council for *Ifá* Religion (ICIR), Idowu Odeyemi, writes,

Figure 10.2. *Ifá* **divination equipment.** *Source***: author's personal collection.**

Ifá is the religion of the Orisas. As the Divine Message, *Ifá* is the Word, which was with Olódùmarè in the beginning. The Word is Olódùmarè, in as much as it cannot be divorced from its owner. In the many aspects which comprise human existence on earth, Yorùbá and other Africans consult *Ifá* in order to know the wishes of Olódùmarè. *Ifá*, throughout the history of Yorùbá over the past several millennia, has always been an essential part of life. The real key to the life of the Yoruba lies in *Ifá*. It forms the foundation of the all-governing principle of life for them. The eight essences of *Ifá* are also, in the main, coincidental with the human essences on planet earth and the non-human essences in the entire universe. They constitute what is also known as "the great mystery system. (2014, 25)

The interpretation of the stated scripture points to one thing; that the spoken word is very powerful (Bewaji, 1983). Every spoken language is a verbalised expression of the human thought; these thoughts are usually made intelligible by reasonable combinations of desired and designated words to express the thoughts, ideas, beliefs, feelings, anxieties, expectations, and speculations, among others. As presented by Bewaji (2013, 219–220), we find the follow-ing clearly reflecting the nature of the efficacy and affective value of words:

Figure 10.3. *Ifá* **divination equipment.** *Source:* **author's personal collection.**

Bewaji (1983), in a special study into these matters, explored aspects of the use of the spoken word in Yoruba society. She found that there are very fine distinctions between even the most esoteric, specialized and casual usage of the spoken word. She was concerned with what is generically referred to as *incantations* in Yoruba orature. Her findings showed that the English language did not have equivalents for these rarefied linguistic typologies, consequently leading to confusion in untutored use and inaccurate translations of the Yoruba language into English and other Western languages.

She found, among other things, that traditional societies, as well as contemporary societies, have what may be regarded as futuristic usage of language to engender actuality of situations in the here and now. She writes, *"Ofo, ogede, ayajo ati aasan fi ara pe'ra die, idi ni wi pe ohun enu ni a n lo fun gbogbo won. A maa n lo won lati mu ki ireti ohun ti a fe ki o ya kiakia. A si n lo won lati mu ki ife inu eniyan se l'ogan"* (Bewaji, 1983, 1). By translation, this can be rendered literally as follows: *"Ofo, ogede, ayajo,* and *aasan* are similar in some minor respects, because we use the word of mouth for all of them. We use them to bring to pass our hopes immediately. We also use them to bring about our wishes and desires on the spot."

In other words, as her study shows, we find that the use of words is important in effecting the desired result. In tracing the origin of the use of words, she found various traditions, but all of them seem to point ultimately to: a) the Yoruba myth of national origin regarding creation of the universe; b) the nature of human beings as advanced language using creatures; c) the place of humans in the scheme of things as conceived by humans; and, finally, d) to the Supreme Being in Yoruba system of religion, Olódùmarè, who grants power to our requests to make our words that we use in requesting them efficacious and ensures that our requests couched in them come to immediate reality.

In a typical communication chain, *words* come after *thoughts*, that is, the thought process is like a progenitor to words and even actions. Oftentimes, what we say or do are the products of our mind-set. For instance, a request in the form of an application is a prayer; either verbalised or textual. The word-content of the prayer creates the efficacy of the request. Discussing the affective nature of communication, Burgoon (1974) observes that,

> Everything we label as communication is affective because it has an impact on someone. The woman who smiles at a man at a party is communicating with him, and that communication will have an impact on the man. Just what that impact will be is difficult to predict, because the man's response will depend on his perception, awareness and experience. (5)

There is no doubt that communication is indeed affective, but we also seek to who that the impact of words in the language of communication is mostly affective. The concept of therapy deserves some explanations, especially as it is applied in this discussion. For our purpose, we use Thomson's definition of therapy:

> Therapy (Latin *therapīa*) literally means "curing, healing" and is the attempted remediation of a health problem, usually following a diagnosis. In the medical field, it is synonymous with the word "treatment." Among psychologists, the term may refer specifically to psychotherapy or "talk therapy." (1973, 325)

Preventive therapy or prophylactic therapy is a treatment that is intended to prevent a medical condition from occurring. For example, many vaccines prevent infectious diseases. An abortive therapy is a treatment that is intended to stop a medical condition from progressing any further. A medication taken at the earliest signs of a disease, such as at the very symptoms of a migraine headache, is an abortive therapy. A supportive therapy is one that does not treat or improve the underlying condition, but instead increases the patient's comfort. Supportive treatment may, therefore, be used in palliative care.

TYPES OF THERAPIES

Examples of healing methods or disease management styles abound. We would list the following among them:

a. Treatment by light phototherapy;

b. by water hydrotherapy;
c. by salt: *speleotherapy*;
d. by heat: *thermotherapy*;
e. by cold: *cryotherapy*;
f. by physical therap/occupational therapy;
g. massage therapy or acupuncture;
h. by lifestyle modifications, such as avoiding unhealthy food or maintaining a predictable sleep schedule;
i. therapy may be by meditation;
j. prayer, as in, *theotherapy*;
k. also by counselling, such as *psychotherapy*; and
l. by education.

As our investigation progressed we were able to observe that *Oriki* (praise singing or cognomen) is a form of *massage therapy*, because it massages the ego of the individual, the family or the community. *Oriki* is an integral part of *Ifá* poetry; and even more than that, it is indeed a form of Yoruba oral history. Orunmila, the first teacher of *Ifá*, is fondly called *"Opitan Elufe"*—the great historian of Ile-Ife, the cradle of Yoruba civilization.

What is very clear from these ideas is the interrelationships between knowledge (episteme) of ontology or metaphysics or genesis of some being, person, thing or entity, appreciation of affiliations, affinities and preferences, and the utilization of these in combinatory performances in language, which allows for affective efficacy (Bewaji, 1992). These many and complicated ideas are a product of keen observation on the part of the leaders of thought and ideas in indigenous Yoruba society, who then synthesize these ideas into transmissible format in language, symbolism and mythologies, and when properly packaged, these constitute very potent affective material for the edification of individuals, communities of individuals and collectives. Even in the constancy of the regularity of consultations of *Ifá* by the diviners, they are aware that uncertainties rule the universe, even if regularities seem to pervade the real of causality in terms of conjoinment of causes and effects; this explains daily divination to find out things regarding all aspects of existence.

Taiwo (2010) has celebrated this as the hallmark of modernity, claiming this as a European forte. But our research for this discussion shows that *Ifá* must be regarded as modern in its effort to continually investigate, and not take for granted anything; while at the same time, it creatively utilizes ideas, old and new, to find better ways of dealing with the uncertainties that pervade the realm of existence. "Modern" science and medicine is coming to the realization of what *Ifá* diviners seem to have known all along, thereby showing that the more things seem to change, the more they remain the same. It is this epistemological fact which constitutes our claim that affective capacity of *Ifá* lores must be harnessed ever more in the present to deal with various palliative health-care needs of individuals, communities and collectives.

DIAGNOSIS

The intricate process of *Ifá* divination, a process similar to mathematical permutation, is usually employed in the quest for the most relevant historical antecedents of the client condition in a holistic manner. The paraphernalia of *Ifá* that is appropriately selected to do the inquest usually determines the style of casting. It may be necessary to take a quick look at the paraphernalia necessary for accessing *Ifá* message, because the message has to be accessed in order to know which story best describes the situation at hand, especially during divination. The materials have been described in detail and illustrated by many scholars, including Bascom (1969, 1980, and 1991), Wande Abimbola (1969, 1975, and 1976) and Yemi Elebuibon (1999) and have been copiously cited by this researcher in related other discussions by this author and in this work.

The essential tool for Ifá divination is "*Ikin,*" the sixteen sacred palm nuts. It is one of the important divination instruments used on special occasions, especially during an annual divination or in resolving very important matters. The sanctity of the palm nut is attested to by the Psalmist in *Psalm* 92:12 of the Christian Bible: "The righteous will flourish like a palm tree."

In reality, no part of the typical palm tree is useless; there are special and critical uses for all parts of the palm tree, from the roots to the leaves, even the fiber of the dead trunk is material for some industrial or domestic products. Investigations have shown that *Ikin* is the most trusted divination tool among Yoruba diviners. Bascom asserts that

> The great oracle of the Yoruba country is Ifá. He (Ifá) is represented chiefly by 16 palm nuts each having from *four to ten eyelets* on them. Behind each one of these representative nuts are sixteen subordinate divinities. Each one of the whole lot is termed an Odù—which means a chief (sic corpus) . . . this makes the number of Odus altogether 256. (1969, 17)

Another essential divination tool, different from *Ikin*, is *Opele*. It is a divining chain containing eight half-nuts stringed together such that when held midway, there would be four half-nuts to either side of the diviner. *Òpèlè* is usually thrown once to reveal a corpus of Ifá. It is however not easy to divine with *Ikin* as one does with '*Òpèlè*' because, while '*Òpèlè*' is thrown once to reveal a book (Odù) it takes a minimum of eight intricate scooping of the *Ikin* nuts, such that one or two left behind (per chance) at every scooping, is recorded in reverse order on the divination tray covered with *Iyerosun*, (the divination powder). Apart from *Ikin* and *Òpèlè*, there are also the "sixteen

Figure 10.4. *Ikin-Ifá. Source:* author's personal collection.

cowries" simply called *Eerindinlogun.* The intricate process is followed to select a book of *Ifá* called *Odù* from which an *Ese Ifá,* a narrative poem is read.

We can see an example of *Ifá* signature of *Eji Ogbe* and *Oyeku Meji* on *Opon Ifá* (divination tray) in figure 10.4.

DEPLOYING *IFÁ* POETRY FOR HYPNOTHERAPY IN *THE GODS ARE NOT TO BLAME*

The Gods Are Not To Blame is Ola Rotimi's adaptation of Sophocles' *Oedipus Rex.* The entire plot of the adaptation is woven with Yoruba *Ifá* culture, as Rotimi attempts to indigenize the Greek philosophy about intractability of human destiny (personal, group and communal) into Yorùbá cosmogony, and which will be applicable to other cultural or geo-social environments. For example, what is happening in the United States of America today can be

Figure 10.5. *Ikin* with five eyelets (marked). *Source*: author's personal collection.

properly investigated through *Ifá* divination, to reveal that Trump is not just a happenstance of bad governance, but a product of a historical and genetic dis-ease from the founding of the United States of America on the theft of land from the indigenous peoples of the Americas, to the forcible destruction of the lives of those people and the criminal importation and enslavement of black in all the walks of life of United States of America, and finally the persistent inequities and injustices of racism, capitalism and religio-cultural oppression domesticated and perfected by bourgeoisie governance system called democracy.

This is the similar trope that Rotimi investigated in *The Gods Are Not to Blame*, with only time and cultural location marking the variation in applicability. The play opens with an *Ifá* priest's prediction about the future of a new-born son of King Adetusa and his Queen Ojuola; a child that will grow up to "kill his own father and then marry his own mother!" The baby's feet are tied with a string of cowries and ordered to be taken to the evil forest for sacrifice to the gods that supposedly sent the evil child.

Years later, the child, Odewale returned, by a twist of fate, given the fact that the persons ordered to dispose of the child, out of empathy, did not carry out the instruction to the letter, is now king and married to his mother,

Figure 10.6.   *Ifá* divination tray. *Source*: author's personal collection

Ojuola. An old man Alaka, half clown, half philosopher, comes to tell Odewale that his "parents" have died. However, Alaka also lets slip that they were not Odewale's real parents. Shamed by the suggestion that he is illegitimate, Odewale brutally forces Alaka to reveal the truth: that he, Alaka, found him, Odewale, in the bush and brought him to the neighboring Ijekun chief to be fostered. Probably this can be paralleled with the historiography of Trump's ancestry, as a way of understanding, through *Ifá* , the reason why Trump is a torment to the peoples of the United States of America, given the fact that his miscegenated ancestry and background should have precluded him from the seat of power. But since there is no way of divining with accuracy the effectuating possibilities attending the crowning of such a misfit into Presidency, *The Gods Are Not to Blame.*

The play, *The Gods Are Not to Blame*, sumptuously feeds on Yorùbá proverbs, which is the primary language of *Ifá* poetry. *Ifá* poems abound generally in proverbs. Oba Adekunle Areje recounts a personal experience in the preface to his book, *Yoruba Proverbs*, "Some time ago, Professor Wande Abimbola, who was the Vice Chancellor of the University of Ife at the time . . . said that Yorùbá proverbs were derived from *Ifá* Oracle. It is

Figure 10.7.   *Ifá* **divination tray.** *Source***: author's personal collection.**

therefore possible that the proverbs might have inherited and acquired the vocabulary of the *Ifá* oracle" (Areje, 1985, iii).

Indeed, not just the vocabulary, Ifá verses are generally rendered in parables usually and deliberately composed of proverbs. The generally accepted style of presentation for *Ese Ifá* is by chanting in musical narrative and recitation format. A well-presented *Ifá* poetic recitation is like musical and lyrical discourse, which music sooths, engages and draws on the mood of the listener, client or patron, thus creating a strong affectation.

Therefore, music lyrics of the verses becomes a tool that can be used to make *Ifá* chants more affective. Like a music art, it can be used in hypnotherapy. Laing, (2013), a therapist of the neuro linguistic programming, observes that hypnosis is a perfectly natural state of complete relaxation which takes place within the physical body and generates a heightened awareness the deep recesses of human consciousness within the mind. This occurs naturally in everyday life and is not very dissimilar to the trance-like feeling you have when one embarks on a reverie or daydreaming. As you enter the hypnotic state you become less aware of your physical and material surroundings and

Figure 10.8.   *Ifá* **divination tray.** *Source:* **author's personal collection.**

you become more acutely aware of your inner feeling. Within this world of mental calm you can automatically direct your attention on the agreed suggestions of the hypnotist or search your own subconscious life for memories otherwise not normally available.

Hypnotherapy uses hypnosis in bringing about the desired effect and change in the target. Mutually agreed positive suggestions are put into the subconscious mind of the target whilst he/she or even group are in the relaxed state of hypnosis. The individual or group will never be out of control or do anything he/she/they disagree with or which is against their normal moral or ethical code.

Ola Rotimi employs the hypnotherapy effect of *Oriki,* as lyrically recited by Asunrara, to suppress the burning anger of King Odewale, when the king was suspecting that a coup was being plotted against him. The situation here supports the argument about the use of catharsis in the reduction of anger. One can probably see a necessary parallel in how a Trumpian presidency would have benefitted from this kind of treatment, to assuage the numerous antipathies manifested by a historical flaw in the individual who assumed

Figure 10.9.   *Ifá* divination trays. *Source*: author's personal collection

such a global power. Unfortunately, humanity has not developed to the level whereby global indigenous knowledge systems of the so-called third world communities of civilizations will be validated and accepted as functionally valuable in the treatment of maladies of the magnitude that threatens to throw the whole world into an omnicidal apocalypse.

Affective use of parables and proverbs in the play makes its language richly poetic. Oftentimes, parables are used to screen the intended meaning of the dialogue, such that an insult woven in parable may not be easily disentangled by the target audience and, by that token, explosive reaction is thereby delayed or avoided. Thus, King Odewale asks Aderopo, "Are you not a Yorùbá man? Must parables be explained to you?" (Rotimi, 1971, 32).

It should be noted that a prescription for healing may also become a dangerous dose, depending on the manner of application. According to Do-pamu, two affective *Ifá* poetry types: Àwure-Ofo Ori Ire—prayer verses for good luck; and Ma Dari Kan—Ofo Isegun—incantation for victory, when not properly coordinated, may work at cross purposes. Both are often called Ohun or Ògede. These two types of *Ese Ifá* were effectively used in the flashback scene, while Odewale engages King Adetusa in a fight (1971, 47–48).

CONCLUSION

Ifá lore is usually rendered as poetry; in chants (song/music), and if music affects the soul, and perhaps heals its wounds, then *Ifá* chants can be employed as a massage therapy to provide some forms of palliative care and relief of the most profound type to a troubles soul or intemperate personality like Trump. In this regard, it would be necessary to find the source or origin of the Trumpian ancestry, the taboos of his family tree, the trajectories of his progenitors, and the fundamental causative and affective background why he has been inflicted on United States of America and the world at this time in human history.

A treatment like this that manages a problem, even of a Trumpian human typology, and which may not necessarily lead to its cure, but which provides treatments which often ameliorates a problem only for as long as the treatment is continued, especially in chronic diseases, may be what is needed for Trump, United States of America and the entire world, so that the whole of humanity will/may not be plunged into an irretrievable self-destruction. For example, there is as yet no cure yet for AIDS, but treatments are available to slow down the harm done by HIV and delay and even prevent the fatality of the disease. Treatments may not always work as desired, but they may have effects which make life bearable for the patient, the client's family and the community of humans at large. For example, chemotherapy is a treatment for some types of cancer. In some cases, chemotherapy may lead to a cure, but not in all cases for all cancers. Hence, as we have iterated in this discussion, the epistemological, ontological and axiological foundations of *Ifá* offers various remarkable affective and palliative measures to address not just individual Yoruba issues, but probably transferable assistance to peoples from other traditions and cultures, to ensure balance in individual psychic and personality displays.

Overall, this chapter is not a study in Western medicine, as the slash and burn principles of Western medicine is understood, and as such has not proposed a cure for any ailment. Rather, the study has identified other uses to which literature, especially its performance, a performative therapeutic utterance, as eminently incorporated in Yoruba *Ifá* traditional lores and verses, can be put. The chapter also concludes that affective communication field, as available in music, poetry, literature, is invaluable in health care management and delivery at the individual, group and communal levels. This is a critical component of the richness of global traditions, as it is one in which the trained encoder understands the language of the text as a necessary literary phenomenon, to improve interaction in the proposed brand of therapy between the practitioner and the target, via *Ifá* lore. This research, in essence, affirms that *Ifá* lore may be employed as hypnotic tool to help someone change an unwanted habit and hence to have improvement in health outcomes.

BIBLIOGRAPHY

Abimbola, Wande (1975). *Sixteen Great Point of Ifá.* Zaria: UNESCO Publications.
———. (1976). *Ifá: An Exposition of Ifá Literary Corpus.* Ibadan: OUP.
Abimbola, Wande (1977). *What is Ifá?* Lagos: Nigeria Magazine Festac Edition.
Adeseye, Femi, and Ibagere, Elo (1999). *Communication and Man: A Theoretical Base for the Student.* Akure: Ola-Olu Enterprises.
Areje, Raphael Adekunle (1985). *Yoruba Proverbs.* Ibadan: Daystar Press.
Bascom, William (1969). *Ifá Divination—Communication between Gods and Men in West Africa.* London: Indiana University Press.
Bewaji, J. A. I. (2013). *Black Aesthetic.* Trenton, NJ: Africa World Press.
———.(2012). *Narratives of Struggle.* Durham, NC: Carolina Academic Press.
Bruscia, Kenneth (2013). (Ed.). *The Dynamics of Music Psychotherapy.* Dallas, TX: Barcelona Publishers.
Burgoon, Michael (1974). *Approaching Speech/Communication.* New York: Rinehart and Winston, Inc.
Elebuibon, Yemi (1998). *The Adventures of Obàtálá.* (Part Two). Lynwood: Ara Ifa Publishing.
———. (2004). *Ifá: The Custodian of Destiny.* Ibadan: Penthouse Publications.
Isola, Akinwumi (1995). "The Role of Literature in the Intellectual and Social Development of the African Child," in *Essays in Honour of Ayo Bamgbose.* Ed. Owolabi, Kola. Ibadan: Group Publishers, 311–322.
Kinni-Olusanyin, Esi (1993). "The Arts as Communication," *Ibadan Journal of Humanistic Studies,*6(August). Ibadan: UI Press.
Laing, Dave (2013). *Hypnosis.* (e-book) www.LNP. Dallas, TX: Barcelona Publishers.
Longe, Olu (1998). *Ifá Divination and Computer Science.* Inaugural Lecture. Ibadan: UI Press.
Lucas, D. W. (1967). *Aristotle Poetics.* Ann Arbor: University of Michigan Press.
Odeyemi, Idowu (2014). "Worship and Sacrificial Essence in Ifa Religion," in *Ile-Ife: Elerii Ipin: A Magazine of the International Council for Ifa Religion,* 6(commemorative edition): 20–26.
Rotimi, Ola (1971). *The Gods Are Not to Blame.* Oxford: Oxford University Press.
Thomson, W. A. R. (1973). *Thomson's Concise Medical Dictionary.* Edinburgh: Livingstone. Yoruba Language Texts.
Abimbola, Wande (1968). *Ijinle Ohun Enu Ifá.* Glasgow: Collins Sons & Co.
———. (1977). *Awon Oju Odu Merindinlogun.* Ibadan: Oxford University Press.
Bewaji, Mary Bolajoko (1983). *Ogede.* Unpublished NCE dissertation at Oyo State College of Education, Ilesa, Nigeria.
Dopamu, P. A. (2000). *Awure—Ofo Ori Ire.* Ibadan: Oluseyi Press Sefer Books Ltd.
———. (2000). *Ma Dari Kan—Ofo Isegun.* Ibadan: Sefer Books.

Chapter Eleven

Colonialism and Homegrown Businesses in Africa

Kehinde O. Ola and David O. Oke

Low economic development in Africa has been a major point of debate in recent times. The question that arises is, why does a continent with enormous resources remain under-developed? There is no doubt that most African countries are endowed with enormous resources—natural and human. All various measures employed to mitigate the problems seem impalpable to bringing the desired target growth. Africa continues to occupy the least place in terms of development and other parameters of assessment. Large numbers of peoples from Africa live in extreme poverty, and Africa has the highest rate of disease occurrence in the world. The national poverty line is two digits, with countries like Nigeria, Zambia, Swaziland, Togo, Madagascar, Gambia, Equatorial Guinea, and Congo Democratic Republic having more than 70 percent poverty coefficients.

This present status of Africa and African countries calls for re-examination of the emergence of colonialism in Africa, because there is no specific account that shows people of Africa living in extreme poverty and dire economic helplessness before of the advent of the European colonization of the continent. Evidence of various occupations and tools used before the colonization can still be seen today in many rural African communities. African descent into poverty began with the advent of colonization and this has shown that colonization entails enslavement of African people and their riches.

Colonialism has retarded African economic development, rather than the various fallacious arguments that colonialism opened Africa to growth and global participation in world economic development. According to Heldring and Robinson, "Africa is poorer today than it would have been had colonial-

ism not occurred" (2013, 1). Colonialism leads to the loss of African industrial and entrepreneurial culture, and the embracing of European lifestyles
has had very pernicious implications on the development on virtually all
segments of African economy. Colonialism has made Africans lose their old
values, their economic identities, their confidence in their own indigenous
knowledge systems, and the utilization of these combination of assets to
develop their own societies. Africa lost sources of wealth with the advent of
colonialism and became dependent on the developing economies of the same
period in Europe. Homegrown businesses are the sources of wealth lost by
Africa and this is the focus of this chapter. Homegrown businesses have been
seen as the backbone of any economy and they are the necessary mechanisms
that will make a country to become self-reliant. The growth of the United
States, Great Britain, Japan, and Germany can be attributed to the promotion
of homegrown businesses.

RESEARCH PROBLEM

Most African countries have been among the most underdeveloped parts of
the world and lots of studies have been carried out to examine the reasons for
this low development. This problem has been addressed historically by such
authors as Ocheni and Nwankwo, Settles, Heldring and Robinson, and Austin. Historical evidence reveals how Africa has lost her riches to Western
countries through colonialism. Colonialism led Africa into producer of raw
materials and consumer of manufactured goods. The physical, human and
economic resources of Africa have been of utmost benefit to the Western
nations without any returns for Africa. All the previous studies only provide
historical account without identifying some of the homegrown businesses
that colonialism have put an end to and destroyed. This study attempts to
identify some of those businesses and to how it may be possible to suggest
the path to their recovery and/or resuscitation.

This chapter will examine how colonialism had destroyed homegrown
businesses in Africa. The specific objectives include, first, to identify businesses that supported African economy before colonialism, and second, to
examine the present state of those businesses in the contemporary Africa.

Entrepreneurship is very important in economic development and it provides a means of generating income. This has made African governments to
emphasis entrepreneurship development. The key to entrepreneurship development is the growth of homegrown businesses. A cursory look at all high-
flying businesses in the world shows that they were once household businesses. Though this is not the case in Africa, no household businesses have
grown beyond cottage industry. This study intends to reveal that there are
businesses in Africa, which had contributed to African economic develop-

ment before colonialism and thereby showing to the government that there is need for revival of these homegrown businesses. African economic development depends on African countries achieving economic self-reliance. This study therefore will demonstrate the importance of developing businesses which indigenous technology can manage.

The most appropriate theory for this study is "dry fish theory"; though it may not have been discussed in any literature, it has some applications to understanding the effects of colonialism on indigenous enterprises in Africa. This theory has three main stages—growing stage, adjusting stage, and redundancy stage. Homegrown businesses in Africa have experienced these three stages. The period before colonialism was an era of continuous growth and they were able to meet the needs of their societies. African households became the center point of economic growth and each household had their share of contribution. This period expired with the emergence of the Europeans. It is like catching a fish in the river, after taking it from the river, its growth stops and start suffocating. The growth of homegrown businesses declined with the advent of colonialism.

This began the second stage which deals with shrinking: the fish caught starts shrinking. All innovations and enhancement in traditional knowledge based occupations stopped, because the people's consumption preference shifted to European goods. As the fish lost its water and other essential nutrients, African traditional businesses declined in artisans and there was migration to other attractive vocations such as clerical works and retail businesses. Therefore, the last stage emerges and this deals with entrepreneurial redundancy. The possibility of reinvigorating a dry fish is zero. The promoters of homegrown businesses suspended production and went into non-primary industries which offered attractive pays, with little risks. This makes promotion of entrepreneurship education in Africa to be far from realization because there are no historical family heritage to support the system.

The foundation for this theory can be found in historical dependency theory. This theory explains that wealthy nations have impoverished the African countries through expropriation of their resources. They took a great quantity of materials such as minerals, metals, and organized cheap labor through slavery. The activities of Belgium in Congo, sponsored by King Leopold II, confirmed how African countries have become dry fish. From the dependency writers, Africa has been turned into structural internal underdevelopment and external dependency. Though Karl Marx never developed a theory on colonialism, his idea could be applied to the activities of European countries in Africa. The Marxist idea revealed that colonialism serves as agent of progress, but the rule must be temporary if the progressive potential is to be realized. This theory showed that colonialism would be of benefit to Africa when the length of rule by the colonial masters is short.

In many of the colonized states, the length of rule was over eighty years, which was enough to complete the exploitation of Africa's diverse resources. The conclusion of the Marxist followers is that international division of labour is structured to benefit the core states and to promote the transfer of resources from the periphery to the core European metropolitan countries. Lenin's theory provided a critical view of imperialism. He showed that imperialism makes European countries to export economic burdens onto weaker states. Hence, the European countries dominated Africa exclusively for economic benefit.

HISTORICAL REVIEW

Colonialism is the practice of domination, which involves the subjugation of one people to another through physical, mental, economic, religious, or other conquest. It is also the implantation of settlements by a group on a distant territory owned by another group (Singh, 2001). The two definitions hold that there must be an attempt by one country/society/group to subjugate another, which involves a deliberate implanting of their administration in the subjugated countries. The term is closely linked with imperialism, in the sense that, imperialism is the idea that drives the practice of colonialism. Both terms involve loss of political and economic control of a country by its people to another. Africa was controlled by the Europeans, with the chief objective of exploiting the lands for economic and political benefits. The conquest began in the nineteenth century, after the abolition and suppression of slave trade which coincided with the expansion of European capitalist industrial revolution.

The end of slave trade did not reduce Europeans' interest in Africa. Hence, the interest shifted to the enormous raw materials Africa could supply, and the new markets available in the regions. The scramble for Africa was motivated by economic, political, and social factors. The dire need to have constant supply of cheap and unpaid for raw materials, guaranteed markets and profitable investment outlets spurred the domination of Africa by the European imperialist. The scramble for African lands came without considering the aspiration and expectation of the indigenous colonized peoples. It was done in the absence of any input from the peoples of Africa. This coming necessitated the need to claim administrative control over the people of Africa, because it fell within the time the European powerful countries had interpower struggles and competition for preeminence. This process of claiming the territories includes the occupation of territories by the European merchants and trading companies and this became the major claim of the European imperialist in acquiring territories in Africa during the Berlin Conference of 1884/1885, initiated by German chancellor Otto von Bismarck.

This penetration into Africa gave the countries in Western Europe the opportunity to establish their own institutions on African lands.

It should be noted that culture establishes the foundation for the growth of economic, political, religious, and social integration of people. Development has never transcended culture. The skills, knowledge, ideas and technology are hidden in the culture of any particular society. The progress of any particular society is interwoven into the culture of the people. Culture has the tendencies to retard or increase development. For instance, industries are created through culture and it is the culture that spread the techniques that suited the people of any particular society, from one generation to another. Innovation cannot take place in the absence of culture of the people. It is the displacement of African culture by colonization that led to the little or no improvement in the lives of the people.

Thus, alienation of African cultures from their lives was the first step in the destruction of homegrown business in Africa. Occupation is an aspect of culture and it is the aspect that determines the economic growth of the society. Occupation makes food, clothing, shelter, trade, manufacturing of tools, art, dance, music, musical instrument to take place. In most traditional African households there usually existed a particular form of occupation that the people are noted for. The entire household concentrates on that occupation and their living are earned from the trade. In Yoruba land, the occupation involved by a household can be identified by mere knowing of the names of those that belongs to that particular household. The various households guard jealously their practicing occupations and entrance into such industries were closely restricted. The society promoted hardworking and thrift. The social status is not restricted to limiting a person from moving to a higher social status; hardworking and prudence can make one to attain some levels of affluence in the society.

The Africa met by the Europeans was not that of scarcity of food or other essential things. Africans were producers of food and other household utensils, as well as arts, crafts and items of luxury for the rich and titled in society. There were small cottage industries where cloth-making, leather-dressing, wood-carvings, silversmithing, blacksmithing, smelting of iron, and saddling were professionally practiced. These industries supply manufactured goods to the African market as well as for export and use by the religious traditions and royalty. The African economy during the precolonial period was highly subsistent in nature, as was the case of most other societies of that period, due to the fact that, there was limited scope for trade and exchange of goods and services. People produced mainly for their households and supplied the excess to the market. This African economy sustained by indigenous technology was short-lived and short-circuited because the Europeans turned Africans into receivers and consumers of their own excess, rather than producers.

Studies on colonialism and African development have shown that the emergence of the Europeans into Africa led to dearth of homegrown businesses. For instance, Ocheni and Nwankwo (2012), in their study "Analysis of Colonialism and its Impact of Africa," found out that the present roles of Africa in international world market could be attributed to long years of colonial dominance, exploitation and imperialism. Their findings showed that Europeans systematically and deliberately destroyed indigenous African economies. They concluded that there is the urgent need for the people and the leadership in various African societies to create their own indigenous identity, culture, technology, economy, education, religion, craft, etc. that would be interwoven in good governance into their capacity building and socio-cultural sustenance. What is implied in this is that the capacity of any society to develop must depend on the agency of that society, based in the internal dynamics and deliberate investment in the cultural foundations of such a society.

Similar findings were obtained by Heldring and Robinson; these authors examined the impact of colonialism on the development in Africa. They categorized the countries in Africa into three, to account for legacy of colonialism. Their finding showed that colonialism has negative effect on economic development of Africa. While Bertocchi built a dynamic model with accumulation as trope, which describes the economy of an underdeveloped country before colonization, during colonization and after decolonization occurs, to explain the impact of colonialism on economic development. His findings showed that colonialism can promote output growth but at the same time depress living standards in the colonies. The African experience showed that colonialism depressed the living standards of the people. One of the factors that accounts for this was the fact that the tailoring of the productive energies towards the meeting of the needs of others automatically leads to ignoring the essential and life-enriching aspects of your own indigenous societies, while what is received in exchange are not necessarily those relevant to the cultures of the domestic societies of Africa.

Liu, using panel data from fifty-one African countries, conducted a study on "Western impact on Africa's economic development and the progress of democracy." He coded selected variables, which include level of democracy, length of years of democracy, British colony, French colony, Portuguese colony, and colonial factor. His findings showed that length of years of colonialism has a negative impact on the development of African countries. Countries that experienced short period of colonization survived economically. The findings further showed that colonialism does not lead to the growth of the colonies. Settles's study also traced history of colonialism in Africa, to ascertain whether it has enhanced economic development or not. His findings showed that colonialism encouraged development in some areas but in many others, severely retarded the optimal progress of the continent. He concluded that Africa would have been better if colonialism had not been imposed on them.

METHODOLOGY

The study adopts historical survey technique, and this allows the researchers to investigate the traditional occupations practiced in the precolonial era. It enables one to track how many of these occupations are out of vogue and those who are the descendants of the people that were involved in the occupations have abandoned them, either because these were regarded as irrelevant, uncivilized or unrewarding occupations. In some other instances, urban drift has affected the improvements that should have taken place on these occupations, to modernize and integrate them into contemporary society.

Historical survey in this study deals with investigation of works done on occupations as it relates to Africa. The researchers considered books on history, journals and, extract from internet. The researchers took note of all works done on precolonial era in Africa. This gave us the insights into the diversity of occupations of precolonial, colonial and contemporary Africa, providing us a basis for the understanding of the impact of European colonization on African economies and development.

Since the interest of the study is on homegrown businesses, which can be derived from the various occupations practiced by the Africans, the researchers ensured that only businesses that were indigenous in nature were considered—carpenters, masons, bricklayers, vehicular drivers, retail traders in building materials, household goods and other imported materials, merchandise such as in trinkets, enamel goods, food processing, and retail trade in local and imported used and new cloths were examined. Occupations that were not initially practiced before the colonial era were not put into consideration. Occupations like bone-settings, cloth weaving, blacksmith, pottery, and so on that were of African origin were taken into account.

DATA ANALYSIS

From historical survey, the following businesses were discovered to have been practiced by the Africans before and during the colonial era.

Table 11.1 reveals some of the industries that were in Africa prior to the conquest of Africa. Some of these industries are no more in existence and few which are in existence operate below optimum level. The information in table 11.1 further reveals the following:

a. Africans manufactured their own medical apparatus, which they used for treatment of different kinds of ailment;

Table 11.1.   Homegrown Businesses in Africa Before Colonialism

Industry	Notable Area	Items Produced	Present Status	Size
iron smelting	Lake Victoria, Tanzania	carbon steel	nonexistent	nil
architectural design	Dogon, Mali	design	nonexistent	nil
decorative	Kiba, Congo	bowls, cloth	nonexistent	nil
measurement	Ashante, Ghana	brass weight	nonexistent	nil
games	Shongo	complex network games	relevant	small
psychotherapy	across Africa	hypnosis, placebo, suggestion	relevant	small
orthopedic	Ogwa, Nigeria	bone settings	relevant	nil
textiles	Iseyin, Nigeria	local textiles	relevant	small
brick	Lake Chad	fire brick	not relevant	nil
plant medicine	Mano, Liberia	all diseases	relevant	small
anatomy & physiology	Mano, Liberia	all diseases	relevant	small
surgery	Banyoro, Uganda	caesarean	nonexistent	nil
ceramic	Igbo-Ukwu, Nigeria	pottery	relevant	small
iron smelting	Nok, Nigeria	terracottas	nonexistent	nil
music (Sufis)	Guajarat, East Africa	Sidis music	relevant	small
natural & traditional medicine	across Africa	herbal medicine	relevant	small
cloth weaving	across Africa	cloth	relevant	small
instruments	across Africa	drums, flutes	relevant	small

Source: a 2013 survey conducted by the author.

b. medical surgery took place in Africa before the advent of colonialism;
c. measurement scales have been invented before colonization, which had provided means of ensuring that all transactions were done with accurate scale;

    d. Africans wore clothes made from local fabrics, using indigenous technology;

    e. Africans had developed a formidable iron industry that produced tools and other artefacts; and

    f. musical instruments were produced for local songs.

DISCUSSION

From the findings, it can be seen that Africans had pioneered inventions on their own, before the advent of Europeans foraging into the continent. These efforts started declining as the length of stay of the Europeans increased. One fact about businesses and innovations are that they grow with time and come to improve with demands. The increase in the number of people demanding for certain commodities will lead to producers developing alternative ways of generating them, simplifying processes and increasing capacity. Increase in demand for a commodity propels the necessity for the producer to increase supply or allow competitors to come into the markets. The necessity will create the technology that will bring about large scale production, moving the production capacity beyond subsistence level to commercial levels.

African entrepreneurs stop thinking about these matters immediately products from European countries enters into their lands, replacing domestic, relevant and useful commodities which they were culturally used to. As foreign, often irrelevant and insensitive but more durable, attractive, and quality European product entered African markets, the people declined their use of locally produced goods. Owners of homegrown businesses such as cloth weaving, pottery, beverages and so on, began to search for alternative occupation, and this happened at the period where there was high need to cultivate more lands for the production of cash crops needed by the European companies. Cash crops production yielded high returns for farmers and the living standard of the farmers rose, but it had the negative effect of luring the African minds away from agency and development of indigenous industries to meet local and external consumer needs.

The earned income was further spent on consumption of manufactured commodities from Europe; leading to reliance on foreign commodities. Nigerian farmers, for example, earned enough to consume foreign commodities and Africa became a market for manufactured commodities from Europe and elsewhere. At the expiration of the era of colonialism, Africa has become a consuming continent rather than a producing continent. The people that once produced enough locally to feed their teeming population, traded the excess with Europe and Asia, now have to depend on foreign commodities for survival.

A critical examination of countries that never had contact with Europeans shows that these countries can experience and have experienced economic growth without influence from the outside. South Korea and North Korea are good examples of those countries. Economic growth can be enhanced through internal restructuring of the existing system to identify the resources available and how it can be put to effective use. No African country has ever done this, because African enlightenment did not come from internal initiatives but from external. Africa never experienced radical transformation that occurred in Western Europe, Russia, Japan, the United States, and Far East countries. Colonialism occurred at a period when Africa's exposures to other countries should have helped in technological advancement, through the improvement of domestic patterns of production and utilization of local resources and capacity.

CONCLUSION AND RECOMMENDATIONS

The survival of any country or society depends on what the citizens of that country or society produce at home. The developed countries of the contemporary times are having large proportion of what they consumed being produced at home. African countries are import dependent and this has weakened their development. Growth in homegrown businesses should have catered for the economy but long time of colonialism has made Africa to lose its entrepreneurial development through excessive campaign by the European countries for activities that retard the growth of home grown businesses. Christian missionaries and promotion of primary European manufactures from their own industries helped in impeding the growth of homegrown businesses. Losing the old traditional cultural values with its attendant of hardworking and prudent management have led to poor perception of African technology that has sustained the African societies before colonialism and embracing the Western culture that produce certificates without technical efficiency. In the beauty industry today, the efforts of indigenous communities to ensure adequate care of African hair, body, and beauty have given way to the fake, bleached, and disgraceful attachment to foreign fashion fads.

There is need for the revival of indigenous technologies and knowledge systems so as to pave way for Africans to produce goods that suit their physiological and cultural needs. In addition, there is need for the governments of the various countries in Africa to encourage development of existing local industries through funding. Lastly, there is need to encourage tertiary institutions and research institutes to investigate ways by which some of the indigenous ideas and inventions can be modernized.

BIBLIOGRAPHY

Austin, Gareth (2010). "African Economic Development and Colonial Legacies," *International Development Policy | Revue internationale de politique de dévelopement*. http://poldev.revues.org/78; DOI: 10.4000/poldev.78.

Bertocchi, Graziella (1998). *Colonialism in the Theory of Growth*. Modena: University of Modena and CEPR.

"Dependency Theories" (2013). Boundless Sociology. https://www.boundless.com/sociology/textbooks/boundless-sociology-textbook/global-stratification-and-inequality-8/sociological-theories-and-global-inequality-72/dependency-theories-428-8541/.

"Colonialism: Africa" (2005). *New Dictionary of the History of Ideas*. http://ic.galegroup.com/ic/suic/ReferenceDetailsPage/ReferenceDetailsWindow?failOverType=&query=.

Heldring, Leander, and Robinson, James A. (2013). *Colonialism and development in Africa*. Accessed June 16, 2013. http://www.voxeu.org/article/colonialism-and-development-africa.

Iweriebor, E. E. G. (2011). *The Colonization of Africa*. New York: Hunter College. http://exhibitions.nypl.org/africanaage/essay-colonization-of-africa.html.

Japan Times (2013). "Spurring Balanced African Growth," *Japan Times*. http://www.japantimes.co.jp/opinion/2013/06/04/editorials/spurring-balanced-african-growth/#.UbouclZrmKE.

Kohn, Margaret (2012). "Colonialism," *Stanford Encyclopedia of Philosophy*. http://plato.stanford.ed/entries/colonialism/.

Liu, Jiaxu (2012). "Western Impact on Africa's Economic Development and the Progress of Democracy." *Graduate Theses and Dissertations*. Paper 12872.

Ocheni, Stephen, and Nwankwo, Basil C. (2012). "Analysis of Colonialism and Its Impact in Africa," *Cross-Cultural Communication*, 8(3): 46–54.

Ogunremi, Deji (1998). "Economic Development and Warfare in Nineteenth-Century Yorubaland," in *War and Peace in Yorubaland 1793–1893* edited by Adeagbo Akinjogbin. Ibadan: Heinemann. 338–348.

Sachs, Jeffrey (2004). *Small Amount Spend on Promoting Africa's Economy Can Save Billions and Make the West More Secure*. http://www.economist.com/node/2685783.

Soetan, R. Olufemi (2001). *Culture, Gender and Development*. A Report submitted to the African Institute for Economic Development and Planning (IDEP), Dakar, Senegal.

Settles, Joshua Dwayne (1996). "The Impact of Colonialism on African Economic Development." *University of Tennessee Honours Thesis Projects*. http://trace.tennessee.edu/utk_chanhonoproj/182.

Singh, Amardeep (2001). *Globalization*. Bethlehem, PA: Lehigh University. >http://www.lehigh.edu/~amsp/eng-11-globalization.htm.

Timberg, Craig, and Halpering, Daniel (2012). "Colonialism in Africa Helped Launch the HIV Epidemic a Century Ago," *Washington Post*. http://articles.washingtonpost.com/2012-02-27/national/35443055_1_beatrice-hahn-aids-epidemic-simian-virus/2.

Udo, Reuben K. (1980). "Environments and Peoples of Nigeria: A Geographical Introduction to the History of Nigeria," in *Groundwork of Nigerian History*. Ed. Obaro Ikime. Ibadan: Heinemann. 1–7.

Uzoigwe, G. N. (1990). "European Partition and Conquest of Africa: An Overview," in *General History of Africa VII* (abridged edition). Ed. A. Adu Boahen. Paris: UNESCO. 10–24.

Chapter Twelve

Postcolonialism and the Emergent Political Culture in Africa

A Literary Study of Ngugi Wa Thiong'O's Fictional Works

Ezinwanyi E. Adam

The way and manner the white people have related with the black people, the levels of reactions of the black population to the invading socio-political values and standards during the colonial era have been the subject of interesting writings in Africa. Of significance, in this class of writing in Kenya, is Ngugi Wa Thiong'O's works. His profound sympathy with his people in their weaknesses, their poverty in the socio-political development in Kenya and particularly his hatred of exploitation, cruelty, and injustice are noteworthy. It is the thrust of this chapter to critically look at the sociopolitical change in postcolonial Kenya, through the literary eyes of Ngugi in his remarkable and compelling work, *Petals of Blood* (1977), with a view to establishing the contributions of the work to real socio-political development in Kenya. This is done through the approaches of textual criticism, interpretation and postcolonial theory. Thus, the chapter examines the sociopolitical development in postcolonial Kenyan society, the lifestyle of people, and the relationships that exist among Kenyan citizens, especially between the rich and poor, the government (ruling class) and the governed (masses). It also establishes the basis for the continued prevalence of the themes of violence, corruption, disillusionment, injustice, decadence and disintegration described in contemporary Kenyan literature, in spite of the transformations and changes taking place in the sociopolitical setting of the state.

POSTCOLONIALISM AND SOCIOPOLITICAL DEVELOPMENT IN AFRICA

It is no longer news that the colonial or imperial powers from Europe and Asia Minor had colonized most parts of the African continent and other parts of the world. It is also indisputable that the colonial masters, including their languages of English, French, Arabic, among others have, in the process of colonization, seriously impacted on and radically altered the socio-political and cultural make-up of the African communities and their populations. What may be in controversy may be the extent or degree of the continuing pointing of accusing fingers at several factors of sociopolitical decadence like corruption, violence, injustice, cruelty, exploitation, and hatred prevalent in many African nations as being a direct consequence of the pervading impact of colonialism. In countries like Nigeria, Ghana, Uganda, and Kenya, the British imperial policies have been held responsible for the delayed or near collapsed socioeconomic and political emergence to levels of developed economies. To what extent this may be true forms part of the thrust of this work.

In Kenya, particularly, the manner and style of the relationship of the white colonialists with the Kenyan population, the levels of reactions and responses of the Kenyan population to the invading socio-political orienta-tions of the colonial officers have formed the subject of interesting writings in literature. Among such writings, the works of Ngugi Wa Thiong'O's occu-py a prominent position. Ngugi's *Petals of Blood* (1977), particularly cap-tures the sociopolitical climate of the postcolonial era in Kenya. It provides a rich avenue through which socio-political developments, and postcolonial-ism, have been creatively documented. It is, therefore, the intention of this chapter to critically analyse the sociopolitical changes in postcolonial Kenya through the literary eyes of Ngugi in *Petals of Blood*.

LITERATURE AND POSTCOLONIAL THEORY

Postcolonial literature, as intended in this essay, refers to writings by people from formerly colonized countries. According to Ashcroft, Griffiths and Tif-fin, the term "postcolonial" covers "all the culture affected by the imperial process from the moment of colonization to the present day. This is because there is a continuity of preoccupation throughout the historical process in-itiated by European imperial aggression" (1998, 2). Postcolonial literary the-ory, according to the observation made by Mark (2007), emerges from the inability of Euro-American theory to escape false notions of "the universal." Euro-American historiography, philosophy and literary study assume that many values and value-assigning practices, epistemologies, characteristics of language, genres, psychological and social models, and the like, apply across time and place. Therefore, postcolonial theory attempts to deconstruct and reconstruct such assumptions, not only through contesting them but also through developing or rediscovering indigenous and valid alternative theories of value, language, and others. However, the study identifies five main models of approaches of postcolonial theory, which are

a. *National or regional models.* These emphasize distinctive features of national or regional history and culture. Examples are the Subaltern Studies group in India, which re-inscribes history from the position of previously silenced indigenous people, and many types of Caribbean studies, which look at shared features, namely, the legacy plantation and slavery, that have shaped literary culture in neighbouring islands (Mark, 2007).

b. *Racial or ethnic models* are not necessarily tied to an essentialist view of race, but rather to the notion that "the idea of race" has been a major feature of Euro-American economic, political, and cultural practice. Examples are writings by African and African diaspora authors.

c. *Comparative models* often stress stylistic and thematic concerns that traverse nation and region. A major concern is language, not only how English or other European languages supplant indigenous languages, but also how English or European languages change into a "nation-language." Another major concern is the struggle oppression. It also focuses on concepts such as exile, education, and treatment of women.

d. As observed, the ethnicity and comparative models are very much applicable to the study of Ngugi's novel, where there is discrimination against the poor and lowly (represented by Wanja, Abdulla, Karega, Nyakinyua, and others) by the rich (represented by Kimeria, Chui, and Mzigo). There is also racial discrimination against blacks by the whites as represented by the students and the principal, respectively, of the high school in the city, attended by Munira. The comparative model is used for the analysis of themes and visions portrayed in *Petals of Blood.*

e. *Colonizers/colonized models* concentrate on the imperial-colonial dialectic. One interesting question such theorists ask is whether decolonization is ever possible. Fanon, the "founding father" of this postcolonial theory, wondered whether "the native intellectual" could escape the hegemony of colonizing, and/or neocolonizing culture.

f. Finally, the *hybridity/syncreticity models* are mostly influenced by post-structuralist theories. They often deconstruct the binary opposition of center/periphery, master/slave, colonizer/colonized, civilization/savagery, rich/poor, etc. The "other" is expedient in this sort of postcolonial theory. According to Ashcroft, Griffiths and Tiffin (1998,

169–171), the "other" is anyone who is separate from one's self. The existence of others is vital in defining what is "normal" and in situating one's own place in the world. In postcolonial theory, as observed, "the other" can refer to the colonized others who are marginalized by the imperial discourse, identified by their difference from the centre and, perhaps importantly, become the pivot of anticipated mastery by the imperial "ego."

The hybridity model is, however, explored in *Petals of Blood*, to show how much influence the colonizers or western culture still has on the colonized or African culture, even as an independent nation. Thus, the ethnicity, comparative, and hybridity models are most relevant to this study and are applied in the textual analysis of the selected novel to bring out the themes of betrayal of love, exploitation, violence, oppression, death, which all depict the high level of decadence and disintegration in most African nations.

NGUGI WA THIONG'O'S *PETALS OF BLOOD*: A SUMMARY

The story in Ngugi Wa Thiong'O's *Petals of Blood,* though narrated mostly in the form of reminiscences rather than in flashbacks, begins in the present with the arrest of the four major characters—Munira, Karega, Wanja and Abdulla. Munira, a school teacher at New Ilmorog Primary School, is the first to be arrested by two police men in what they claim to be a routine questioning about a murder case in Ilmorog. Next to be arrested is Abdulla who lives at New Jerusalem in Ilmorog, Wanja then follows, and finally, Karega, who works at the Theng'eta Brewery in Ilmorog. They were arrested as suspects in the murder case of three African directors of the Theng'eta Brewery—Mzigo, Chui, and Kimeria.

The story is narrated in the form of Munira's recollections as he sits in his cell, writing notes in the form of a dairy, in order to keep his mind clear about the importance of the incidents, past and present in Ilmorog and to satisfy the probing mind of the police investigator and his several demands. This, according to Adam (2013), affects the narrative technique, as the story moves from the present (told in the omniscient point-of-view) back to the past, twelve years to Munira's reminiscences of his first arrival in Ilmorog, events and stories that lead to change and development of Ilmorog (told in the first-person point-of-view).

Munira, at his first arrival to Ilmorog, a village that was inhabited by peasant farmers and their uneducated children, who only stay to help their parents in farm work and cattle rearing, tries to reorganize a school for the children. He is met with difficulty, as the children refuse to come to school and hatred, perhaps, because he is seen as an agent of social change that comes with colonialism and postcolonialism, as well as imperialism.

The school was a "four-roomed barrack with broken mud walls, a tin roof with gaping holes and more spiders' webs and the wings and heads of dead flies" (Ngugi, 1977, 5). Many teachers who had been sent to Ilmorog before the arrival of Munira had encountered similar challenges and gone away without notice. Munira, therefore, is expected to leave like the others, but he does not. He shares his experiences with Abdulla, Wanja, and later on, with Karega, who had all come to Ilmorog, a deserted homestead, for reasons well known to them as individuals.

Abdulla is handicapped and relies on his donkey for his movement. He lost the use of one of his legs during his involvement as a Mau Mau fighter in the fight for "Mhuru"—freedom of the Kenyan people from white colonialists. He and his friend, Nding'uri, who happens to be an elder brother to Karega, are betrayed by Nding'uri's girlfriend's brother, who they later found out to be Kimeria, one of the directors of Theng'eta Brewery. It is also Kimeria who destroys Wanja. Wanja is impregnated by Kimeria, a married man with two children, who denies the pregnancy. She gives birth to a baby who she later drops into a pit toilet. She is hunted by the memory of her past and, in order to forget her past and live a new life, she comes to live in Ilmorog with her grandmother, Nyakinyua who is a strong-spirited, friendly and influential old woman. She counsels Munira, Abdulla, Karega, and Wanja, and also gives them all the support they need during the journey to the city on an account of the drought in Ilmorog.

Munira is seen as a big failure in his own family and a coward by his friends as he refuses to take the right actions but always chooses to sit on the fence. He is seen as an outsider. His siblings happen to be very successful people. They are all doing well in their respective endeavours of life. Munira's father, Ezekieli is "tall, severe in his austere" manners and is "a wealthy landowner and a respected elder in the hierarchy of the Presbyterian Church." He believes that children should be brought up on 'boiled maize grains sprinkled with a few beans and on the tea with only tiny drops of milk and no sugar, but all crowned with words of God and prayers" (Ngugi, 1977, 13–14).

To whom much is given, much is expected. Ezekieli, therefore, expects so much from Munira, his eldest child, whom he had given much. Munira disappoints his father when he is expelled from school for taking part in a revolt. While his siblings (except for Mukami, Karega's girlfriend who commits suicide) become successful professionals and financially independent, Munira still wallows in poverty as he cannot attend to his needs and wants with his little earnings as a teacher in a "village-turned-city," Ilmorog.

Munira, however, enjoys his work and experience as a teacher. After all, he is not a total failure, as his father thinks, since he contributes so much to the society by giving education to impoverished children of Ilmorog. He teaches them the names of the parts of flower, "the stigma, the pistil, pollen, the petals" (21). It is while Munira is teaching the children about fertilization that a child cries out, "Look. A flower with petals of blood," referring to a solitary red bean flower in a field dominated by white, blue and violet flower.

Munira falls in love with Wanja, a strong, resourceful, intelligent, and dynamic woman whose ugly experiences in her early age as a beautiful young girl turns her to prostitution. He is attracted by Wanja's beauty and often sees her in his dreams. Wanja sleeps with Munira, not out of love, but in order to be impregnated by him. But that does not happen as she did not conceive. Wanja meets Kimeria again, after a long time, during their journey to the city. He forces her to sleep with him, thereby humiliating her once again. This experience hurts Wanja, who then swears to get back at Kimeria. During the journey, so many personal secrets are revealed by Abdulla, Karega, Wanja, and Munira. It is at this time that Wanja reveals her relationship with Kimeria, as well as with other men like Kalasingh, a white man who wanted her to sleep with a dog. She explains how Kimeria, like his contemporaries, had taken advantage of her as a maid in his household. Abdulla also reveals how he fought as a woollen, a fighter; he worked with Ole Massai who was killed in the fight for freedom and also with Dedan Kimathi.

The journey, therefore, becomes a journey of discoveries of self, potentials, abilities, strengths, talents and weaknesses. They meet with several challenges, hunger and thirst, as well as with self-centred, arrogant, abusive and power drunk Rev. Jerrod Brown Kamau, Raymond Chui, Kimeria, and Nderi Wa Riera, the member of parliament (MP) for Ilmorog, but at last, overcome. They experience victory through the help of the lawyer in Nairobi West, Wanja's friend who is an embodiment of truth, self-sacrifice, kindness, honesty, and true patriotism.

Karega and Wanja start a relationship during the journey, and for the first time, Wanja falls in love with a man, Karega, who she wants to spend the rest of her life with. Munira gets envious of Karega and gets him dismissed from his teaching job in Ilmorog. Karega also finds out that Wanja is a mistress to Kimeria Wa Kamianja, the man who betrayed Nding'uri, his brother and Abdulla; the man who is responsible for Abdulla's crippled state. He leaves Ilmorog unannounced and later returns a different and experienced man. He comes back to find a fast developing Ilmorog, with so many changes on the people and the entire town.

The change affects everybody—Abdulla, Wanja, Munira, Njuguna, and Nyakinyua whose death is as a result of the change that has come to Ilmorog. Munira explains that, "Indeed, changes did come to Ilmorog, changes that drove the old one away and ushered a new era in our lives. And nobody could tell, really tell, how it had happened, except that it had happened" (p. 280). The change affects Munira psychologically, spiritually, economically, and physically. He becomes a religious fanatic after his unconvincing and rather too sudden conversion, and after an encounter with Prophetess Lillian, his former lover. The story ends with Munira's confession to setting Wanja's whorehouse on fire, in order to save Karega from the claws of Wanja. In the process, he kills Chui, Kimeria and Nderi, the symbols of imperialist government in Africa. He also hurts Wanja (Adam, 2013).

POSTCOLONIAL ISSUES AND SOCIOPOLITICAL CHANGES IN KENYA: AN ANALYSIS OF *PETALS OF BLOOD*

Ngugi Wa Thiong'O's *Petals of Blood* has been said to be his most representative, ambitious and comprehensive novel, because it incorporates all the major thematic preoccupations of his novels, and African novels, from the pioneers; that is, from the first generation, to the contemporary novelists; that is, including twenty-first-century African novelists (Palmer, 1979). The novel is concerned with the first stage of the colonial African historical development, with its dominant themes of cultural imperialism, racial discrimination, and exploitation of the African continent by white colonialists. It focuses mainly on the disintegration and disillusionment caused within the indigenous African society by European "civilization," through the introduction of foreign or strange educational, political, and religious systems by the white colonialists (Ngugi, 1977, 68–69).

Ngugi weaves into his story the Kenyan history of the first white colonist to bring the so-called civilization. Lord Freeze Kilby comes with his wife to civilize Ilmorog. He employs the use of force, aggression and oppression, on one hand, and religion and education, on the other hand. Munira explains:

> Cambridge Fraudsham came to the scene. Before we had any time to know him, he changed our lives. Fresh from the war, he already had firm notions how an African school had to be. Now, my boys, trousers are quite out of the question in the tropics. He sketched a profile of an imaginary thick-lipped African in a grey woollen suit, a sun-helmet, a white starched stiff collar and tie, and laughed contemptuously: Don't emulate this man. (28–29)

Education and religion are described as powerful tools of western civilization not just in Kenya but in the entire Africa during the colonial period. Ngugi employs the use of historical facts to tell the story of how whites came to settle in Ilmorog and how they introduced strange things, including food and motor car in Ilmorog (120–122). The novel also projects the second stage of Kenyan history, that is, the Mau Mau fight for freedom. Ngugi tells the story of historical figures, like Dedan Kimathi, Ole Massai, and other Mau Mau fighters and their struggle for liberation. Thus, he projects the themes of oppression, war, and struggle for liberation of African nation and people, revolution, man's inhumanity to man, disillusionment, as a result of unrealized dreams and hopes, betrayal and disintegration of the indigenous African society (Ngugi, 141).

Petals of Blood reveals the third stage of historical development in Kenya and, by extension, Africa as a continent, with its attending themes such as poverty, prostitution, class, corruption, exploitation, betrayal, social injustice, decadence, hypocrisy, feminism, imperialism, and many other postcolonial issues. The novel presents, according to Palmer (1979), "the most comprehensive analysis to date of the evils perpetrated in independent African society by black imperialists and capitalists" (1979, 288). For example, it is observed that things in Ilmorog and Kenya, as a nation, have not been better even as African governors and chiefs take over the leadership of the state. We are told that since they took over the people suffer from absence of basic facilities.

Ngugi's novel also focuses on the resourceful and courageous African women, old and new, as represented by Nyakinyua and Wanja, respectively. Wanja is the most significant female character in the novel. She is also seen as the most influential woman in Ilmorog. Munira tells Karega that "She is the most powerful woman in all Ilmorog. She owns houses between here and Nairobi. She owns a fleet of matatus. She owns a fleet of big transport lorries. She is that bird periodically born out of the ashes and dust" (Ngugi, 1977, 281). Wanja's driving force, as discovered throughout the novel, is the need to be independent and not to enslave men. She channels all energy, courage, resourcefulness, dynamism and strength toward making herself independent. It is her energy, initiative, resourcefulness, creativity and drive, which we admire so much in the novel, that bring development in Ilmorog. She learns from her father that "money moves the world. Money is time. Money is beauty. Money is elegance. Money is power" and that with money one can buy freedom for all people because "money is freedom" (233). Therefore, Wanja works hard to bring progress, not just for herself, but for the whole of Ilmorog and the change did come. The text affirms:

> Indeed, changes did come to Ilmorog, changes that drove the old one away and ushered a new era in our lives. And nobody could tell, really tell, how it had happened, except that it had happened. Within a year or so of the New Ilmorog shopping centre being completed, wheat fields and ranches had sprung up all around the plains: the herdsmen had died or had been driven further afield into the drier parts, but a few had become workers on the wheat fields and ranches on the earth upon which they once roamed freely. (Ngugi, 1977, 280)

The growth and development of the community resulted to the creation of several phases of Ilmorog, which completely changed the communal way of living of the people of old Ilmorog and brought the individualistic, class, and exploitative style of living that often come with capitalism. The change affects everyone in Ilmorog, as well as the community itself. Nyakinyua's death is as a result of the change in the society; she could not reclaim her land that was taken away from her by the bank. Abdulla loses everything, including his donkey and bar. He becomes a road-side seller of oranges. Munira becomes a religious fanatic. Karega becomes a trade union activist, organizing workers and the masses to restore the lost African societal values.

In Part I, Ngugi presents a community that represents a typical small traditional rural community, with its innocence and purity intact. In Part II, at the start of the journey to the city in search of solution to the drought, Ngugi, making use of African oral traditions, celebrates the heroes of Ilmorog revealing the gradual social change from a nomadic to an agrarian culture, and presenting their source of pride, joy, unity, and contentment. The introduction of imperialism and capitalism by not just whites but also blacks (indigenes) was the first blow to Ilmorog's pride, joy, and unity; this consequently led to the death of cultural and traditional values, the social, moral, and political decay and disintegration of Ilmorog community (Adam, 2013).

At the beginning of the novel, Ilmorog is described as a desolate, unattractive, and unprogressive rural community "with broken mud walls, a tin roof with gaping holes and more spiders' webs and the wings and heads of dead flies." No wonder teachers refuse to come to Ilmorog and those who came "ran away at the first glance." Even the young people of Ilmorog are happy to run away from the community.

The general comment was "Who would want to settle in this wasteland except those without limbs—may the devil swallow Abdulla—and those with aged loins—may the Lord bless Nyakinyua, the old woman" (5). It is, therefore, noteworthy that the only young people who stay in Ilmorog are the spiritually maimed ones, as symbolized by Abdulla's lame leg. Munira is staying in Ilmorog to hide from the competitive capitalist society; Abdulla is maimed during the Mau Mau fighting for liberty and he is disillusioned by the result of the *Uhuru* independence of Kenya. Wanja is running away from her life as a prostitute and searching for self-fulfilment in motherhood, and Karega who is expelled from school and is unable to survive the oppressive capitalist Kenya, and finally, the wise old people, as represented by the strong—spirited Nyakinyua and Njuguna. Ilmorog is described as, "a 'deserted homestead,' 'a forgotten village,' an island of underdevelopment which after being sucked thin and dry was itself left standing static, a grotesque distorted image of what peasant life was and could be" (184).

The journey to the city finally brings about rapid development and evident transformation in Ilmorog, which is suggested by the symbol of rain—the rain that falls immediately after their journey to the city is, to the elders of Ilmorog, an answer to their sacrifice. Ngugi makes use of images of the earth's reception of the rainfall to suggest productiveness, bountiful harvest and fruitfulness. Some of the images are got from oral traditions of folktales (196).

Even the maimed souls of individuals are revived by the rain-spirit. "Wanja was possessed of the rain-spirit. She walked through it, clothes drenched, skirt-hem tight against her thighs, revelling in the waters of heaven" (196). Despite all the happiness and joys that came with the rain, people still had their doubts about what would follow or happen afterwards, whether it would be favourable or not. Their doubts are, therefore, justified as capitalists move into Ilmorog with their industries, banks, roads, factories, shops, breweries, hotels, and estate management. The old small village of Ilmorog is completely and irredeemably destroyed by the change that comes with modernity and "civilization."

The people of Ilmorog, who are mainly peasants, unable to compete or contest with the business insights and expertise of the capitalists, painfully lose their lands and inheritances, and finally, disintegrate dependently into labourers or worse, for example, becoming roadside orange sellers like Abdulla. Some courageous ones, like Nyakinyua, who are determined to fight all forces of capitalism and exploitation, are discouraged by the lack of support they get. We, therefore, agree with Killam (1973), Moore (2000), and Palmer (1979) that Nyakinyua's resolution constitutes the last failing attempt of a once venerable and protected society to resist the encroachments of strange men (Adam, 2013).

However, this attempt fails because of the lack of support received from others as well, which signifies the degeneration that has taken over the whole of Ilmorog as a result of corruption, social, and moral decadence and all other attendant problems of capitalism, including lack of housing (shelter), water, clothing, security and food—the primary needs of decent human beings globally. Ngugi also emphasizes the point that this degeneration was caused, first by the white imperialists during the colonial stage, and the black imperialists after independence. These people pile up wealth and neglect the needs of the people and their responsibilities toward them. They rather invite the masses for a cultural programme and for teas which they are taxed financially in order to participate (84–89).

CONCLUSION

This chapter has considered postcolonialism and its impact on sociopolitical development in Africa as reflected in Ngugi's *Petals of Blood*. It has identified the sociopolitical crisis prevalent in postcolonial Africa such as violence, corruption, insecurity, unemployment, nepotism, imperialism, among others. This crisis is contradistinguished from the high political, economic and social expectations at the point of attainment of sovereignty from the

British colonial masters. Ngugi captures these political and economic failures in his novel, where he clearly shows that colonialism and postcolonialism have impacted greatly and negatively on sociopolitical score card of nascent African nations after the attainment of independence. Thus, it is implied in Ngugi's work that the expected positive change in the living conditions of Africans as represented by the people of Ilmorog in postcolonial era is still a mirage than reality. Therefore, it would take more deliberate actions intended for the growth and development of the people and nation than mere taking over power and governance by the indigenous African leaders.

BIBLIOGRAPHY

Adam, Ezinwanyi E. (2013). "The Foundations of Literary Excellence in the Selected Novels of Fyodor Dostoyevsky, Leo Tolstoy, Ben Okri and Ngugi Wa Thiong'O's". Unpublished PhD thesis, Department of Languages and Literary Studies, Babcock University.

Ashcroft, Bill, Gareth Griffiths, Gareth, and Tiffi (1989). *The Empire Write Back.* London and New York: Routledge.

———. (1998). *Key Concepts in Postolonial Studies.* London and New York: Routledge.

Griffiths, Gareth (2000). *African Literatures in English: East and West.* Harlow, Essex: Pearson Education.

Irele, Abiola (1981). *The African Experience in Literature and Ideology.* London: Heinemann Educational Books Ltd.

Killam, G. D. (1973).(Ed.). *African Writers on African Writing.* London: Heinemann.

Mark, E. O. (2007). "Decadence and Disintegration: A Postcolonial Study of Selected New Nigerian Novels." Unpublished MA dissertation, Department of English, University of Ibadan.

Moore, Gerald (2000[1962]). *Seven African Writers.* London: Oxford University Press.

Palmer, Eustace (1979). *The Growth of the African Novel.* London: Heinemann Educational Books.

———. (1974). "The Criticism of African Fiction: its Nature and Function" in *International Fiction Review.* (Spring): 112–119.

Said, Edward (1993). *Culture and Imperialism.* New York: Vintage Books.

Wa Thiong'O', Ngugi (1981). *Writers in Politics.* London: Heinemann Educational Books.

———. (1986). *Decolonising the Novel.* Nairobi, Kenya: East African Educational Publishers.

Wa Thiong'O's, Ngugi (1989). *Petals of Blood.* London: Heinemann Educational Books.

Chapter Thirteen

The Body in Personal Identity Development

An Exploration Utilizing Jamaica Kincaid's
The Autobiography of My Mother

Roxanne Burton

The Western tradition has generally discounted the role and value of the human body. As Oyewumi notes, this tradition has created the idea that "bodylessness" is a "precondition of rational thought" (Oyewumi, 1997, 3), which has generally been theorized as one of the crucial markers of person-hood. This is usually accompanied by a disregard of the social aspects of personhood. Western philosophy is replete with attempts to privilege the so-called interior rational self, and separate it from the physical material exterior self through which the self relates and develops, while placing the body in the exterior context. Furthermore, "all those who are qualified for the label 'different' in varying historical epochs have been considered to be embodied, eliminated, therefore, by instinct and effect, reason being beyond them" (Oyewumi, 1997, 3). Anyone who does not meet the paradigm of the physically and mentally able-bodied white male would generally be labeled as different. However, as I will argue in this chapter, the body is inherently social and is an integral part of the conception of the person and one's sense of self. I stress that we cannot reasonably conceive of ourselves as disembodied as this does not reflect our lived reality. Instead, it is through the body that one can, and does, have a world, as the human body is the site for interaction and communication, through which one's physiological, social and psychological capacities (crucial components of personhood) are realized. I also defend the view that our bodies are therefore crucial to both our understanding of our-selves and to our personhood. We are who we are because we interact with others and other aspects of the environment in the social space. In so doing, I discuss how there has been differential assessment of different types of bodies, and some implications for one's sense of self. I demonstrate these issues using Jamaica Kincaid's *The Autobiography of My Mother* (1997).

AKAN PHILOSOPHY AND HUMAN PERSON

It should first be noted that the value of the body has consistently been recognized within African philosophical thought, unlike in the Western tradition. The Akan, for example, in theorizing about persons and personhood, argue that the body is a necessary component of the person. Wiredu argues that the Akan language reflects the idea that there cannot be a disembodied notion of the self (the kind that has been seen in western philosophy). In the Akan language, "to exist" is "*wo ho*," which translates as "to be at some place" (Wiredu, 1996, 49). Therefore, for the Akan there is necessarily a material dimension to the person, the *onipa*. At the metaphysical level, the *onipa* is comprised of three components: *ōkra, sunsum,* and *honam/nipadua* (Gyekye, 1995; Wiredu, 1996). The *ōkra* is the life force, which allows one to be alive, and which gives all human beings intrinsic value. The nipadua is the body, the physical component of the individual, with Wiredu observing that the literal translation of nipadua is "person tree" (Wiredu, 1996, 126). The third element, the sunsum, is the foundation for the individual's personality or character. The Akan view is that "person" at the metaphysical level cannot be defined by either purely physical or mental features. While recognizing the value of the body, the onipa is an integrated being and to attempt to remove or privilege one aspect distorts the person. So we are never purely biological organisms, but "biologico-cultural" entities (22). While we may have some instinctive biological reactions, these impulses are shaped and understood within the context of a society or culture.

Philosophy as practiced within the African diaspora has also embraced the value of the body, which is unsurprising given the way in which non-white bodies have been treated. At the same time, given the influence of European philosophical thought, the lack of value given to the body and its role in the development of the sense of self has created a schism such that, as Mills asserts, it is generally considered that the "mind is located in Europe and body in the Third World" (2010, 3486). Work in African Diaspora philosophy, therefore, necessarily involves overturning the attempt to present some persons as disembodied when considering the person and her sense of self, a view that permeated Western philosophical thought until recently when the phenomenological turn resulted in a rigorous discussion of the body in Western thought. Phenomenologists were the first group of theorists to seriously consider the value of the body for persons. Phenomenological theories see the individual as being embedded and embodied in the world (Alcoff, 2006) and argue that the self should not be theorised as being a purely rational being which has no value for its body. However, the typical white male phenomenologist still does not engage in questions about bodies that are deemed "different." African diaspora philosophers such as Lewis Gordon have utilized phenomenology to examine such questions.

Lewis Gordon notes that the body can be seen as having three dimensions: "the body as one's perspective on the world . . . the body as seen by others, and the body's (consciousness') realization of itself as seen by others" (2000, 120). All three of these dimensions highlight the socially embedded nature of the body. In discussing the first dimension, Gordon notes that each person has a specific perspective on the world, a perspective that cannot be overcome though it can be enhanced, so that "I, in effect, *live* my perspective" (120; emphasis in the original). With respect to the second dimension, Gordon argues that the body can be experienced by others as "the locus of possibilities in the world," while it also "signifies different meanings in different situations" (122). The third dimension of Gordon's discussion of embodiment, consciousness of being seen by others, is especially salient when considering race and gender. Alcoff can be seen as examining dimensions discussed by Gordon in commenting on Lakoff and Johnson's (1999) examination of how reason itself is embodied. She postulates that "the fact that we conceptualize the mind and its operations of thought in bodily terms means that the body is always present in our perception and assessment of our own and others' intelligence" (Alcoff, 2006, 105). However, the way that the body is assessed by oneself and others goes beyond associations of levels of intelligence; since our personal identities are linked in significant ways to our bodies. As Alcoff notes, our everyday understanding of the term "identity" "implies a recognition of bodily difference" (105), and race and gender, as visible identities, function based on their bodily markers and affects how we perceive ourselves, others and the world. Similarly, the main language(s) that one uses, which is also based on our bodies, though maybe not as obviously as race and gender, can affect how we use our bodies and how we perceive the world.

I contend that all our major social identities (that is, the variety of positions that we occupy in our social space) are in significant ways marked on the body, and shape our subjective and intersubjective identities, and our perceptions of our sociocultural-historical space. Any identity that an individual possesses, whether embraced by the individual, or imposed in the social space, is grounded in and mediated through the body, since identities are always material, that is, possessed by lived bodies. Furthermore, since social identities are understood within a particular sociocultural-historical context, one's bodily identity is ultimately shaped by and within that space in which one operates. As Alcoff therefore argues, it is not possible to separate a "real self" from our social identities—grounded in our bodies—since they provide the framework for us to understand the world (Alcoff, 2006). One's subjectivity is influenced by the social identities which "constitute the necessary background from which I know the world" (126) since "the practices and meanings that are intelligible to me are ontologically grounded in group interactions, which are themselves structured by political economies of social structures" (121). To that end, those characteristics that we normally associate with who we are—"moral agency, subjectivity, and reasoning capacity"—cannot be understood outside of the interpretive horizon that develops within the social context (112). This point by Alcoff is reminiscent of the Gyekye's discussion of the Akan view of the person. Even while stressing the individuality of the person, Gyekye argues that the capacities to realize that individuality, that sense of who one is, is developed and facilitated in the social context. Since our social identities shape us from an early age, they are part of each person's interpretive horizon, even if we are not always aware of their role.

Our bodies are, therefore, not purely descriptive but are also pregnant with normative meaning. So, a body is not simply a material object, but a sociocultural historical object that is pregnant with meaning. By looking on a particular body, assessments are made about a person's age, gender, race, ethnicity, social status, and so on. A judgment is consequently made about the expected mode of behaviour that is likely to be exhibited by that person. Our identities are therefore, in significant respects, marked on our bodies, and with those identities are judgements about the value that should be attached to that person and the capacities and characteristics that the person is likely to possess. These expectations may be based on stereotypes, and may be passively processed, but they infuse how we interact with other persons, as well as how social institutions treat different kinds of bodies or members of social groups. The result is that descriptions of a person's body are not purely descriptive, but will have embedded a normative dimension.

MERLEAU-PONTY, GORDON, MILLS, AND HUMAN PERSON

It is evident from the forgoing that every aspect of the person and their understanding of themselves and the world is grounded in one's bodily identity. Merleau-Ponty insists that it would be impossible for someone not to recognise the importance of the body in the positing of objects, intentions of behaviour, and consciousness/subjectivity and consequently impossible to view the bodies of others as objects. This approach is certainly applicable when two paradigmatic bodies interact or are assumed. Within the Western context, such a body is white, male, and able-bodied. Someone who possesses such a body has the possibility of rejecting or downplaying their incorpo-reality, hence Mills' assertion that the white body can disappear, such that the European can be associated only with mentality, not corporeality. A similar assertion is made with respect to gender, where a man's body is allowed to disappear, while a woman's body is not. Once a non-paradigmatic body becomes involved, the meaning of the body changes for both persons since the paradigmatic body and the non-paradigmatic body have very differ-ent meanings attached to them within the society.

So, what happens when the body which one inhabits, and which is a tool for meaning formation and identity creation is one that is deemed non-para-digmatic and systematically maligned? Audre Lorde notes that the "mythical norm" for the body is "white, thin, male, young, heterosexual, Christian, and financially secure" (Lorde, 1984, 116). One can argue that those bodies as the norm have traditionally been allowed to become invisible in theorising (as Mills notes), so non-corporeality of theory is possible. This is supported by what Weiss calls the "hegemony of the anticorporeal" (Weiss, 1999, 56). While the mythical body is allowed to disappear, nonmythical bodies be-come even more visible. One can argue that it is due to this need to decide which bodies become salient and which will not—whether in our everyday interactions or in theorising—that Alcoff notes that "racial and gender iden-tities that are not visible create fear and consternation" (2006, 102). Alcoff further argues that "we conceptualise variously marked bodies very different-ly, with different 'natural' movements and abilities" (105). The visibility of the body, therefore, can create problems because of the labels and concepts that are associated with different types of bodies, which operate at both the level of a group's identity, as well as an individual's identity. Oyewumi similarly argues that the body within the Western conceptual framework, especially the visible body, plays a prominent and crucial role, and the "gaze is an invitation to differentiate" (Oyewumi, 1997, 2).

Gordon argues, in relation to race, that while there is an ambiguity that is inherent in one's subjectivity, an "expression of the human being as a mean-ingful, multifaceted way of being that may involve contradictory interpreta-tions, or at least equivocal ones" (1997, 72), this ambiguity is evaded for the black body. Ambiguity exists, Gordon asserts, because human beings are neither purely objects nor purely subjects, but involves shifts between the two, especially in interactions with others, which are mediated by the body. Because of this ambiguity, one's body image is necessarily fluid, since one necessarily shifts perspectives between being object and being subject. How-ever, this fluidity is not generally recognised in the African/black body, the black body being perceived purely as an object, and not as a signifier of human presence. From this practice, Gordon argues, comes the evasion of the black person as a consciousness, who would therefore be unable to enter into a relationship with another subject and so create meanings. So, Fanon argues,

"I am given no chance. I am overdetermined from without. I am the slave not of the "idea" that others have of me but of my own appearance" (1986, 116). By treating the black body as an absence of human subjectivity, the black perspective would also be absent. Fanon argues that the black person suffers not simply because she is not white, but because of what not being white means. It means that she is viewed as an object, one that is discriminated against, based on the color of her skin. She will lose all individuality because to see one black person is to see all others, since this view involves anonymity.

Mills also highlights the normative dimension of the body when he argues that the body is used as a marker for being seen as being admissible to the moral community, and so the body itself should be seen as a "philosophical object." Kant, for example, argues that all humans are persons because they have the capacity for consciousness and so should be treated as ends because they have intrinsic moral worth, grounded in human rationality and autonomy (Eze, 2003, 432). However, when his anthropological views are examined, it is evident that Kant's view is that non-whites cannot develop rationality and so will not have autonomous wills. For example, he claims that Africans "can be educated but only as servants (slaves), that is they allow themselves to be trained," and by training he means being whipped or being otherwise physically coerced (439). Mills notes that the hierarchy based on race created a distinction between persons and subpersons, and a subperson could not have "the moral development necessary for being a responsible moral and political agent" and so could not be accorded "full membership in the polity" (Oyewumi, 1997, 60). The result is that non-whites have a "different and inferior schedule of rights and liberties applying to them" (56). The body of the black person takes on a significance that the white person's body does not: "unlike the white (male) body, normative ('flesh-coloured,' after all), unproblematic, vanishing from philosophical sight, invisibly visible, the black body is visibly invisible, deviant, nonneutral (unflesh-coloured?), and problematic. . . . The body, then, is what incarnates one's differential positioning in the world" (Mills, 1998, 16). A similar view can be applied to other visible identities, including persons who are visibly differently abled. It becomes even more challenging when one considers the intersectionality dimension, with Mills noting that black women have it especially hard because of the combination of sexism and racism, sexism that "values women primarily for their bodies and a racist norm that makes the Caucasoid somatype the standard of beauty" (16–17).

In the Caribbean, the influence of Western ideas of race and gender permeates the lived experiences of persons, coming through the colonisation and creolisation processes. Though the majority of the population is phenotypically black (except in Guyana and Trinidad and Tobago), the associations of blackness with goodness are still rare. In Jamaica, there is, for example, a well-known saying, "nutten weh black nuh good" (nothing that is black is good). It is also reflected in a proverb used by Nettleford, "Every john crow tink him pickney white" (Nettleford, 1998, 173), which highlights the view that whiteness is associated with what is good. Mills (2010), in discussing this issue in relation to Nettleford's work, contends that "smadditisation" (Nettleford's term used to refer to the recognition by oneself and others of one's moral and social status as a person) is not simply aimed at improving the social status of the person, but at changing the negation of blackness. Smaddisation is a process that requires changing the way in which the black body is viewed so that the mechanisms used by persons to have their bodies approximate whiteness no longer have to be utilized:

> The body, the flesh, is the sign of sub-personhood, the signal of inferiority, and this body must register its inferiority in the postures that it takes up and the body-languages that it speaks. So one must recover and re-valorise the body, relating to it differently. One unlearns the imposed body; one reinvents and reincorporates the body; one teaches it a new body language; and to a certain extent one is unlearning the metaphysics, challenging the ontology. (3611–3615)

One aspect of this process of revalorising the black body is related to the use of the body for artistic representations, including clothing, jewelry, and hairstyles and adornment. While clothing is functional, it has aesthetic, political, ontological, and social ramifications because they are used to both make assertions and be used as a basis for making judgments about the person. Our worn art selections function as a significant part of the way that we project our bodies and therefore ourselves into the world, and so our clothes tell a story about how we want to be seen. The question that arises then is what kind of story do we want to tell with our clothing? How many of our choices—and assessment of the choices made by others—are based on cultural or religious factors, on beliefs about the message (and sometimes subsequent fear) that certain types of clothing will project, etc.? We have to, subsequently, consider whether, in making these judgments, we are working with a particular set of assumptions about how clothing ought to look. So when natural black hair is deemed "inappropriate" for work contexts, there is a clear underlying assumption about the difference between black bodies and white bodies. In the Caribbean, serious consideration has to be given to the way in which clothing and bodily adornments, as part of the way in which the body is understood, can be used to teach "a new body language." While some of the revalorisation of the black body through clothing is evident, it is an ongoing process and needs to be treated as such.

JAMAICA KINCAID'S *AUTOBIOGRAPHY OF MY MOTHER*

Revalorization of the black body ultimately means giving value to all aspects of one's body, given the crucial role that the body plays in intersubjective identity, one's sense of self, and one's understanding of the world. This process is evidenced in Jamaica Kincaid's *The Autobiography of My Mother* (1997). The novel is set in Dominica, an island which, like all others in the Caribbean, has a history of European genocide of the indigenous peoples, enslavement of Africans, and colonialism. The events in the novel begin under the period of post-slavery colonialism. The novel's first-person narrator, Xuela Claudette Richardson, presents her story in the form of a memoir, as the reader sees the seventy-year-old woman reflecting on her life, and, in so doing, trying to piece together the life of the mother who died while giving birth to her.

In *The Autobiography of My Mother*, Kincaid clearly highlights the value of bodily identity in the development of both the narrator and main character Xuela's subjective identity and her understanding of other persons' identities. She demonstrates this value through her use of bodily descriptions offered by Xuela, of herself and significant people in her life. It is therefore appropriate and feasible that I use this text to support and show examples of the claims that I have been making. Xuela describes several persons throughout her narrative, descriptions that are infused with her feelings about (and therefore, would treat) the person, highlighting how the descriptive and normative aspects of one's bodily identity are inseparable and the importance of the body in developing one's identity and ascribing a particular set of characteristics to others. In offering her descriptions, one sees how she aims to subvert the limited body image that is paradigmatic within the colonial and postcolonial Caribbean space and, shows a path to smadditisation.

Given the significance of the mother-daughter relationship for Xuela, it is not surprising that one of the persons that she describes is her mother, though she never met her. Xuela nonetheless offers a description of her mother, though the source for that description is not clear: "She was tall (I am told—I did not know her, she died at the moment I was born); her hair was black, her fingers were long, her legs were long, her feet were long and narrow with a high instep, her face was thin and bony, her chin was narrow, her cheekbones high and wide, her lips were thin and wide, her body was thin and long; she had a natural graceful gait; she did not speak much" (198). This first description offered is a relatively empty one, compared to the descriptions that Xuela offers of other people, in part because she did not know her mother and so could not describe her in such a way that reflected Xuela's understanding of her character. But even in describing her mother, one can infer that body image is vital for Xuela. She says, for example, that her father would not have liked her mother's skin (197). Xuela had earlier offered a description of her father which was not too salutary (Kincaid, 1997, 49).

Note here that Xuela reflects on the shade of one's skin color, a major issue within the Caribbean space, and appears to reject the valorising of these characteristics that her father possesses, which in the Caribbean would be seen as part of the ideal body because they approximate whiteness. Instead, even at a young age, Xuela seems to have more appreciation for the aesthetic beauty of darker skin tones. This appreciation contrasts with the description of her father's, which takes on a more sinister description when Xuela later describes him: "my father's skin was the colour of corruption: copper, gold, ore; his eyes were grey, his hair was red, his nose was long and narrow" (181). Associating his skin color with corruption resulted from how he lived his life: "he was a thief, he was a jailer, he spoke falsehoods, he took advantage of the weak" (53). Here, one can see how Xuela reverses the beauty norms that have generally operated within the Caribbean space, assigning more value to phenotypically African physical features, including one's hairstyle. Furthermore, her descriptions highlight how she fuses the descriptive and normative dimensions of one's bodily identity with character of the individual.

Xuela similarly emphasises her husband Philip's skin: "thin and pink and transparent, as if it were on its way to being skin but had not yet reached the state that real skin is" (152). She further notes that "he did not look like anyone I could love, and he didn't look like anyone I should love, and I was determined then that I could not love him and I determined then that I shall not love him" (Kincaid, 1997, 152). Here Xuela uses Philip's bodily identity to determine how she would treat him. So while she would have sex with him, and eventually marry him, she would not love him, reinforcing the significance of one's bodily appearance in ascribing characteristics to someone, and consequently how one will treat that person. The person that she does love, Roland, is one who she sees as being the opposite of Philip, and her description of him bears this out. Her description of Roland is the most extensive in *The Autobiography of My Mother*, though interestingly there is no exhaustive description of the color of his skin. There is a passing comment about his skin color ("twig-brown") but it is part of a description of his mouth—his first feature that she notices—which captured her attention and triggered her love for him (163–165). She further describes his hands, legs, and the hair on various parts of his body. Her descriptions are active, showing the positive feelings that she has for him. Though she labels him as being someone who "did not have a history, he was only a small event in somebody else's history" (167), she notes that he "carried himself as if he was something precious" (168), and this may be part of the appeal that he has for Xuela, that sense of being valuable without being in a position of power like her father or Philip.

Of Philip's wife Moira, Xuela says, "she was very pleased to be who she was, and by that she meant she was pleased to be of the English people," which is reflected in how she assesses her physical appearance. Xuela, however, does not see Moira's body in a positive light, describing her complexion as "waxy, ghoulish, without life" (Kincaid, 1997, 156). Instead of seeing features associated with whiteness as beautiful, she views them negatively. One may question whether Xuela develops a negative image of the body that is white or approximates whiteness, one that Weiss would say is too coherent. However, I believe that this approach is one where she is in fact claiming a more fluid notion of body image and the resulting identity, rejecting the mythical norm or paradigm that operates in her sociocultural historical space.

Xuela also reflects on introducing Moira to a hallucinogenic tea to which she becomes fatally addicted and which causes her skin to turn black before she died. Through Xuela's comment on Moira's dislike of black people, one can see how the phenotypical racial identity that one has is sufficient for being hated by some persons. Unlike Moira, Xuela has a negative reaction to those persons with white skin or skin that approximates whiteness. So, while she seems to criticise Moira for her hatred of black people, Xuela seems to have a similar tendency. However, Xuela's dislike can be interpreted as a conscious and political one, because Xuela associates the colour of one's skin with power, and she sides with the powerless.

Of her brother, who she notes only became her brother at his death, Xuela thought that he looked more like his mother than his father, though she was encouraged to see more of her father in him (Kincaid, 1997, 53). Xuela's cynical view is that her father's walk and gestures were not natural. So the mimicry that is being observed is only reflective of the desire on the part of the son and the mother to be like his father, including being given his name. Xuela's sister, Elizabeth, resembles her father, having the same color hair, eyes, and skin (Kincaid, 1997, 52), but because she is a girl and so could not start a dynasty, she is not as favored as her brother is (Kincaid, 1997, 53). After her brother died, Elizabeth's mother, in Xuela's view "could not look at [Elizabeth], for what a waste she was, she was the wrong one to be alive, [while] her father had never really looked at her" (Kincaid, 1997, 113). Though his son did not have red hair, he is seen as the next link in a possible dynasty. So, it is not simply one's physical appearance, but the gendered interpretation of one's appearance that matters.

Xuela's reflections also highlight the intersection of gender and race when she compares herself with Moira (Kincaid, 1997). In drawing a distinction between "woman" and "lady," one sees a class dimension, but there is also a clear racial (and colonial) component, since Moira is white and English, though it should be noted that in the Caribbean space race and class are usually blurred. Xuela, by grounding her identity as a woman in her body and its appearance seems to be suggesting that in a significant way all women are alike and so are likely to have some shared experiences, including how they experience their embodiment, though Moira would reject that based on race, class and culture. By seeing her definition as an act of "self-possession," however, it can be argued that for Xuela, one has to embrace one's bodily identity, which Moira does not appear to do, in order to be able to fully understand oneself.

Xuela's definition of a woman has some affinity with Alcoff's, since she defines "woman" in relation to those aspects of the woman usually associated with biological reproduction, as Alcoff does. Alcoff conceptualises gender as positionality, "gender is, among other things, a position one occupies and from which one can act politically" (2006, 148). An important aspect of that positional consciousness is an objective basis, where *"women and men are differentiated by virtue of their different relationship of possibility to biological reproduction, with biological reproduction referring to conceiving, giving birth, and breast-feeding, involving one's body"* (Alcoff, 2006, 172; emphasis in the original). Alcoff notes that one does not have to become pregnant or have a child to have a gendered identity based on the "differential relation to biological reproduction" since the way in which one interacts in the world will still be shaped by it.

Xuela had her first abortion at around sixteen years old, after which she goes to work on road construction, and says she began to worship herself. At that point she offered one of the most exhaustive descriptions of herself (Kincaid, 1997). Here one can see how Xuela uses her body as a way to get back a sense of self that she lost because of the loss of the trust she experienced with Lise Labatte (who basically treated her as a prize for her husband and a source for a child). In the final chapter of the book, she again describes herself, highlighting how she has aged, but notes that what she "had lost in physical appeal or beauty I had gained in character. It was written all over me; I did not fail to arouse curiosity in anyone capable of it" (206).

Xuela has a clear sense of herself as a woman, a recognition of the challenges that she faces as a girl/woman, but also the power that comes with being a woman—the power to choose to conceive, to bring a child into the world, and also stop a child from coming, and to help others in stopping potential children from developing, including her sister Elizabeth.

She has a positive view of her own body, which she embraces from a young age. One way in which Xuela exhibits her bodily identity, arguably the strongest way, is through her sexuality and sexual behaviour. Xuela uses her sexuality as a means of learning about herself, the world, and others. The female is usually the one presented as the object in the sex act, the submissive member. However, Xuela's approach to sex precludes her objectification. Furthermore, if one conceives sexual encounters as a symbolic relationship between the powerful and the weak, Xuela is the powerful. Therefore, though she is a non-white female, through sex and her body, she is able to see herself in a positive light, to overcome the role of the weak that would have been automatically assigned to her. Even in her first sexual encounter with Philip, which sees her hands tied together in a sado-masochistic posture, she is the person in control. "I made him" is repeated by her three times as she describes the various positions that they assumed during their sexual encounter. She is here even rewriting the colonial relationship. In these sexual encounters that Xuela describes, she destroys the façade of the powerful/powerless, subject/object. Sexuality for Xuela is therefore a reordering of the landscape of relationships in her environment, and also a tool through which she can acquire a further understanding of herself and others.

She also indulges heavily in autoeroticism, describing her masturbatory practices initially as a means of quietening her feelings of loss and loneliness, her body being a source of comfort. Two of the three significant sexual relationships that she discusses begin with an autoerotic scene. Though the eroticized body is an important aspect of the development of her subjectivity, she places primacy in self-reliance and does not locate pleasure solely in the interaction with others. Her autoeroticism and masturbatory practices are also ways of giving herself love. She did not feel loved by anyone, so she developed narcissistic tendencies, all of which were located in the body. Merleau-Ponty argues that one, in the process of meaning formation, may take a meaning that is based in sexual desire and assign a more general meaning to it. In Xuela's case, she takes her sexual desire and the pleasure that she gets from smelling, seeing and touching herself and extrapolates that to a more general love for herself.

Xuela therefore embraces her bodily identity and actually uses it positively in the development of her sense of self. In the process, she does what Mills advocates in terms of his process of smadditisation. She chooses to embrace her sexuality in a way that would generally be frowned upon as being inappropriate behaviour for a woman and utilises it in a positive way to move beyond the identity that would have been expected of a black woman in colonial Dominica. Further, she identifies with subordinate groups—patois-speaking, poor, female, black and/or Carib—as she realizes that there is value in such an identification. Through it, she is able, just as standpoint epistemologists argue, to see the injustices of, and inconsistencies in, the position assumed by the powerful, male and white (or those approximating whiteness). She is also able to see why other black Dominicans find themselves caught in the trap of being seen as the other, as objects, a result of the colonial system and the hate and despair it produces. With respect to gender, Xuela realizes that the society tends to treat her, as a female, in a different way from a male solely due to her gender and is scathing in her commentary on it. But Xuela—though constrained by some societal standards—is also able to subvert some of those norms or reach beyond them.

CONCLUSION

Though the situation into which Xuela was born automatically conferred a subordinated social position (being seen as an object rather than a subject), she is able to subvert this label and, starting with the body as the point of perception and the means of interpretation, Xuela is able to reflect on and interpret her experience and those of the other persons on the island on which she resides. Her sense of self is firmly grounded in her body, both at the physiological and the phenomenal levels. Her body, as a point of interaction, is useful for understanding others and herself, and through it, she is able to affirm her subjectivity. She chooses to identify herself with the weak, the defeated. Yet she does not have a sense of self that is grounded in a distorted body image. While one may be judged by others, this judgement is not absolute; there is the freedom to choose to reject these labels and create meaning for oneself. This is what Xuela does and the sense of self that she develops is one that she creates for herself. The sense of self that Xuela derives at the end of the text involves an evaluative process, stimulated primarily by painful life events that force her to reflect on what she wants to be, strengthens her to make tough choices, and allows her to question the dominant societal views.

BIBLIOGRAPHY

Alcoff, Linda Martín (2006). *Visible Identities: Race Gender and the Self.* New York: Oxford University Press.

Bewaji, J. A. I. (2012). *Narratives of Struggle.* Durham, NC: Carolina Academic Press.

Eze, Emmanuel C. (2003). "The Colour of Reason: The Idea of "Race" in Kant's Anthropology," in *The African Philosophy Reader: A Text with Readings* (2nd edition). Eds. P. H. Coetzee and A. P. J. Roux. New York: Routledge. 430–456.

Fanon, Frantz (1986). *Black Skin, White Masks.* Trans. Charles Lam Markmann. London: Pluto Press.

Gyekye, Kwame (1995). *An Essay on African Philosophical Thought: The Akan Conceptual Scheme.* Philadelphia, PA: Temple University Press.

Gordon, Lewis R. (2000). *Existentia Africana: Understanding Africana Existential Thought.* New York: Routledge.

Kincaid, Jamaica (1997). *The Autobiography of My Mother.* New York: Plume/Penguin.

Lakoff, George, and Mark Johnson (1999). *Philosophy in the Flesh: The Embodied Mind and Its Challenge to Western Thought.* New York: Basic Books.

Lorde, Audre (1984). "Age, Race, Class and Sex: Women Redefining Difference," in *Sister Outsider: Essays and Speeches,* 114–123. Freedom, CA: Crossing Press.

Merleau-Ponty, Maurice (1962). *Phenomenology of Perception.* Trans. Colin Smith. London: Routledge and Kegan Paul.

Mills, Charles W. (2010). "Smadditizin," in *Radical Theory, Caribbean Reality: Race, Class and Social Domination.* Kingston: University of the West Indies Press. Kindle. 3310–693.

———. (1998). *Blackness Visible: Essays on Philosophy and Race.* Ithaca, NC: Cornell University Press.

———. (1997). *The Racial Contract.* Ithaca, NC: Cornell University Press.

Nettleford, Rex (1998). *Mirror Mirror: Identity, Race and Protest in Jamaica.* Kingston: LMH Publishing.

Oyewumi, Oyeronke (1997). *The Invention of Women: Making an African Sense of Western Gender Discourses*. Minneapolis: University of Minnesota Press.

Weiss, Gail (1999). "The Abject Borders of the Body Image," in *Perspectives on Embodiment: The Intersections of Nature and Culture*. Eds. Gail Weiss and Honi Fern Haber. New York: Routledge. 41–59.

Wiredu, Kwasi (1996). *Cultural Universals and Particulars*. Bloomington and Indianapolis: Indiana University Press.

Young, Iris Marion (1994). "Gender as Seriality: Thinking about Women as a Social Collective," *Signs*, 19(3): 713–738.

Chapter Fourteen

Sexual Predators or Prey

The White Male in Jude Dibia's Novels

Ifeyinwa Genevieve Okolo

Predation generally refers to the strategizing, capturing, killing and devouring of organisms by other organisms, but it also metaphorically covers some human behaviors. Predation has systemised mechanisms and is a calculated process involving aggression. Sexual predation in humans has, over time, been associated with, or taken to simply refer to, child sexual abuse, rape, or sex related domestic violence. However, so many other behaviors which are subtly aggressive also qualify as sexual predation. Staik (2011) opines that the negative cultural understanding of masculinity, wherein dominance is eroticised in sexual relations, has led many men and women to believe in and build their lives around men adopting unhealthy behaviors and ideals:

a. Sex is a weapon for personal gain to prove superiority, via dominance (versus a key aspect of emotional intimacy in a couple's relationship).
b. Primary goal is to "win" by overpowering the will of another, to ensure they know "their place"—and sex is a secondary goal.
c. Main pleasure is derived from causing (emotional) pain to the other, i.e., tricking or manipulating them for own gratification.
d. The other is seen as a weak or defective "object" without feelings, thoughts, opinions, etc., of their own.
e. Love is regarded as overall sex-focused, sex is equated with intimacy, and emotional intimacy is tactically avoided.
f. Women only respect men who dominate them, and respect is associated or equated with obedience.

The above list is a compilation of sexually predatory behaviours and ideals. But, while Staik (2011) sees these as basically emanating from men, Carroll (2005) shows that these behaviors are not gender specific. Women can exhibit the same unhealthy sexual behaviors as men and for the same reasons too. Again, given the evolution in sexual identities and the blurring of gender roles in recent times, pegging specific sexual behaviors on a particular gender type proves problematic.

In three novels, *Walking with Shadows*, *Unbridled*, and *Blackbird*, Dibia is concerned with sexuality and sexual relationships between or among individuals and groups. His efforts to ensure the sexual presence of white males in his novels and to pitch them against the blacks (both males and females) are remarkable. Dibia gives two angles to viewing the white male in his novels. Sometimes he is the prey; at other times, he is the predator; and in some occasions, he is both prey and predator or neither. His black counterparts are also given the same treatment, which goes to say that the role of prey or predator is not domiciled in any particular race, and can be viewed as a human trait—probably no different from basic animal instinct toward gratification of sexual desires.

THEORETICAL FRAMEWORK

When Eagleton (1983) summarizes Jacques Lacan's angle to psychoanalysis as that which "permits us to explore the relations between the unconscious and human society" (173), the picture of social relations ordered by the workings of the mind was concretised. Lacan reinterprets Freudianism in terms of language—a predominantly social activity—and in so doing, the unconscious becomes "a particular effect of language, a process of desire set in motion by difference" (173). This difference/otherness is occasioned through naming—language use—and John Storey (1993) adds, "the cultural repertoire we encounter in our everyday existence" (90). This goes to say that what is called the unconscious and the human behavior stemming from it are informed by the environment (society). Eagleton (1983) captures the human relationship with this otherness through the unconscious manifesting in actions thus

> our unconscious desire is directed towards this Other, in the shape of some ultimately gratifying reality which we can never have; but it is also true for Lacan that our desire is in some way always *received* from the Other too. We desire what others—our parents, for instance—unconsciously desire for us; and desire can only happen because we are caught up in linguistic, sexual and social relations—the whole field of the "Other"—which generate it. (174)

In essence, the differences in humans create in them a longing for or revulsion towards that which differentiates them. It is based on this understanding of the push-and-pull force of difference that communities are formed: likes/ sameness attracts and maintains a bond which keeps "unlikes"/"unsameness" out, making them spectacles to be treated specially or handled separately. The bond creates a "we" and/versus "them/other" way of classification. This psychoanalytical concept of "othering" is utilised in teasing out the meanings of the frictions in the sexual relationships in the novels examined, especially those of interracial nature where what draws attention to the sexual relationship is the difference in the races of the characters.

HOMOSEXUALITY AND PREDATION
IN *WALKING WITH SHADOWS*

The gay relationships between the blacks and whites in *Walking with Shadows* show that predatory practices are not fixed to any particular environment. Dibia is not subjective or biased in his views about homosexuality. On the larger scale, however, the West is presented as being more tolerant of homosexuality, hence, the gay protagonist, Adrian/Ebele Njoko, is forced to relocate to London where he hopes to live the life that is free of sexual discrimination. Before this, the Nigerian society, both men and women, and the church form a formidable opposition to his chosen sexual orientation, preference or lifestyle. Ebele suffers gay bashing, social alienation in his work place and rejection from his family. Although his family later begins to tolerate him, he relocates: what he needs is not their tolerance but their understanding, acceptance and full integration into their lives.

While Ebele seeks healing by migrating to the West, Dibia does not give the impression that all is rosy with gay relationships there or with the ones between the blacks and whites in Nigeria. Ebele's relationship with Antonio, his Spanish lover in Nigeria, does not turn out well. Antonio betrays Ebele and leaves him broken hearted. To cure his broken heart, Ebele gets married and tries to get along with Ada, his wife and their daughter, Ego.

Antonio gets reckless after he parts with Ebele, has multiple partners and sex without protection. He is HIV-positive and is slowly but surely dying by the end of the novel.

The picture of Antonio does not subscribe to either prey or predator in the text, even when he is the one that breaks Ebele's heart. Relationships fall apart every day and since the text does not go into details on what transpired to make Antonio leave Ebele, it is best taken as a gay relationship gone sour. There is nothing to suggest that either Antonio or Ebele was using the other. Therefore, in their relationship, none is prey or predator. They had it rosy while the relationship lasted. That Ebele goes to see Antonio before leaving the country to offer him forgiveness for breaking his heart is an evidence of their quality time together.

Antonio can also not be strictly classified as a predator in his other relationships with black men. His reason for multiple partners: "Too many beautiful black men, so little time" (247), portrays him as reckless and not as calculating, scheming or predatory. He is simply attracted to that which is different from him and goes after it with his eyes closed to the precautions he could have taken to safeguard his life. So, in the end, he pays for his recklessness and not for moving out of his "we" to the "other" circle. Ironically, being a Spanish in Nigeria questions his being a "we" and his Nigerian sex partners the "other."

Dibia uses George and Johan to examine the opportunistic tendencies of some people who are or who profess to be gay and who try to live out their dreams against all odds, by moving away from a country that is homophobic like Nigeria. George runs away from Nigeria with his German boyfriend, Johan. They get married in Germany and live happily for ten years. George's mother dies, and he is in Nigeria for her burial with complaints of being tired of Johan. He wants to get a new relationship with another foreigner because Johan is becoming too old for him. Suddenly, the fifteen years age difference means much to him only because he has used Johan to get out of the country, get German citizenship, and a good job in Germany. The complaints he gives of being marginalized because of his color sounds hollow since they only come up as an excuse for him to leave Johan. Suggestions from Abdul and Adrian to come back to the country are not welcome—he misses the Nigeria of his dreams where everything worked well, and the citizens are contented and happy. He would rather stay in Germany (where he claims to suffer from racial discrimination/marginalisation) and find a new lover/partner.

It is obvious that Johan is the prey while George is the predator. Johan, like Antonio, is drawn into the relationship by George's difference—his beautiful black body. Interestingly, George takes Johan to his own country to exploit him there and runs home to Nigeria to re-strategize on how to find the next prey. George is not like Clarence in Camara Laye's *Radiance of the King* whose role as the prey is enhanced by his strange African environment.

UNBRIDLED: MIGRATION AS PANACEA FOR PREDATION?

In *Unbridled*, the use of migratory trends in destabilising the location of the predatory behaviour is seen in the protagonist's, Ngozi's, movements. Continuously raped by her father, Akadike Akachi, from when she is six years old on, Ngozi had to be sent away to live with her uncle in Lagos. So, her first movement is from her village, Ezi, to the city of Lagos. At this level, the popularly held idea of pristine rural life which is usually destroyed by the malevolent city (Obiechina, 1975; Palmer, 1979; Hassan, 1995; Jimoh, 2004; and Weinstein, 2007) proves untrue. Ngozi's life is already destroyed in the village before she ever thought about the city. She is not lured to the city of Lagos by its charms and bright lights, like Jagua Nana in Cyprian Ekwensi's *Jagua Nana,* but comes there to escape the sexual horrors of the village. In Lagos, Ngozi develops a crush for Gerald Okoro, a rich boy in her neighborhood. Unhappy with the diversion of attention from her to her brother, Tiffany (Gerald's sister) brings Ngozi's aunt to know of the sexual relationship between Ngozi and Gerald. Consequently, Ngozi is sent out of the house and gets to stay with Precious and Uloma by a stroke of luck. Dark memories from the village still haunt her and send her off to London to marry James.

In the Ngozi-Gerald relationship, it is difficult to define or differentiate who is the prey or who the predator is. This is because Gerald uses Ngozi as a plaything, a sex pet to occupy his time when he is away from school and the class of girls he is used to while Ngozi enjoys being his pet. Ngozi is captivated by George's charms and awed by the very fact that the rich boy, who is the dream of all the girls on their street, singles her out for sexual attention. She is aware that theirs will never be the fairy tale where Cinderella marries the prince but goes along without being pressurised into the relationship. Both of them arrange their secret meetings and look forward to them. In essence, she has no problems with being George's sex machine, so theirs is a relationship of mutual understanding. She says, "I have since come to realise that it was as much my choice what happened between us, as it was Gerald's pleasure. It was a dangerous game we were playing and I could see he relished it completely" (140). This takes away the label of predator from George, although it can be argued that his social standing, his difference from Ngozi, gives him an oppressive powerful bargaining chip which Ngozi could not have resisted.

With James King, right from the prologue, a predator is presented. Ngozi/Erika King mistakes a passenger for James, her British husband, and the response this elicits from her is, "I found myself momentarily frozen as cold fear formed goose bumps across my arms and the back of my neck. *JAMES,* my head kept screaming. James, James, James. He had finally found me. He had come to take me back. His green eyes bore into me like red hot coal" (12).

Given this introduction, expectations all through the novel are fixed on finding out what it is about James that chills Erika's blood. His role in the novel has been defined. His gentlemanly manners at the airport when he comes to receive Ngozi/Erika soon give way to the monster within. But, how monstrous is James really when we consider that both he and Ngozi lied to each other about their true identities while chatting online. Instead of twenty-two, Ngozi claims eighteen years old and James twenty-eight, instead of his twenty-two. James also has lied about his financial status and family. So,

Ngozi, on getting to London, has to deal with James' housemates: English-Jamaican Thomas and Nigerian-fortune-seeker-in-London Providence. These share his apartment in order to raise money for the maintenance of the apartment. Ngozi's desires for difference and dreams of a London with the streets of gold are shattered. Her reality is a British husband who is always high on drugs and alcohol and cheats on her too. She is simply his African trophy, a prize won for being a smart internet user. It is not enough that James beats her up and generally treats her badly after stealing all her money and confiscating her passport, Ngozi endures Thomas' exhibitionism and Providence's twisted sexual attraction. Her routine of tiptoeing around the house and hiding from the three men living in the house with her rightly confers the status of predators on the three men.

All three have sexual takes on her and use her as their field for measuring their masculinity. For James, the promise of a marriage certificate, with which he holds Ngozi captive, is his winning chip. For Thomas, it is the huge size of his penis which he loves to show off and which Providence describes as "the only black thing he inherited from his black father" (96). Providence relies on his kinship with Ngozi, being a Nigerian.

Providence's reference to Thomas' penis as his only African endowment calls to mind myths of the virile, hyper-sexed African male and sexually loose female; notions strongly influencing the classification of non-white races as exotic when brought up in sexual discussions (Agustin, 1988; D'Emilio, DeMillo, and Freedman, 1988; Carroll, 2005). This is also the same myth Dibia draws on in *Walking with Shadows* when Antonio cannot seem to get enough of beautiful black men until he gets HIV. It is also noticed that Thomas treats his women differently, based on the color of their skins:

> It was certainly better than watching Thomas bring in his women from time-to-time or having to endure the noise they produced while in his bedroom. It got to a point when I believed the rumpus they made was intentional, to get my attention. It had its patterns. With white girls he was more discreet, almost quiet. But when he came with a black woman or a woman who was mixed race like himself, there was an effort to make a show for me. (149)

Thomas utilises racial difference in establishing his masculinity and in the fight for Ngozi's sexual attention.

In *Unbridled*, what is seen is a lady running from one predator (her black father) to another (a British James) and then from/to others (hybrid/mulatto Thomas and Nigerian Providence). With Ngozi/Erika King running to/from predators—black, white, and mixed blood—Dibia makes it clear that any race can be predatory. Again, Erika's Ghanaian neighbour in London, Bessie, confirms with her relationships with her two husbands that predatory habits are not racial. Her first husband, Kwesi (Ghanaian), has abused her both psychologically and physically until she leaves him. She remarries to a white/Romanian, Nicolas, who treats her with love and respect.

MECHANISMS OF SEXUAL PREDATION IN *BLACKBIRD*

Blackbird partly shares the same kind of migratory trend in *Walking with Shadows*, only this time it is an American that is involved in the journeys. Edward Wood's presence in Nigeria is initiated by business and not the need for some sort of sexual asylum. Hence, his sexual involvements feature in the novel as part of the philandering life of a sexually overcharged male. His role fluctuates from predator to prey all through the text, showing that in his base elements, man (irrespective of race) is capable of either being predator or prey. In the end, however, when his predatory involvements backfire, he migrates back to his own country, leaving a sorry mess behind.

Their differences (racial and financial) bring Edward and Nduesoh together. American, Edward is fascinated by Nduesoh's plain African looks and marries her. Nduesoh overlooks the generation gap between them, because her family makes her feel she is fortunate to have seen somebody interested enough in her to ignore her plain looks and marry her. Nduesoh and her family see Edward as their ladder to social heights. In this regard, Edward is preyed upon for financial purposes. However, when he begins to encroach on Omoniyi's territory by taking a sexual interest in Maya, he becomes the predator and the cumulative effect of his actions destroys almost all that he holds dear—his wife (Nduesoh), Oasis Hotel, which he manages, and his stay in Nigeria. In the end, he has to leave the country, since it no longer holds anything of joy for him.

Othering works in multiples in the Nduesoh-Edward relationship which touches on so many other relationships in the novel. Nduesoh has lived under the anonymity that the lack of a pretty face bestows on women. Her marriage to Edward, according to her family, was her only chance of ever getting married, considering her looks. Edward's money and white color confer on her a status she ordinarily would not have had in a place like Nigeria that is controlled by the othering occasioned by racial difference. So, when Edward's attention begins to get captured by beautiful black women, especially Maya, Nduesoh knows she cannot allow anybody to take Edward, her source of power and social relevance, away from her.

She seeks vengeance and reaffirms her existence, at least to herself, by raping Maya's husband, a man the text describes as beautiful. Nduesoh finds her raping of Omoniyi exhilarating, liberating and a lease of new life. Her satisfaction from the rape is multifaceted: first, her victim is the husband of the woman Edward is trying to displace her with; second, he is handsome/ beautiful and as such hers is the triumph of gaining power over the beauty which nature has denied her and for which she has suffered neglect from men (especially good looking men like her victim); third, the feeling of reversal of the traditional/patriarchal roles of who is in control of sexual acts confers on her "a true sense of freedom and control. And rapture" (220).

Omoniyi is attacked in his place of discharging his duties as a housekeeper by a woman who is socially and economically more powerful than he is. The fact that his penis betrays him by having an erection makes the rape more humiliating for him, especially as Nduesoh abandons him the moment she is satisfied while his erection is still in need of satiation. After the rape, he does not mean anything to Nduesoh and it becomes his obligation to ensure that Edward does not slip away from Nduesoh's grip by his setting up structures to keep Maya on the leash.

This sets off a chain of events that leads to several deaths in the text, including Nduesoh's death. It is noteworthy that much of the feeling of worthlessness which Omoniyi feels from the rape arises from the reversal of roles in the act: he has been made by a woman to feel powerless and "as helpless as a woman being violated against her will. . . . How unlike a man he felt in her arms" (222).

Omoniyi is clearly Nduesoh's prey. His position here is heightened by his understanding and interpretation of masculinity as being a correlate of violence, as Mekgwe (2007) observes in Ayi Kwei Armah's *Fragments*. It is clear that Omoniyi does not react to his rape like the white lady whose rape opens the novel's prologue. Hired by her black husband, Scorpion and his men come to this unnamed white woman's house to murder her and rid the husband of her presence. Her show of fear sexually excites Scorpion and he settles down with his men to rape her in turns before murdering her. While fear paralyzes the white woman, it is shame that takes over Omoniyi.

Like Antonio and Johan, Edward is captivated by the black skin:

> He loved black. He loved the feel and smell of the African skin. He refrained from using the word *exotic* to describe the beauty of it. Exotic sounded like a term he would use to describe a rare bird or flower. It also had the ring of old colonial condescension. He had no such notion of Africans; rather he was inexplicably drawn to them. He had been drawn to Nduesoh in this same manner... He could not control his weakness for African women and, like Emmanuel, the night porter, his libido was insatiable. (199–120)

Edward has money to back up his taste in black women and enjoys the attention his money gets him when women come running to him for what they believe he can offer them. So, his heightened interest and determination to get and conquer Maya is rooted not just in her skin but also in her refusal to run after him like the others. His predatory techniques with Maya include taking an interest in her while she sings at Segun's restaurant, *SìGun Restaurant;* hounding her even after she gives up the job at the club on Omoniyi's order to stay at home and take care of her sick son, Deji; giving her a job to sing in his own hotel; giving Omoniyi a job in Oasis Hotel; taking over Deji's hospital bills; and planning and obtaining international passports and travelling papers with which to take Maya and Deji abroad, where she will be available to him alone. They gradually but surely destabilise Maya's marriage and incur Nduesoh's wrath. Although Omoniyi's hard-headedness and misplaced male ego contributes to the crippling of his marriage, Edward's machinations serve as the distraction Maya falls back on in the face of Omoniyi's unreasonableness.

CONCLUSION

Othering/difference—racial, financial, cultural, and social—is seen to be a key factor in aligning the sexual relationships and identities in *Walking with Shadows*, *Unbridled*, and *Blackbird*. Jude Dibia, in developing his stories and characters, first draw the attention of the reader to their apparent differences before going on to show that these differences are not primarily responsible for the characters' positions as preys or predators. Dibia consistently shows in his novels, through juxtaposition of the white men against the black men, that rigid definitions of sexual involvements/relationships are not possible.

BIBLIOGRAPHY

Agustin, Laura Maria (1988). *Sex at the Margins: Migration, Labour Markets and the Rescue Industry*. London: Zed Books.
Carroll, Janell L. (2005). *Sexuality Now: Embracing Diversity*. Belmont, CA: Wadsworth/ Thomson Learning.
D'Emilio, J., DeMillo, J., and Freedman, E. B. (1988). *Intimate Matters: A History of Sex in America*. New York: HarperCollins.
Dibia, Jude (2005). *Walking with Shadows*. Lagos: Blacksands Books.
———. (2007). *Unbridled*. Lagos: Blacksands Books.
———. (2011). *Blackbird*. Lagos: Jalaa Writers' Collective.
Eagleton, Terry (1983). *Literary Theory: An Introduction*. Oxford: Basil Blackwell.
Ekwensi, Cyprian (1961). *Jagua Nana*. London: Hutchinson.
Hassan, Ihab (1995). *Rumours of Change: Essays of Five Decades*. Tuscaloosa: University of Alabama Press.
Jimoh, J. B. (2004). "Trends and Causes of Rural-Urban Migration in Nigeria," *Pacesetter: Journal of Oyo State College of Education*, 2(2): 157–175.
Laye, Camara (1956). *The Radiance of the King*. Glasgow: Fontana Books.
Mekgwe, Pinkie (2007). "Constructing Postcolonial Maleness in Ayi Kwei Armah's *Fragments*," in *Gender and Sexuality in African Literature and Film*. Eds. Azodo, Ada Uzoamaka, and Eke, Maureen Ngozi. Trenton, NJ: Africa World Press. 49–56.
Obiechina, Emmanuel (1975). *Culture, Tradition and Society in the West African Novel*. Cambridge: Cambridge University Press.
Palmer, Eustace (1979). *The Growth of the African Novel*. London: Heinemann.
Staik, Athena (2011). "Eroticized Dominance—Emotional Grooming, Predatory Behaviours as Cultural Norms?" *Neuroscience and Relationships*. Retrieved on May 29, 2013 from http://

blogs.psychcentral.com/relationships/2011/10/eroticizing-dominance-grooming-sexual-predatory-behaviors-as-norms/.

Storey, John (1993). *An Introductory Guide to Cultural Theory and Popular Culture*. Athens: University of Georgia Press.

Weinstein, Arnold (2013). *Soul and the City: Art, Literature, and Urban Living.* (audio book). Chantilly, VA: The Great Courses.

Chapter Fifteen

Human Trafficking in Ifeanyi Ajaegbo's *Sara House*

Akinbimpe Akintayo Akinyele

The social, political, economic, and utilitarian functions of literature in Africa cannot be over-emphasized. The reason for this is because the concept of "art for art's sake" is secondary in Africa; the belief is in "art for life's sake" philosophy. According to Obafemi (2008),

> It is difficult for a Nigerian writer, or any postcolonial writer, to either take a definite, Kantian art-for-art sake position or an inviolable ideological bent, in a society that is in a permanent state of flux and ideological doldrums. In the Nigerian experience, since the ravages of colonialism and the reality of neo-colonialism, the fortunes of politics have been inextricably bound with the fortunes of literature. (70)

This is why it is very impossible to detach a literary text from the cultural milieu in which it is produced. Kehinde (2007, 87) states that, "Actually, all works of art signify the relationship between the individual and his society." That literature is a humanistic field of scholarship is an indubitable fact. By humanistic, we mean literature focuses attention on the human experiences and condition. Literature is considered life, because it deals with human beings in every conceivable relation with other humans, relating their joys and woes, tragedies and comedies, fears and hopes. A literary writer is, therefore, a humanist, whose intention is to represent the world of reality. For this reason, literature cannot be separated from society (Obiechina, 1975, 324). Kehinde (2005) submits that

> The modern novel is an attempt to confront reality in a period of change, an effort to foreground the disagreement among writers on the old side and those

pleading for the new. This gives rise to definite experimentation with content and form. The modern novel has a tone of disillusionment; it is signified by the post-world war philosophy of existentialism which is marked by alienation, despair, cruelty, absurdity, urban terrorism, crime, pain, dissonance, espionage, poverty, dislocation, disintegration, famine, frustration, anarchy, atheism, misogyny, misanthropy, betrayal, nihilism and all forms of anomie. (338)

Kehinde (2005) is, therefore, of the opinion that if there is anything special in the modern novel, it is the fact that it is fraught with the issue of pains. It dwells on the social disorder, injustice and human failures and frailties. Kehinde contends further that the most widely employed literary canon the African critic deploys in the evaluation of the African novel is that of social realism.

In Nigeria, and Africa in general, one of the menaces of the twenty-first century is the problem of human trafficking. This menace has caught the attention of contemporary Nigerian writers, in order to conscientise the general populace on the inhumanity and dehumanisation of this horrific trade. Section 50 of the "Trafficking in Persons (Prohibition) Law Enforcement and Administration Act" (2003), enacted by the National Assembly as it applies to the Nigerian situation, defines trafficking as

> All acts involved in the recruitment, transportation within or across Nigerian borders, purchases, sale, transfer, receipt or harbouring of a person, involving the use of deception, coercion or debt bondage for the purpose of placing or holding the person whether for or not in involuntary servitude (domestic, sexual or reproductive) in forced or bonded labour or in slavery-like conditions. (NAPTIP Act, 2003, 11)

According to the United Nations Office on Drugs and Crime (UNODC, 2012),

> Trafficking in persons is a global crime affecting nearly all countries in every region of the world. Between 2007 and 2010, victims of 136 different nationalities were detected in 118 countries across the world, and most countries were affected by several trafficking flows. About 460 distinct trafficking flows around the world were identified during the reporting period. (14)

This shows that human trafficking is a global phenomenon. This crime has assumed a transnational trade status, encompassing all the continents of the world. Human trafficking is reported to be "the fastest growing criminal industry in the world" and "the world's third largest criminal enterprise, after drug dealing and gun running" (Lipede, 2007, 3). This lends credence to the contention that the uncontrolled and wide spread of this phenomenon in the twenty-first century is one of the most serious cancerous ailments troubling contemporary human society.

Lee (2007) views trafficking in humans in various conceptions namely: slavery, prostitution, forced migration and abuse of human rights. As a form of slavery, it is often viewed as a temporary ownership, debt bondage, forced labour and hyper-exploitative contractual arrangement in the global economy (Bales, 2000, 2005). Austin et al. (2012) situates trafficking in the larger pattern of contemporary slavery. Also, contemporary slavery is better understood as an extension or reconfiguration of enduring historical themes of exploitation and greed, rather than as distinctively modern developments (Austin et al., 2012).

The menace of human trafficking is a global challenge; it affects virtually all the nations of the world. Its presence and effects are, however, differently felt from country to country. While some countries deny the magnitude of the phenomenon as it affects their nationals, it cannot be denied that human trafficking has become a worrisome social malaise, which affects the contemporary human society (Lipede, 2007).

Statistics shows that there are around 190 million people around the world living in a country not of their birth—about three per cent of the world's population. As many as 100 million people are "on the move" across international boundaries, one in every 60 human beings. Most of this cross-border migration is not a matter of choice, as people are forced to move for many different reasons. These reasons include war, civil conflict and persecution; nevertheless, millions try to escape hunger or the consequences of environmental degradation. Economic systems that have failed to provide for people's most basic survival needs, or that are simply unable to fulfil expectations of decent living standards, also drive people to look outside their country of birth for a better life (IOM, 2006).

Troung and Angeles (2005) identified trafficking in human beings as an age-old practice found in nearly all human societies. The complexity and spread of the phenomenon attained an alarming magnitude since the cold war. In a similar view, in Ifaorumhe (2003), the wife of the former vice president of Nigeria, Mrs. Titi Abubakar was cited. She was of the opinion that when nationalist founding fathers fought the independence war against colonialism, we thought they had won when we attained flag independence, but the colonialism bounced back with neocolonialism and new forms of enslavement of black people in the form of human trafficking. This shows the ugliness of this modern slavery. Some of the factors identified to have fuelled human trafficking include poverty, social imbalances, uneven development, official corruption, gender discrimination, harmful and barbaric cultural practices, civil unrest, natural disaster, and lack of the political will to curb the menace (UNO, 2012, 2).

That the post-independence Nigeria is drenched with poverty is an indubitable truism. Thus, poverty is one of the veritable push factors responsible for human trafficking. Nigerians do not need to read about poverty, for their lives is a replica of what poverty is. However, the case of the Nigeria is pathetic. This is because Nigerians can be described as people who have abundant wealth but live in lack. This means that the level of their lack is beyond measure. Meanwhile, the problem of poverty is not unconnected with the myopic political leadership with which the nation is beleaguered. Lipede (2007, 6–7) is of opinion that "poverty, manifested in illiteracy, unemployment and poor living standard, therefore appears to be at the heart of human trafficking. It sparks the push factors in urban and rural communities and is one of the reactions of women and girls to persistent and endemic hardship."

The many factors aiding the proliferation of human trafficking can be conveniently categorised into two: push and pull factors. Push factors are those that force people into human trafficking trade, either to be trafficked or to be traffickers. Push factors are trafficking inducing. In the context of Nigeria, poverty is one strong push factor that has fuelled this modern slavery and conditions close to it.

The high level of poverty in Nigeria cannot be overstressed. Uzoma (2003) identifies poverty as the major push factor in the proliferation of human trafficking. We may not be wrong to say that 80 percent of Nigerians live in abject poverty. Poverty, defined in absolute terms refers to a state in which an individual lacks the resources for subsistence. Studies show that low-income countries live in absolute poverty. Nigeria cannot be excluded from the low-income countries considering the low standard of living among the employed Nigerians. This means that what the people earn as take-home cannot take them home.

Also, the legalization of sex work in some countries of the world, especially such countries as Italy, which invariably serve as the final destinations of human trafficking victims, has continued to promote the menace. According to Olaniyi (2009, 155), police are prevented from deporting immigrant sex workers as they are protected by Merlin law of 1958 in so far as they have necessary documents. Thus, many traffickers do use this law to have total control over trafficked women with threat to exposing them to police for deportation.

Furthermore, the endless sociopolitical unrest in the country has been a push factor aiding human trafficking. Nigeria is no doubt confronted with security challenge. This is, however, the outcome of inequality, anger, and bitterness among the people. Nigeria has been reduced to a dystopian state, due to hellish living situation.

There are pull factors which continue to lure people out of their cultural and political polity. One major pull factor seems to be the law of demand and supply. There is consistent increase in the demand for cheap labor and sex workers of different kinds in the developed world. European countries always advertise for both skilled and unskilled labor. This kind of offer tends to provide opportunity for the depressed and disillusioned Nigerians. Corrupt governments leave slavery unchecked, and slaveholders continue to skirt the law and hold people in bondage.

Women and children make up the majority of the world's slaves. In many countries, women are at particular risk due to their oppressed and marginalized position in society. They are vulnerable to sexual harassment and violence. Women are enslaved to work as domestic servants, farm workers, and forced prostitutes in countries around the world. Because women are also often responsible for raising their children, if a woman becomes enslaved, her children could likely follow her into bondage.

NO FREEDOM, NO RIGHT
IN IFEANYI AJAEGBO'S *SARAH HOUSE*

In *Sarah House*, Ajaegbo remonstrated about the trafficker's deception which lured the ignorant but greedy victims of human trafficking into modern day slavery:

> He did that to all of us. He showed us a different world from that which we lived in. He told us what was possible. He made us believe in what was beyond our limitations then, and that we could achieve those dreams. He gave us hope that even he did not have . . . it is the life of prostitutes. The life of slaves. You do what they ask you to do. (2012, 31)

Sarah House chronicles Nita's slavish experience in an entirely new world where she finds herself. She wakes up from her sleep and discovers that she is in a strange land full of strange things. She describes the room in which she is put in this manner: "The room was tiny. Two small beds took up what little space there was, and I was lying on one of them" (1). This attests to the spacelessness with which the place is characterised.

To her bewilderment, all the occupants of the room are "young girl-women," who either dress half-naked or are completely naked. Although Nita is not familiar with the nature of life in this place, other girls are used to it. The room offers no comfort and the occupants are impervious to physical pains. For, "The bed springs poked through the thin threadbare mattress against my skin. They pinched like vengeful bedbugs each time I tried to adjust my sitting position" (2).

Not only that, Nita discovers that the other girls are naked. She settles that they must been adapted to exposing their bodies. The names of other young girls whom Nita meets in the strange environment are Tega, Matti, Mary, Ibiwari, and Ibiso. It is, therefore, clear that she has been trafficked. She has been uprooted from her home to another land different from the serene, though poor, one she used to know. When she can no longer subdue her emotion, she voices out by asking the other girls "where is this?" (4). Fear, however, grips all her listeners as they lack the capacity to answer the question:

> Tega stiffened beside me. For some reason, my question made her afraid. The smile on her face slipped for a second and then came back, but it was not the same. I had seen a dark fear jump momentarily into her eyes before she reasserted the smile. Tega turned towards the other girls and a silent message passed across the room with each glance. (4)

This means that they have been devoiced, instead of communicating through speech, silence becomes their means of communication. The girls are thus *subalternized*. In other words, they are treated as minors who are not capable of reasoning.

The trafficked girls do not sleep in the night; they have to go to "work." Fatty announces to Tega, Matti, and Dumi to prepare for "work." No one tells Nita the kind of work the girls do. They look very tired, lifeless, deflated and defeated as they haggardly move to resume their normal duty. Having dressed up, Fatty says, "That's right girls, working time. Money-making time. We can't keep the mugus waiting. They pay the cash, you know" (14).

Mugus are those who pay for sex. The girls are, therefore, sex-machines that gives satisfaction to mugus' sexual urges. After the day's work, all the girls come back looking so depressed. Dumi cries in low, body-shaking sobs. Nita tries to placate her, but Tega asks her to leave the crying girl alone, because she cannot do anything about her plight.

The identity of Slim is disclosed when Tega asks Nita, "Who brought you here?" to which Nita replies, "Slim. He is my boyfriend." Tega let Nita know the truth about Slim: "Slim is not your boyfriend. That little worm is no one's boyfriend" (15–16).

It is very clear that Slim has masterminded the trafficking of all the girls. They have been duped by his lies that he loves them. Hearing this, Nita cannot hold her emotion as she sheds tears profusely and cold from nowhere descends on her. Nita, therefore, comes to the realisation that, no doubt, she has been trafficked. They are subjected to psychological trauma and pains and physical torture.

In reports like those above, an image of the "typical" trafficking victim becomes evident. Even in these few examples, we can begin to see an emphasis on certain words and phrases: "young," "naïve," "beauty," "better life," "lured," "deceived" and "forced into prostitution." These words show us the youth and beauty of the victims, their desperate economic plight, their lack of knowledge as to the fate that awaits them, and their transformation from the hopeful to the hopeless, "naïve" to "hardened," as the "life on the streets" takes its toll.

Nita is not allowed to go out. She is being imprisoned. She has no sense of day and night except when Fatty comes to take the girls away and when they return from work. Nita keeps on wondering over the kind of work the girls do, as no one is ready to disclose this to her. She is, however, familiar with the use of violence in the house. It seems that everyone is ruled by violence and the men seemed to cause pain without much thought (Ajaegbo, 2012, 19).

Nita has to accept her fate, since there is nothing she can do to liberate herself from the prison-like world in which she finds herself. Living in this nameless house is not in any way different from being in the prison-yard. The victims are made to eat watery porridge in a plastic bowl. It is obvious to Nita that the girls are subjected to sexual exploitation. They are to satisfy the sexual urges of certain oppressive men who are referred to as Fatty's friends, while Fatty is paid in turn.

The girls are always taken out and brought in by Fatty, after which he immediately locks up the room. They have no right on how they live their lives. They are like animals in captivity whose lives are determined by their captors. They have no right to what they do, how they feel and even their fundamental human right is dehumanized.

Deception is a veritable weapon human traffickers use to lure their unsuspecting victims (preys) into sex trade. After a long silence, Tega declares the reality of the city where they are: "It is the life of prostitutes. The life of slaves. You do what they ask you to do" (31). It is now that Nita understands why the girls would come in the morning, look so tired, bruised, despondent and robbed of words. Nita wonders if it is the girls that have given their informed consent to the kind of work they do. However, they have no say in the matter, as Tega reveals further their complete lack of control over their own personal affairs (32).

Anyone who proves stubborn is eventually beaten, raped, and killed by the keepers of the house. The story of a girl whose recalcitrance they cannot withstand serves as a warning to others who may want to follow her path.

The picture being painted here is that of subjugation. The trafficked victims are dispossessed of their personhood. They cannot lay claim to anything in life, as they live in both physical and mental anguish. The pains of the girls become a source of gain to their exploiters and heartless captors. Nita begins working for Slim when a man who appears to be drug addict is brought in to where she is and sleeps with her. She does not know what to do as she prayerfully expects a messiah perhaps in the form of a *deux ex machina*. She is mentally disturbed while recounting her first encounter with heartless men in the new world; "The hell I was running away from had come home to me. I struggled against the grip of his hand. I knew then that every effort I made was useless" (46).

In Sarah House, the girls have diverse experiences, depending on whom they are made to sleep with. Nita's experience is no doubt, painless compared to other girls. For instance, Miko stays with Lothar, a German pornographic-film-maker. Lothar uses belts, whips and other bizarre things in bed. Thus, the unfortunate girls who stay with Lothar are both physically mutilated and sexually violated.

Ajaegbo frequently reveals the psychological milieu in which the characters-victims find themselves, especially through psychological posture of the protagonist-narrator, Nita. Her mind swerves between Sarah House, Fatty and Slim's house, and her village. Nita often plunges into reminiscences of the past experiences in such a fashion that narration is rendered in her vivid explanation of the actions in the narrative. Besides, Nita and her fellow captives lack freedom of expression. They are made to hear, not to speak. Thus, their voices are faintly heard, and the author aptly conscientize the readers on the effect of harrowing experience the victimised young ladies are subjected to in the text. Nita attests to this by indicating how they have been stripped of the right to make decisions; such rights belonged to someone else now (Ajaegbo, 2012, 106).

The implication of this is that the girls are forced to abandon their normal ways of life and are compelled to adopt the new life offered them by their superior captors. The politics of othering, viewing those who are different from oneself as inferior beings, is being illustrated in the text. The girls are "othered," that is treated and seen as the inferior others, which can still be referred to as the demonic other. This is not different from master-slave relationship on the slavery plantation. The girls have been enslaved and their slave masters force another life upon them. It is enslavement in one's land. The girls are not taken out of their own country. This fact underscores perennial reality of poverty and exploitation in post-independence Nigeria, and Africa by extension.

Nita vividly captures an experience at the golden cave. The girls parade themselves in complete of nudity while they fling their brassiere and pants on any man who has interest in them. It is not as though the girls like this kind of life, but they are physically, psychologically and emotionally imprisoned. They are subjected to dehumanisation and enslavement. Nita reports thus:

> I followed the progress of the girls as they moved from one table to another through the cheering crowd. The men adored them, touching their breasts and public area with naira notes before either sticking them into their hairpins or dropping them at their feet. The girls move on while a man followed discreetly, picking up the money. (109)

The picture that is being painted above can be likened to that of a farm labourer and harvester. As the girls disgracefully labor, their pimps rake in the money for themselves.

CONCLUSION

In a compassionate engagement with issues of human and sex trafficking, it is vital for us to recognize the re-emergence of slavery in the twenty-first century and corruption and poverty as the fundamental socioeconomic and political issues that plague Nigeria and other societies of the world today. The business of modern slavery today is very much like that which dominated the Atlantic slave trade 350 years ago. Yet, while there was then the existence of the Underground Railroad of freedom to assist the abolition of slavery, this is today replaced by an underground criminal network that entraps and sells people into slavery. This, indeed, is a tragic paradox in our time, one which continues to be a hidden crime. Yet the core focus of our discussion here has been to analyse the push and pull factors in Nigeria as the major cause of this inhumane act, and how the fundamental right of the captives are been violated by their captors on a daily basis for monetary gain.

The large-scale immigration waves to European countries brought about by poverty and the seeming lack of opportunities at home for many youths and the lure of "good life" in Europe has given rise to this menace. Although the case of some immigrants is paradoxical, in the sense that they have alternative means of survival at home; they are, however, lured by the "European Dream." Other factors pulling perpetrators and victims of human trafficking alike include religious intolerance and relative peace abroad. Usually, human traffickers threaten their victims with juju that, should they reveal any information about their identity, they would either die or run mad. However, despite the fact that various bodies, both governmental and non-governmental have assiduously taken steps against the proliferation of this inhuman act, the evil keeps on growing. This is why contemporary Nigerian novelists have also delved into conscientising the people about this modern slavery, in order to arrest the situation.

BIBLIOGRAPHY

Ajaegbo, Ifeanyi (2012). *Sarah House*. Johannesburg, South Africa: Picador Africa
Allwell, Abalogu Onukaogu, and Ezechi Onyerionwu (2009). *Twenty-First-Century Nigerian Literature: An Introduction Test*. Ibadan, Nigeria: Kraft Books.
Bewaji, J. A. I. (2013). *Black Aesthetics*. Trenton, NJ: Africa World Press.
Ezeigbo, Theodora Akachi (2008). *Artistic Creativity: Literature in the Service of Society*. Lagos: University of Lagos Press.
International Organisation for Migration (2006). *A UNISON Discussion Paper*.

Kehinde, Ayo (2005). "Rethinking African in the Era of Globalisation: A Contest of Text and Context," *Journal of the Nigeria English Studies Association*, 11(1): 87–100.

———. (2005). "The Modern Novelist and the Historical Sense: The Example of D.H Lawrence and Virginia Woolf," in *Perspective on Language and Literature*. Eds. Olateju, Moji, and Oyeleye, Lekan. Ile-Ife: Obafemi Awolowo University Press. 337–349.

Ifaorumhe, M. (2003). "The Socioeconomic Implications of Human Trafficking on Nigeria," *FERET: Bi-annual Magazine of Defense Intelligence Agency*, 2(1).

Lipede, Abiola (2007). "Women Trafficking and Insecurity in West Africa: Character, Trend and Scale in Nigeria," in *Human Trafficking and Economic Crimes across Nigeria's International Borders*. Eds. Barkindo, M. Bawuro, and Lipede, Abiola. Ibadan: Spectrum Books.

NAPTIP (2003). Trafficking in Persons (Prohibition) Law Enforcement and Administration Act.

Oko, Chinedu C. N., and Donald, Ukachu D. (2010). "African Culture and Nigeria Literature: Echoes and Departures in Twenty-First-Century Creative Enterprise," *Journal of Nigerian Languages and Culture*, 12(2): 164–173.

Omotere, A. (2011). *Child Trafficking in Nigeria: Causes, Effects and Remedies*. Ogun: Ego Booster Books.

Osiki, Omon Mercy (2009). "The Face of Trafficking and Human Smuggling across the Nigeria-Benin Border," in *Globalisation and Transnational Migrations: Africa and African in the Contemporary Global System*. Eds. Adebayo, G. Akanmu, and Adesina, C. Olutayo. Newcastle: Cambridge Scholars Publishing. 162–180.

Thanh-Dam, Troung, and Maria Belen Angeles (2005). "Searching for the best practices to Counter Human Trafficking in Africa." A *Focus on Women and Children* report commissioned by UNESCO.

Tiffin, Helen (1997). "Postcolonial Literatures and Counter-discourse," in *Postcolonial Studies Reader*. Eds. Ashcroft, Bill, Griffiths, Gareth, and Tiffin, Helen. London and New York: Routledge.

Unigwe, Chika (2010). *On Black Sisters' Street*. London: Vintage books.

United Nations Office on Drugs and Crime (2006). *Trafficking in Persons: Global Patterns*. New York: United Nations.

United Nations Office on Drugs and Crime (2012). *Global Report on Trafficking in Persons*. New York: United Nations.

Uzoma, R. C. (2003). "The Sociocultural and Economic Implications of Human Trafficking in Contemporary Nigeria." An essay submitted in partial fulfilment for the Membership of the National Institute for Policy and Strategic Studies.

Chapter Sixteen

Representation of Human Trafficking in Ifeoma Chinwuba's *Merchants of Flesh*

Solomon O. Olaniyan

Despite the fact that trade in humans was officially abolished in 1807, over two hundred years ago, the inhumane trade has continued. Both the old slave trade and its (re)emerging new form—human trafficking—have quantitatively led to the indiscriminate dispersion of people of African ancestry across the globe. Today, there is hardly any continent where blacks are not present in high numbers. The history of the black race is replete with the motifs of displacement and dispossession.

Slave trade marked the genesis of involuntary displacement and dispossession of peoples of the black race, as they were carted away to other lands. The history of displacement and dispossession in what is known as Atlantic slave started as early as 1619, when the first set of Africans, twenty in number, were delivered to Jamestown, Virginia, as indentured servants, to work for whites (Bigsby and Thompson, 1981). Between 1619 and 1860, some 400,000 blacks were transplanted from Africa to what is now known as the United States of America.

J. E. Inikori (1978) opines that the slaves were dispossessed of their personhood and liberty, and were sold as slaves to the Arabian and European merchants. Arabians and Europeans are, therefore, the first set of "merchants of flesh" to come to the African soil. Some of the factors which contributed to the earlier displacement and dispossession of Africans included religious institutions and extreme economic distress.

Postcolonial theory, which offers theoretical assumptions and political concerns on the experience and literary production of peoples whose history is characterised by extreme political, social, and psychological dislocation and oppression (Tyson, 1999, 363) is adopted as the theoretical framework for the study. Emerging in early 1990s, postcolonial theory presents an exposition of the domination of the formerly colonised peoples as being subjected to the political domination of another population. The theory has been popularised through the writings and publications of such scholars as Gayatri Spivak, Bill Ashcroft, Homi Bhabha and Edward Said. The birth of postcolonial theory can be traced to the 1961 publication of the Martinique-born psychiatrist, Frantz Fanon's *The Wretched of the Earth* (1961), in which he declares that the colonised of the world should reclaim their past for their voice to be heard.

Fanon counters the domin(eering)ated Eurocentric literature, which sees the history, culture and progress of the world as being coterminous with the advent of the Europeans. The idea is, therefore, "to erode the colonialist ideology by which . . . past had been devalued" (Barry, 1995, 192). That over three quarters of the contemporary world has been directly and profoundly affected by imperialism and colonialism; and by extension, neocolonialism, is an indisputable truism (Tiffin, 1997, 95). This means that the history of the world would be incomplete without talking about the different phases of colonialism and imperialism.

It is observed that the post-independence nations (in Africa) are still very much characterised with gamut of sociopolitical breakdown, economic stagnation, cultural erosion, religious bigotry and moral decadence. The milieu is, therefore, replete with post-independence disillusionment; angst and pangs; and dissonance. The new leaders are not in any way different from the colonial ones, from whose hands power had been wrestled. All these issues are addressed by the postcolonial theory which has been chosen as the theoretical framework for the study. In other words, the "post" in postcolonial theory does not mean the *pastness* of the experiences; rather, it means *continuousness* of colonial harrowing experiences.

The notion of place, according to Ashcroft (2001), is the interactive convergence of language, history, spatiality, and environment in the experience of colonised peoples. In the same way colonisation disrupts the colonised subject's sense of place, human trafficking brings about dislocation to the trafficked subject. In most cases, identity and an actual place have been totally severed and all attempts to identify oneself with the original location have generally resulted in frustration and more displacement. Displacement has been an experience of the postcolonial nations of the world. Displacement may occur as a result of transportation from one nation to the other through slavery, imprisonment, invasion, settlement or a consequence of (in)voluntary movement from a known location to the unknown one. In the recent time, human trafficking has proven to be a means of displacement and dispossession of citizens of postcolonial nations. The phenomenal challenge of human trafficking, otherwise known as modern-day slavery, is not new, though it has lately caught the attention of contemporary Nigerian writers.

Researches have shown that trafficking in persons is increasing day-by-day (Moffat, 2009; Olaniyi, 2009; Osiki, 2009; Akanle, 2009; Lipede, 2007; and Okoro, 2007). While women are more vulnerable, it cannot be said that only women are victims of human trafficking. Anybody can be trafficked—women, children and men alike. The main aim of this chapter is to critique the depiction of human trafficking in Ifeoma Chinwuba's *Merchants of Flesh.* The exploitative, cruel and dehumanising nature of modern-day slavery has propelled various governmental and non-governmental agencies and concerned individuals to challenge the persistent proliferation of this brutal institution against human race. For instance, United Nations in its Universal Declaration on Human Right strongly abnegates any inhuman act which may lead to violation of human right. Gloud (2010) reports that international organisations have abolished practices that create circumstances of servile status which include debt bondage, serfdom, unfree marriage and exploitation of young people.

HUMAN TRAFFICKING: MEANING AND CAUSES

The contemporary world is faced with various problems. The continuing flourish of many trans-border crimes globally cannot be disputed. Trans-border crimes include human trafficking, drug trafficking, money laundering and smuggling of contraband goods. All these are resultant effects of globalisation. A crime is considered trans-border if, "committed in more than one state; in one state but a substantial part of its preparation, planning, direction or control takes place in another state; or is committed in one state but has substantial effect in another state" (Oni, 2006, 134).

The phenomenon of human trafficking can also be referred to as human smuggling. Human trafficking is a trans-border or transnational crime, though it is not unconnected with other transnational crimes, such as drug trafficking, drug smuggling and money laundering. The history of human trafficking is long; it can be traced to antiquity, during the obnoxious slavery introduced by the Europe and embraced by Africa. However, while slavery can be said to have been abolished, it re-emerged in new form in the twenty-first century.

Omon Mercy Osiki (2009) posits that human trafficking can be seen as, both an overt and clandestine, criminal activity involving a network of individuals whose motive is to make profits out of their victims. In other words, one cannot deny the fact that human trafficking is a lucrative venture, although it is a criminal act. The desire to amass profit, therefore, leads to the 'thingification' and commodification of human beings. Nagle lends credence to this position, when he argues, "The danger of globalisation is that as long as there is a profit motive, human beings have become just another commodity to trade and to move across borders into nations that depend on cheap labour and profit from sexual exploitation" (Nagle, 2007, 10).

The primary motive of human trafficking is exploitation. The Protocol to Prevent, Suppress and Punish Trafficking in Persons, Especially Women and Children, supplementing the United Nations Convention against Transnational Organized Crime (2000), sees trafficking in persons as the recruitment, transportation, transfer, harbouring or receipt of persons, by means of the threat or use of force or other forms of coercion, of abduction, of fraud, of deception, of the abuse of power or of a position of vulnerability or of the giving or receiving of payments or benefits to achieve the consent of a person having control over another person, for the purpose of exploitation.

Meanwhile, there are several factors which aid the persistent proliferation of this twenty-First-century challenge. These factors can be conveniently categorised into two: push and pull factors. Push factors are those that force people into human trafficking trade, either to be trafficked or to be traffickers. Push factors are trafficking inducing. In the context of Nigeria, poverty is one strong push factor that has fuelled this modern-day slavery. The high level of poverty in Nigeria cannot be overstressed. Uzoma (2003) identifies poverty as the major push factor in the proliferation of human trafficking. Nigeria cannot be excluded from the low-income countries considering the low standard of living among the employed Nigerians. This means that what the people earn as take-home cannot take them home.

Nigeria produces thousands of graduates every year without any hope of gainful employment. The desire to be gainfully employed, therefore, pushes many into this inhuman trade in human body. The unemployed and underemployed people seek various means to alter their poor status and by so doing, meet their financial needs. One of these means is human trafficking; others include prostitution, robbery, panhandling or mendicancy (Lamidi, 2006). Many helpless and hopeless Nigerians seek succour in trans-border crimes to cushion their financial mishap.

Furthermore, the endless socio-political unrest in the country has been a push factor aiding human trafficking. Nigeria is no doubt confronted with security challenge. This is, however, the outcome of inequality, anger and bitterness among the people. Nigeria has been reduced to a dystopian state due to hellish living situation. Therefore, many Nigerians are arrested in psychological limbo which does not merely result from some individual psychological disorder but from the trauma of the psycho-cultural displacement within which one lives. Homi Bhabha has coined the word *unhomeliness* to refer to this situation (Tyson, 1999). Tyson goes further to expound the coinage, "Being 'nhomed" is not the same as being homeless. To be unhomed is to feel not at home even in your own home because you are not at home in yourself: your cultural identity crisis has made you a psychological refuge so to speak" (Tyson, 1999, 368).

The *unhomely* situation of the country has, therefore, reduced people to hunters and preys of this merchandise in human flesh. Many of the victims of human trafficking fall victims out of their desire to escape the unliveable situation of the country. The socio-political history of Nigeria is replete with civil unrest, religious violence, political riot, civil war, inter and intra-ethnic crises and electoral violence. All these scare even the patriotic citizens away from the polity.

Besides, the porosity of Nigerian borders cannot be dissociated from the growth of modern slavery. Many of the law enforcement agents that are supposed to curb the menace only contribute to it. Lipede declares, "rogue elements in the immigration, police, customs and other border patrol agencies act as powerful push factors in the evil trade, similar elements in destination countries facilitate the entry of victims into their countries" (Lipede, 2007, 10).

The legalisation of sex work in some countries of the world helps in the persistence of second slavery. Though there is domestic legislation and moralisation that criminalises sex work, which frowns at the immorality of the work, this legislation has not been harmonised with international standard (Fwa, 2006). It is considered a crime to enter European cities without a regular visa issued by a European Embassy and also illegal to transport a person for forced prostitution and sex exploitation. Nevertheless, prostitution as a business itself is legalised. Lipede (2007) reports that in the city of Rome, prostitution is not only legal but also taxed, thus generating income for the government. This implies the legalisation and commercialisation of this immoral act.

Furthermore, there are pull factors which continue to lure people out of their cultural and political polity. One major pull factor seems to be the law of demand and supply. There is consistent increase in the demand for cheap labour and sex workers of different kinds in the developed world. European countries always advertise for both skilled and unskilled labour. This kind of offer tends to provide opportunity for the depressed and disillusioned Nigerians who have been longing to leave their *unhomed* home.

However, despite the fact that various bodies, both governmental and non-governmental have assiduously taken steps against the proliferation of this inhuman act, the evil keeps on growing. This is why contemporary Nigerian novelists have also delved into conscientising the people about this modern slavery in order to arrest the situation.

REPRESENTATION OF HUMAN TRAFFICKING
IN CHINWUBA'S *MERCHANTS OF FLESH*

Human trafficking is a social malady that affects human race from time immemorial. The essence of literature in African context, however, lies in its sociology. The story begins on a gruesome note. A lifeless body is discovered by a Good Samaritan. The corpse is almost naked. The policeman that comes to check the scene does not hesitate to declare that the victim must have been a "road worker." It is, however, assumed that the victim, who is later recognised as Lovett John must have been murdered. The police file a report and immediately decide to get in touch with her country's mission to inform her next of kin for burial abroad or repatriation of the corpse. The first encounter in the narrative is a ruthless experience of Nigerian immigrants to Italy, all in the name of searching for a greener pasture. The narrative thus, relays the unknown pains immigrants are liable to in overseas.

The Consular Officer is perplexed, together with her boss, due to the increase in the incessant rapid and mysterious death of prostitutes in recent days. Ironically, the police care not to investigate. The kind of calamity that befalls Nigerians (especially females) who, by all means, travel abroad without any particular aim in mind is exposed here.

Thus, the life of the victims amounts to nothing. Italy is known for its notoriety in accommodating Nigerian girls for prostitution. One major contributory factor to this is the legalisation of prostitution in Italy. In other words, prostitution is professionalised and even taxed by the government (Lipede, 2007). It is, therefore, impossible for a government that collects taxes from prostitution to criminalise it as a result of pecuniary gain.

Eventually, the Consul decides to contact the victim's Nigerian community. From the records available, it is found that the late Lovett John is from Benin City. Lipede (2007) lends credence to the fact that women trafficking and the international sex trade have been a feature of life in Benin City for nearly twenty years. Mr Ufot orders the Consular Officer to deport all the girls, while she notes that, "deporting alone may not do the trick, sir. The effects are not felt. How can they be when these girls are arriving from all angles, from every corner, through all sorts of ports? You deport fifty a week while everyday ten arrive. The effects are not felt" (13).

Here, the Consular Officer identifies the problem of the nation's border porosity. This has led to the indiscriminate immigration of Nigerians abroad.

Mr. Ufot expresses his displeasure about the recent cases of supplying of prostitutes to Europe. This has made the black race lose respect in Italy, for instance. Again, Western thirst for Africans' "flesh" exposes the barbaric and dehumanising nature of the Europeans, who engage in the "merchandise of flesh."

It is not only adult women that do sell their body to survive; children are also abused through street hawking. This is what we see in the family of Faith Moses Ugiame. The little children have to sell bread after school hours in order to keep body and soul together. Okorie Uka Okoro (2007) makes a distinction between 'child work' and 'child labour'. According to him, child work is any work carried out by children which does not involve risks and danger but contributes to the welfare of the children, especially their self-esteem and their ability to be integrated with their families. However, though child work is not seen as something anti-child in Okoro's definition, it does have negative effect on the well-being of the children. Although this act is against the child right, one may not condemn it outright when one looks at the level of poverty in which the people live, "there was only one double-sized bed a carpenter had knocked together for Faith. Osas got her two little sisters to lie on it. She herself lay at the edge. That way, they would not fall off it. She got an old faded bed sheet reeking of urine and covered them all with it" (34).

The above shows the pang of poverty on the people. Faith's family is such a poor one that the children often go to their neighbour's house to watch television. Faith herself decries her poor condition and contemplates various ways of ridding herself of it, even though these seem difficult to realize.

One may not, however, blame some of the victims of human trafficking. The reason for this is not far to see. The political leaders in the country are not ready to make life in the country comfortable for the citizenry. Poverty, therefore, pushes people to foreign land where they are more frustrated. Lipede (2007) opines that one major effect of poverty is an increase in the rate of crimes, such as armed robbery, prostitution, Advance Fee Fraud otherwise known as "419" and drug trafficking.

That the country is fraught with an amalgam of malaise is indubitable. Chinwuba thematises the issue of untimely death, especially of the family's breadwinners. Many of the victims of human trafficking depicted in the novel do not have anyone to sponsor their education. Akanle (2009) maintains that a lot of Nigerians that immigrate into the United Kingdom are the educated, young and ambitious who consider their chances of furthering at home irrelevant and needless since they do not trust the educational system in Nigeria to be of standard among the best in the world. Faith is a victim of several tragic circumstances. She is fatherless and husbandless; thus, she has no one to cushion her life of permanent want and insufficiency. As a ward-maid, Faith is exposed to untold and unwholesome experiences. Doctors often use her to do some delicate work, like carrying out abortion and operation. This is an unethical practice among the contemporary Nigerian physicians.

Faith comes Lizzy's way while trying to look for Okada that would convey her home after the day's work. Lizzy attends the same school which

Faith also attends. There is a wide gap between the duos. Lizzy looks richer, better, more civilised and socialised. Eventually, she offers her complimentary card to Faith should she need assistance regarding better employment before she leaves for Europe. She promises to help Faith by getting her a more lucrative job in Italy. Lizzy is, no doubt, one of the 'madams' in Italy who engage in the "merchandise of flesh". She succeeds in luring three young ladies: Faith, Dons and Amaka. They are to make minimum wage for themselves and maximum wage for her (Lizzy). She has to pay huge amount of money to process the arrangement for their transportation to Italy. She, however, deceives them by saying that the "market" calls for young girls—between twelve and sixteen, preferably virgins.

Some parents (especially mothers) sell their own children to prostitution. An example is the case of Faith. When she has cold feet regarding Lizzy's pressure, her mother encourages her, despite the fact that her mother is aware of what will become her (Faith's) fate in Italy. Okoro is of opinion that, "Parents consent to the placing of their children in foster homes or work places, most parents, on their own volition, arrange for foster homes for their children. Parents agree, and sometimes earnestly solicit, to place their children or wards in the homes of richer or more connected individuals" (Chinwuba, 2011, 50–51). Faith's experience validates Okoro's (2007) assertion, as shown in the foregoing excerpt.

The story of Tina shows the highest form of inhumanity meted out to victims of human trafficking. Tina is one of the very few victims who prove stubborn by refusing to cooperate with their inhumane madams. Thus, she refuses to be merchandised even though she has been purchased by Lizzy. She would not bring Lizzy any money, which makes Lizzy threaten her but to no avail. Eventually, Lizzy hires Ali, a drug addict and AIDS virus carrier to forcefully rape her, while other prostitutes hold her down. Afterward, Lizzy plugs pressing iron and presses on Tina's back, leaving her back badly wounded. This makes Tina desert her eventually. This establishes the fact that trafficked victims are subjected to physical assault, not only sexploitation, which is the ubiquitous reason for the proliferation of the crime, "The other girls held Tina down when Ali was raping her. Lizzy had plugged on her pressing iron. When Ali emptied his virus-ridden sperm inside the hysterical girl, Lizzy branded her back with the hot iron and pushed her out of the flat" (Chinwuba, 2011, 79). The scene painted here is much more tortuous than the real slavery. This is to show the inhumanity of this modern-day slavery.

It is, however, disheartening to note that the people that have been saddled with the responsibility of curbing human trafficking are actually the ones promoting it. This shows the level of moral decadence and unethical practices in the post-independence Nigeria. Thus, a member of staff at the embassy alerts Lizzy (a madam) that there is going to be a raid and that she should disallow all are girls from going to the "market" for some days. Hearing this, Lizzy heads to one of her seniors' place, Aunty Helen, to acquaint her with the news. Lizzy suggests that they should also go on strike—"prostitutes' strike", so as to protest incessant raids which have been spoiling "market" for the madams. She lampoons the police officers and politicians who make sanctimonious attempts to eradicate prostitution; yet they still patronise prostitutes at the night, "Don't mind them. It's pretence. They do all these raids, as if they do not patronise the prostitute. Pretenders all. . . . Yet at night, you see them sneaking around looking for that prostitute. Pretence. Hypocrites. God will punish all of them" (Chinwuba, 2011, 83).

In the same vein, the narrator exposes some unwholesome and unethical practices among the diplomats. Many of them engage in importation of contraband. We are informed about one of them thus, "Each weekend, he had ferried across the border, bags and bags of rice, hot drinks and tobacco, frozen chicken and other consumables, some bought tax-free and duty-free in the name of the mission" (19).

Also, wives of the diplomats do engage in human trafficking. A typical case is that of Mrs Mercy Ufot, whose husband is after the human traffickers. On several occasions, Chief Godson would leave his home to avoid domestic violence and go to Milan where he can enjoy some peace of mind. He eventually engages in illicit sexual affairs in hotel. This is the ambassador that is supposed to curb prostitution; he himself indulges in it.

When the Nigerian government can no longer condone the bad image resulting from the illegal migration of her citizens who are involved in "street walk", a delegate is sent to the Nigerian Consulate in Italy. Police Commissioner Kurma informs the diplomats that the Federal Government wishes to collaborate with the Italian government on how to curb human trafficking, Advance Fee Fraud (419) and drug trafficking. For instance, back at home, there are two bodies that have been working assiduously against these social maladies—Women Trafficking and Child Labour Eradication Foundation (WOTCLEF, an NGO founded and funded by the wife of the vice-president and Idia—Renaissance which is founded by the wife of Edo State Governor). It is estimated that the total number of Nigerian prostitutes in Italy is over eleven thousand. It is unfortunate to note that many of the victims of this heinous act of "flesh merchandise" are high school dropouts. Many of them have no one to sponsor their education following the untimely death of their breadwinners. A typical example is Faith.

Faith recounts the horrible experiences the ever-zealous migrants go through before they secure visa. They queue for days; they would not be attended to unless they "see" (bribe) the embassy officials. This shows the extent of moral decadence and corruption in postcolonial polity, "You have to "see" the quite men, someone informed. With five hundred naira, you will not need to queue up or spend the night here" (Chinwuba, 2011, 158).

One of the aspiring migrants, a graduate of Medicine, narrates his ordeal to Faith. His words, "Look, I am a medical doctor. I graduated since four years ago, no job. They say there is embargo on employment. What should I do? I have been driving taxi for two years now, just to feed. I have a brother in Italy. He says I should come" (Chinwuba, 2011, 159).

This is one of the genuine reasons many talented Nigerian youths troop to other countries in search of non-existing greener pastures. There is no doubt in saying that Nigerian leadership has disappointed her citizenry; hence, the youth resort to travelling abroad as a result of post-independence disillusionment, "I left the University nine years ago. I have not got a job. I tried to teach for eighteen months, teachers were not paid salaries? Eighteen months. Tell me, what am I to do?" (159).

In solving the problem of dehumanisation confronting the illicit immigrants, an embassy officer suggests that the prostitutes should be liberated from their madams, rehabilitated and allowed to continue to stay in Italy without deportation. Meanwhile, many of those prostitutes prefer staying in Italy to coming back home. For instance, Precious Isaac pleads with the Consul, "Please Sir, do not send me to Nigeria. My people are suffering. My father is dead and my mother has seven children. Please we are suffering. Do not make paper to depot me. I beg you in the name of God" (173).

The foregoing foregrounds the earlier claim that the problems in homeland push the migrants away from home. Unfortunately, their case is like someone who is rootless and roofless. In other words, they are just floating as they neither belong here nor there, especially psychologically.

Faith relates how she and other aspiring migrants are made to swear an oath before a very powerful medicine-man that they would pay their madam whatever the amount she spends on them and that should they be arrested, whether in Nigeria or Italy, they would not divulge the information about their madam (Lizzy). Not adhering to the oath would result in madness for them, as well as their mothers' death and their children's untimely death. However, fear of poverty and suffering in Nigeria makes them sign the undertaking.

Mama Tayo is surrounded by two of her male companions when her phone rings. Lizzy calls to inform her that there will be a meeting of the madams tomorrow, at Helen's. The main message Lizzy has dropped is that there is going to be "prostitutes' strike". The strike declared by the madams due to the unfavourable, unbearable and incessant raid and harassment by the police does not go on well even with some "big men" in the society. A politician calls the police chief to soft-pedal in the raid, harassment and subsequent deportation of the "road workers". The argument of the politician is that: "It seems they have a role they play in the economy too" (199).

The chief medical director of the general hospital also calls the commissioner of police to express his displeasure regarding the incessant increase in rape cases in the hospital, "My dear Commissioner of Police. What is happening to your tour. . . . Nine rape cases in one weekend. Four by family members. Even a teenage immigrant was gang-raped by a group of boys. What is happening?" (Chinwuba, 2011, 200).

Meanwhile, the chief medical director's opinion is that the recent increase in rape cases is not unconnected with the prostitutes' strike to protest police harassment, raid and deportation. In other words, these immigrant prostituting Nigerian girls have been *thingified* and *commodified*. Their host country now uses them to control their economy and health system. This also foregrounds white men's barbarism and inhumanity.

Freedom is usually accompanied with some measure of *stubbornness*. Faith refuses to eternally suffer dispossession having been displaced by Lizzy. She is taken out by Lovett to show her necessary joints and routes she needs to know before she would eventually resume work after the prostitutes' strike is called off by the madams. Eventually, Lovett and Faith are arrested by a police officer. They are raped by the same policemen without paying them. Lovett later runs away to Rome, while Faith organises other prostituting girls to embark on strike just as their madams have done. The next news Faith hears of Lovett is that she has been murdered. It is this inhumanity meted out to the prostitutes that makes Faith sensitise and conscientise her fellow captives to rise in their own self-defence.

This brave attempt by the victims is both a historic and metaphorical one. None of the prostitutes ever thinks of liberation from their bondage. At the same time, this action is to serve as an attack against (s)exploitation which has become the order of the day especially among the trafficked girls. The liberation is, therefore, not meant for them alone, but also for the generation to come after them just as Faith declares that they should never have gone into this business in the first place; they should never have succumbed to the lure to come to Italy. But the mistake had been made. It was now up to them to salvage their lives, or whatever was left of it and struggle to rescue future generation from this hell. Human trafficking is likened to "this hell". This is not unconnected with the kind of trauma, assault and pains these victims have to pass through.

They protest the huge amount their madams demand. Lizzy is surprised when she sees all her girls carrying placards; she calls them, but none responds to her threat. This is when she realises that she has been denounced. The placards read:

STOP SEXUAL SLAVERY NOW. SAVE OUR SOULS, DOWN WITH PROSTITUTION, WE WANT FREEDOM. (259)

Meanwhile, there is a religious organisation whose main work is kicking against road work, prostitution and human trafficking. It aims at the liberation and rehabilitation of the enslaved girls from their madams. Thus, Faith, having collected the addresses of all the madams from the prostitutes, goes straight to the priest who listens to her story. She hands over the list of the madams to him, which he later takes to the police officer. Thus, all the madams are raided and prosecuted.

With their inhumane madams arrested and carted away, the liberated girls troop to the Community Centre. Many of them that are physically sick are taken to the hospitals for proper medical treatment. Meanwhile, there others whose life has been damaged physiologically beyond repair. Some of them become mentally ill and are thus, repatriated. Eventually, their stay in Italy is regularised. Normal jobs are secured for them. For instance, Faith gets a job as a welfare clerk at the commune.

Back at home, Faith's mother dies a mysterious death, leaving behind Faith's two children. A man comes to assist the family in taking care of the two children left behind, saying, "My name is Kaine. Sorry about what happened. . . . I have sisters in Spain and Italy. If you like, I can arrange for Osas to go and work there" (Chinwuba, 2011, 265). Meanwhile, the people do not hesitate to reply another visiting human trafficker who has come in the name of sympathising with the people, "No. No more Italy for us. The elders met and decided. None of our children will go there again. If they hear mention that country, you are in trouble. Better leave now" (65).

The people have been sensitised about the menace of human trafficking. Kaine is not allowed to go as he is arrested and is set ablaze by the angry people. The killing of Kaine is symbolic of complete eradication of human trafficking through the concerted effort of the people. The inescapability of this visiting trafficker, therefore, implies that end has come to human trafficking.

In the foregoing analysis, the factors that push immigrants away from home in search of a green pasture abroad and above all, their ignoble experiences abroad emphasise the writer's intension as she canvasses for collaborative effort in combating this ignoble, heinous, dehumanising practice are revealed. Therefore, Chinwuba has not only diagnosed the social problem of human trafficking with which her cultural milieu is fraught, but she has also prescribed the pragmatic antidote that can practically eradicate the heinous act.

CONCLUSION

Displacement and dispossession are two inseparable realities of the post-independence and postmodern Africa. When someone is displaced, the person would be dispossessed. As a matter of fact, displacement is a kind of dispossession on its own. Victims of human trafficking are first of all displaced as they are moved, usually, to other country. This further exposes them to be prone to dispossession. Through sexploitation, they are psychologically, physiologically, physically and emotionally dispossessed and *commodified* by their madams. In fact, their personhood is turned to a commercialised object. Their madams and other people involved in this heinous trade *thingify* them. In other words, they are reduced to ordinary things that have no feeling. They are nothing but chattels to the madam. From every indication, Chinwuba has been able to engage in self-criticism by looking inward as she does not point an accusing finger to outsider for her race's *self-recolonisation*. Without prevarication, this writer has revealed the social malaise of modern-day slavery, with its attendant psychological, emotional and physical effects on the victims.

BIBLIOGRAPHY

Achebe, C. (1975). *Morning Yet on Creation Day*. London: Heinemann.

Akanle, O. (2009). "Immigration Cultism and the Nigerian Migrants: Tidal Dynamism in the Age of Globalisation," in *Globalisation and Transnational Migrations: Africa and African in the Contemporary Global System*. Eds. Adebayo, G. Akanmu, and Adesina, C. Olutayo. Newcastle: Cambridge Scholars Publishing. 181–200.

Ashcroft, B. (2001). *Postcolonial Transformation*. London: Routledge.

Ashcroft, B., Griffiths, G., and Tiffin, H. (1997). "Introduction," in *Postcolonial Studies Reader*. Eds. Ashcroft, Bill, Griffiths, Gareth, and Tiffin, Helen. London and New York: Routledge. 1–4.

Bigsby, C. W. E., and Thompson, R. (1981). "The Black Experience," in *Introduction to American Studies* (2nd edition). Eds. Bradbury, Malcolm, and Temperley, Howard. London and New York: Longman.

Caws, P. (1995). "Identity: Cultural, Transcultural, and Multicultural," in *Multiculturalism: A Critical Reader*. Ed. Goldberg, David. Cambridge, MA: Blackwell. 371–386.

Chinwuba, I. (2011). *Merchants of Flesh*. Ibadan: Kraft Books.

Ezeigbo, T. A. (2008). *Artistic Creativity: Literature in the Service of Society*. Lagos: University of Lagos Press.

Fanon, Frantz (1961). *The Wretched of the Earth*. New York: Grove Press.

Fwa, K. L. (2007). "Money Laundering in West Africa: An Overview of the Threat in Nigeria," in *Human Trafficking and Economic Crimes across Nigeria's International Borders*. Eds. Barkindo, M. Bawuro, and Lipede, Abiola. Ibadan: Spectrum Books. 142–180.

Gloud, A. J. (2010). *Modern Slavery: A Regional Focus*. New York: University of Nebraska.

Inikori, J. E. (1978). "The Origin of the Diaspora: The Slave Trade from Africa," in *The African Diaspora*. Eds. Asiwaju, A. I., and Crowther, Michael. United States: Longman. 1–19.

International Criminal Court, Rome Statute: Article 7: (2003). *Crimes Against Humanity*. International Labour Organisation (ILO) (2005) *Human Trafficking Report*. International Organisation for Migration. (2006). *A Unison Discussion Paper*.

Kehinde, A. (2006). "Postcolonial Writings and Transgression of Boundaries: Reading Caryl Phillips' *Crossing the River as a Dialogic Text*." Paper presented at the conference, "Caryl Phillips: 25 Years of Writing," held at the University of Liege, Belgium, November, 1–2, 2006.

Lamidi, M. T. (2006). "The Rhetoric of Panhandling in Two Cities of Western Nigeria," in *Wole Soyinka @ 70 Festschrift*. Eds. Adelugba, Dapo, Izevbaye, Dan, and Ifie, Egbe. Nigeria: LACE Occasional Publications and Data and Partners Logistics Ltd. 879–922.

Lipede, A. (2007). "Women Trafficking and Insecurity in West Africa: Character, Trend, and Scale in Nigeria," in *Human Trafficking and Economic Crimes across Nigeria's International Borders*. Eds. Barkindo, M. Bawuro, and Lipede. Ibadan: Spectrum Books. 3–43.

Márquez, G. G. (1979). *No One Writes to the Colonel, and Other Stories*. New York: Harper and Row.

Nagle, L. E. (2007). "Curbing Human Trafficking Globally." *The Nation*, June 17: 10.

Okoro, U. O. (2007). "War Against Child Trafficking across Nigeria's International Borders: The Need for a Re-focus," in *Human Trafficking and Economic Crimes across Nigeria's International Borders*. Eds. Barkindo, M. Bawuro, and Lipede, Abiola. Ibadan: Spectrum Books Limited. 44–75.

Olaniyi, R. (2007). "'We Asked for Workers But Human Beings Came': A Critical Assessment of Immigration Policies on Human Trafficking in the European Union," in *Globalisation and Transnational Migrations: Africa and African in the Contemporary Global System*. Eds. Adebayo, G. Akanmu, and Adesina, C. Olutayo. Newcastle: Cambridge Scholars Publishing. 134–161.

Oni, S. I. (2006). "Transport-Induced Crimes and Border Control in the African Union," in *African Integration, Images and Perspective*. Ed. Akinyele, R. T. Lagos: University of Lagos Press. 134–143.

Osiki, O. M. (2009). "The Face of Trafficking and Human Smuggling across the Nigeria-Benin Border," in *Globalisation and Transnational Migrations: Africa and African in the Contemporary Global System*. Eds. Adebayo, G. Akanmu, Adesina, and C., Olutayo. Newcastle: Cambridge Scholars Publishing. 162–180.

Peter-Omale, F. (2005). Human Trafficking: Nigerian Jailed in UK. *Bradford.* February.

Scott, J., and Marshall, G. (Eds). (2005). *A Dictionary of Sociology.* Oxford: Oxford University Press.

Spivak, G. C. (1997). "Can the Subaltern Speak?" *Postcolonial Studies Reader.* Eds. Ashcroft, Bill, Griffiths, Gareth, and Tiffin, Helen. 1997. London and New York: Routledge. 24–35.

Tyson, L. (1999). *Critical Theory Today: A User-friendly Guide*. New York and London: Garland Publishing.

United Nations Office on Drugs and Crime. (2012). *Global Report on Trafficking in Persons*. Vienna: United Nations.

Uzoma, R. C. (2003). "The Sociocultural and Economic Implications of Human Trafficking in Contemporary Nigeria." An essay submitted in partial fulfilment for the membership of the National Institute for Policy and Strategic Studies.

Chapter Seventeen

Cultural Crisis of Widowhood Inheritance and Maltreatment in an African Society

Taofiq Olaide Nasir

The subservient position of women and the level of discrimination that accompanies widowhood practices and maltreatment is an acknowledged social problem in many African societies. In many societies, widowhood, resulting from natural in many instances, but especially in the sad situations of sudden death of husbands, leaves no room for a will or other preparations. A widow is a woman whose spouse has died and has not re-married while a widower is a man whose wife is dead. In the same vein, widowhood refers to the period in a woman's life when she is a widow and widowhood, the period during which a man remains a widower.

The phenomenon of widowhood is attributed to death of a husband whose causes are varied. In contemporary societies like Nigeria, the first notable variety of death worth considering due to its profound and immediate impact on widowhood in terms of creating many widows at a given time is war or armed conflict. Typical examples are World War I and II, the Ibo pogroms of 1966, the violent political crisis in Western Nigeria in the mid-1960s, the Nigerian civil war of 1967–1970, all produced more widows than any period in modern Nigeria (Agena, 2008). Added to this are ethnic and religious conflicts such as the Tiv riots of the 1960s; the Tiv-Jukun crises of the early 1990s and 2001; the Ife-Modakeke crisis of 2000, the Amuleri-Aguleri in South-Eastern Nigeria in 2001; the Maitatsine religious crisis of the 1980s that erupted in Kaduna and spread across northern Nigeria with flash points in states like Kano, Bauchi, and Plateau; the recurring religio-ethnic crises in

Jos, Plateau State, and Kaduna metropolis since 2000; these have all combined to produce additional widows in huge numbers (Alubo, 2006, Hembe,
2003; Suberu,1996 and Anifowose, 1982). In between these are unreported
cases of violent conflicts between minority ethnic groups that result in male
causalities. Since 1999 the Niger Delta crisis, electoral related violence and
the Boko Haram menace have caused substantial deaths in Nigeria. The
group has carried out heavy attacks since 2007 in Maiduguri, Kano, the
Police Headquarters in Abuja, churches in Abuja and Suleija in Niger state
and at the United Nations house in Abuja, media houses in Abuja (*ThisDay*
newspaper) and Kaduna (*The Sun* and *The Observer* newspapers) (Adeyemi,
2012; Akogun et al., 2011; Onojovwo, 2012; Alli, 2012; and Adamu, 2012).
Boko Haram killings is still going on though on a reduced scale, while
another incursion in the name of Fulani herdsmen has joined the fray and
claimed many lives. Undoubtedly, majority of those who lost their lives in all
these wars and crises and bombings are men, many of whom were married.
Those left behind include widows and children in a sizeable proportion.

Widowhood is one of the most distressing life events, more common with
women than men. Widowhood experiences are generally traumatic, but in
some African societies, they are considered more as an experience of deprivation, subjugation, humiliation and stigmatization. This last one, stigmatization, has been discovered to be the norm, as the disorganization and trauma
that follows the death of a spouse seem to be greater on the women than on
the men, whenever either loses his or her spouse. In the case of the loss of the
husband, the wife, at times, becomes the primary suspect of the cause of the
husband's death and is thus treated accordingly by grieving relatives of the
dead man. On the other hand, where a man loses his wife, the man is almost
immediately offered a substitute woman as wife to comfort and lessen the
impact of the grief of bereavement. The cause of this is not far-fetched. As
observed by Ahosi (2002, 2),

> the differentiation between men and women's role in Nigeria as with other
> African societies is one of complementary and superior relationship in favour
> of men. It involves a hierarchy in which men are given greater leverage over
> decision making and resources than women. The result is a cultural setting that
> invariably promotes male domination and female subordination.

Women maltreatment goes beyond mere verbal, physical and psychological
battering. It includes other forms of violence such as female genital mutila-
tion/cutting, violence against refugee women, sexual harassment, and
widowhood rituals and so on. Some of the rituals may include seclusion,
sexual cleansing, or other forms of encounters with the spiritual world to
avert further tragedies for the family of the diseased male

The 1995 Platform for Action of the Fourth World Conference on Women in Beijing was perhaps one of the major conferences ever organized, committed to a critical reflection on any negative filial action resulting from widowhood against women. As informed by Merry (2006, 76), the conference explicitly defined violence against women as "any act of gender-based violence that results in, or is likely to result in, physical, sexual coercion or arbitrary deprivation of liberty, whether occurring in public or private life".

Beyond this, it also took account of any act of gender-based violence perpetrated by the family, community or state, and leading to physical, sexual, and psychological harm and suffering of women in both private and public life. The document states further that any violence against women both violates and nullifies the enjoyment by women of their human rights and fundamental freedoms in a modern society.

As it relates to many communities in Nigeria, some of the customs relegate women to the background and clearly rob them of their rights and privileges. Sufficient evidence suggests that widowed women are severally affected financially, psychologically, sexually, and socially. The severe effects of widowhood in Nigeria are rooted in cultural and traditional practices, as well as the socialization processes that condition women to passivity and dependence (Stillion, 1984; Afolayan, 2011).

The most painful void left by the death of a spouse is felt after the funeral of the deceased, when relatives have departed and the bereaved is alone. In many instances the bereaved becomes preoccupied by memories of the deceased, sometimes even talking to the departed person, as though he or she were still alive. The widow or widower is not only isolating him/ herself from the living but is making it harder for him/herself to face the reality of the spouse's death. Their actions often lead to difficulty in concentration, lack of appetite and reliance on medication, such as sleeping pills or tranquillizers.

By declaring the right of women (including widows) to protection from violence as an important international women's right issue, the Beijing conference reaffirmed this intense statement of women's rights as human rights. From the interpretation of Beijing declaration, one can conclude that these rights have been and are still being trampled upon, especially in the case of widows, all in the name of culture/customs.

Against this background, the chapter is devoted to examining the traditional practice of widowhood and maltreatment often suffered by women in selected parts of Nigeria as an example of similar practices in Africa, *vis a vis* the influence of modernization and religion on this practice. Our effort in this chapter is anchored on three theoretical platforms that are considered most germane to the issues reflected upon: Radical Feminist Theory, Cultural Theory and the Rights Theory

RADICAL FEMINIST THEORY

According to Roberts (2006), the historical roots of radical feminism can be traced to the United States' Civil Rights Movement, particularly the Student Non-Violent Coordinating Committee. Many feminist pioneers of the second wave (Shulamith Firestone, Kathie Sarachild, Carol Hanisch, Judith Brown, and others) were active as volunteers in the struggle against racism in the early and mid-1960s. Using a method called "testifying" and "telling it like it is," they developed consciousness arising directly from experiences in the black-led Civil Rights Movement.

Randall (2003) postulates explicitly that radical feminist arose as a reaction to violence against women. In their epistemology of violence against women, the radical feminists have explained much in terms of heterosexual relationships as a product of the disproportional appreciation of the feminine gender as an epistemic being. However, they have glossed over the problem of economic disempowerment of women through practices property inheritance as violence against women. Malley-Morrison and Hines (2004, 75) assert that radical feminist theories blame patriarchy for violence against women in society. An interpretation of this violence in Africa is aligned to pervasive gender inequality and criticizes the patriarchal order subordinating women in virtually all aspects of life, but more significantly in the economic sphere.

Patriarchal theory maintains that the primary element of patriarchy is a relationship of dominance, where one party is dominant and exploits the other party for their own benefit. At the center of exploiting the subordinate group is the use of patriarchal tools such as culture, tradition, and norms that members of a given dominated group are obliged to observe.

As observed by David (2003, 37), radical feminists have claimed that men use social systems and other methods of control to keep women suppressed. He maintains that the investment of intellectual capital of radical feminism believe that eliminating patriarchy and other systems which perpetuate the domination of one group over another, will liberate women from an unjust society. The theorists critically postulate that institutionalization of inequality remains common in many countries, and in many African cultures and customary laws, which must be abolished. They highlight how even the United States of America strives to address pay inequality among men and women at the work-place, which culminated in Obama signing the equal pay law during his presidency. However, they did not critique property inheritance within the institution of customary law in many other societies, where women have no right to inherit from their husbands, are not regarded as sharing ownership of marital property, are excluded from ownership of land, and are almost without remedy upon divorce.

CULTURAL THEORY

It may be argued that the history of any society pave way for how people conduct themselves in the future. This may be attributed to the fact that history may have a strong bearing on the values and behavior of the people concerned.

Mate (2002) informs that some observers attribute part of the blame for domestic violence, and violence against women in general, to an alleged "culture of violence" in many modern African societies. Cultural theory emphasise that violence is accepted as a way to resolve disputes, and many links are drawn to the colonial heritage. This, perhaps, informs Randall's submission that Africans were treated coercively and violently by their colonizers and hence inherited the harsh treatment towards others from the colonial masters' practices. Lengthy civil wars and the repressive practices of many postcolonial regimes continue this culture of violence in family situations, with women suffering the most.

Inherent in the ideologies of colonization are power inequalities and oppression of one powerless group to the advantage of the other. The powerful group controls the less powerful and manipulates it with the intention of gaining and acquiring resources to the detriment of the colonized.

The concept of power inequalities and oppression of one group (usually women) has been fiercely criticized by the radical feminist intellectuals, who usually attribute it to patriarchy as the chief system for entrenching inequality in society. From this standpoint radical feminist theory could be expected to conceptualize the act of wife battering and women as part of property inheritance as an act of violence against women.

Cultural theory emphasizes the power of tradition and norms within African culture to explain the widespread incidence of violence against women in general and widows in particular. The term "culture" is often used to describe patterns of beliefs and behaviors shared by a social group. According to Nayak and Anna (2003), culture observes particular traditions and norms that control the behavior of people built upon, cemented and inherent in patriarchal attitudes and beliefs.

Theorists such as Heath view the connection between traditional norms and violence against women as a direct one, arguing that some perceived violence such as wife battering is regarded as normal within traditional African culture. The cultural theory finds its basis for explaining violence against women in traditions and norms within the patriarchal system so criticized by radical feminist theories. Culture so criticized is within a patriarchal society and hence this cultural theory augments the classical argument of radical feminist theory to which this chapter also subscribes.

THE RIGHTS THEORY

Women's protection rights and the rights theory fit together well when trying to explore the problem of women and the hardship they go through in many societies, including societies in Africa. The rights theory fundamentally explores women's rights. The rights theory is entirely based upon individual rights. Randall (2003) explains that most African countries have ratified numerous international covenants that either explicitly or implicitly interprets violence and rights of women as a form violation of human rights. At the basic ontological level, these treaties urge that the identities and agencies of women are compromised when the rights and privileges appertaining to their humanity are compromised simply on gender grounds. These further carry collective moral opprobrium with them to challenge the integrity of whatever structures of human relations are instituted at the domestic, national and international levels; thereby calling on collective moral courage of humans everywhere to stand up for the equality of all human beings, whether in bereavement or in ordinary filial relations.

Despite this fact, theories about violence against women based on the assertion of individual human rights are minimal in many African society. In many African societies, while a link may be drawn between freedom from violence and human rights guarantees in various international charters, the rights-based arguments often appear to be tacked on and to be weak and fit uneasily with the continent's sociocultural problematic. For example, Fitnat Adjetey, as quoted by Randall (2003), discussed domestic violence in Ghana as one small part of a much larger pattern of violence against women, including female genital mutilation, rape, child marriage, widowhood rites, widow inheritance, and female religious bondage.

He gives advice about how specific provisions of international human rights conventions may be used to accomplish piecemeal legal reforms. Yet if violence is just one manifestation of a much larger phenomenon of gender inequality and violent treatment of women (Anglophone Africa, 2004), then surely piecemeal legal reforms are unlikely to provide an effective remedy for women in many African societies, as there is likely to be continuous conflict between the law and culture.

CONCEPT OF WIDOW INHERITANCE

Widowhood inheritance has been aptly categorized as one of the consequences of death upon marriage. When a married man dies in many African societies, his marriage contract is not automatically discharged. His surviving wife is still regarded as married to him. This marriage is, in fact, still subsisting, but in order to achieve its social purpose, there are some formalities as well as legal rights and duties attached to it, which are to be performed or executed for normal life to continue for filial relations.

The marriage subsisting after the husband's death may end up in three ways, depending on the wife's choice. First, the marriage may be formally dissolved, through the process of divorce. The plaintiff, as the wife of the deceased, could seek formal dissolution of the marriage from a competent court, especially if relatives of the deceased does not care and maintain her. If she is able to prove her case beyond reasonable doubt, the court can grant her wish and rule in her favour.

This case re-emphasizes the fact that the death of a husband does not automatically discharge the marriage contract. Hence, the normal divorce proceedings must take place, and in the appropriate circumstances, the bride-price must be refunded.

The second way in which the problem of female dependency, aggravated by husband's death may be resolved begins the same way as the above; that is, by regarding marriage as subsisting, though in a fictitious sense. There seems, however, to be another basic assumption in this regard. Once a woman marries a man, she is deemed to be married to the same man until she dies. It makes no difference whether the man is dead or alive, unless, of course, the marriage has been terminated by divorce. When the man dies, the marriage is deemed to continue as if the man is still alive. His "brother" is required to play the role of a sexual partner, but he does this on behalf of the deceased man. Any children born out of this relationship are regarded as the children of the deceased man. They are entitled to inherit the property of the deceased man, and to have mutual rights of the deceased ma. They are entitled to have equal rights with his other children. This practice is known as "levirate." This is a form of widow inheritance.

According to Holleman (2007, 83) the customary law states that the first and foremost problem is the one of terminological inexactitude. The concept of widow inheritance is not easily translatable into the English language which does not have the same concept. Holleman therefore submits that the African concept of the word estate has a much wider range of meaning than the latter. It classes inheritance and self-acquired property together and makes no distinction between rights over things and rights over persons.

Hence, when one uses such terms as widow-inheritance and estate-wife as understood within the cultural context, they are in no way derogatory. It is only when one understands them in a strange and foreign sense that they can be regarded as derogatory.

MALTREATMENT OF WIDOWS

Widows' maltreatment practices in many Nigerian, African, and other human societies could be said to be steeped in the people's culture. Culture being the totality of societal beliefs values, attitudes, customs and traditions by which people within a society organize themselves and conduct their day to day activities cuts across all society and assist greatly in societal intra- and inter-relations (Bewaji, 2013, 2014, and 2016). There is no society without culture. Culture is dynamic and diverse and embraces the material and non-material experiences of the people.

When a husband dies, irrespective of the age of the wife, she automatically goes into widowhood and, depending on the cultural background of the marriage; the widow's conduct and activities are, henceforth, regulated by customary practices and norms. In general, according to Ewuluka, in Vanessa Emery (2003) "widowhood rites include isolation and confinement, restrictions in movement and association and hair shaving." Among the people of Edo in Edo state in South Western Nigeria conspicuous practices include a seven days period of mourning under restricted movement and association. Shaving of the head, eating from unwashed plates, compulsory wailing, and washing the dead man's body and drinking the water (Emery, 2003) are some of the dehumanizing practices that widows are subjected to.

Among the Hausa-Fulani community and tainted with Islamic religious elements, mourning and purification rites are also imposed and adhered to. A Muslim widow in Kano undergoes a four-month mourning period and observes reasonable number of days in seclusion. In Plateau and Bauchi states, Muslim widows observe forty days of mourning and thirty days of seclusion which run concurrently (Emery, 2003). Among the Igbos of South-Eastern Nigeria, a widow's head is shaved immediately upon the death of her husband. In addition, a widow is expected to use sticks in scratching her body from time to time during the mourning period. Besides, she is restrained from washing herself. These practices are rooted in the belief that every death is unnatural. Therefore, a widow must pass through these rituals to prove her innocence and purify herself and at the same time protect herself from further defilement (Okoye, 1995). At the death of a husband, the mourning period ranges from one week to a year with activities that differ from one community to another.

In most Igbo communities, a woman is expected to dress in the mud cloth called "Ogodo Upa" for a period of seven days to a year, depending on the emphasis of the community. In other communities, a woman is expected to wail three times a day or once in a day for three or seven days. In addition to the woman's hair being entirely shaven, she would sit on a mat surrounded by sympathizers and clad in black attire for seven months during the mourning period (Breeze Magazine, 2012).

Among the Yoruba of South-Western Nigeria, widowhood practices are generally characterized by some level of human filial greed, superstitious beliefs and religious rites (Afolayan, 2011). This assertion holds true for other ethnic groups in Nigeria and Africa as well. The extent and intensity of these practices are influenced by changes brought about by foreign religions and modernity; the teachings of Islam and Christianity and the economic status of the deceased and the personal means of the widow. Among the Yoruba people, widowhood in its simple cultural manifestation, without the moderation of modernity, "is an enduring period of deep-rooted agony, exclusion, anxiety, as well as a period of restriction, isolation, trauma, insecurity and pain" (Afolayan, 2011, 28).

These widowhood practices also vary from community to community throughout Yoruba land and Africa. In some communities, widows are required to recite incantation in thick forests at night for the purpose of self "cleansing" (UN, 2001, 8).

Many cultures in Nigeria share similarities in widowhood practices. Many of the other African ethnic groups as Yoruba, Igbo, and minority groups as the Tiv, Idoma, Urhobo, Ishan, and including those in Edo and Delta states, observe a mourning period that differ only in degree. This may range from a few days to a year. During this period the widows' appearance is distinct from others by dressing in white or black attire, accentuated by a grieving expression. The Igbo's shave the widow's hair while the Tiv only cut the hair low. In most of the cultures, the widow is a suspect in the death of her husband and is made to undergo widowhood rites in atonement, purification, and self-immolation.

There are two other elements in widowhood practices that are widely shared by many ethnic groups in Africa, and perhaps globally; these are levirate marriage and disinheritance for the widow. After the mourning period, the widow in Yoruba, Igbo, or Tiv and many other ethnic groups is expected to remarry to a relative of her late husband. In general, this practice is on the decline due to the influence of social and cultural changes, modernity, Christian, and Islamic religious influences (Akumadu, 1998).

Akinade and Suleiman (2005, 153) inform that the cultural milieu in which people operate, and the effect of gender role stereotype, gives the notion that widows are failures and are unfulfilled in the society. Thus, when the death of a husband occurs, the woman is faced with the feeling of guilt or failure and the negative stigma of being a widow. It has been observed that across cultures, religions, regions, class and caste, the treatment of widows in many developing countries, Nigeria inclusive, is harsh and discriminatory.

All human societies have sought ways to make death acceptable and to provide opportunities for expressing grief and showing respect to the dead person. In societies where the status of a woman is secondary to male status, the mourning and burial rites are inherently gendered; the widow is expected to grieve openly to demonstrate the intensity of her feeling.

In some societies, the widow is kept in solitary confinement without access to members of the public, friends and associates. She can be prohibited from washing her body even if she is menstruating. For several months, she is forced to sit naked on a mat and ritually scream at specific times of the day and night. In addition, hairs in every part of the widow's body are shaved and she's allowed to dress only in black cloths.

John and Maurice (2009, 65) inform that in the eastern region of Nigeria, a widow is forced to drink the water with which the corpse of the husband is washed before burial to prove that she was not involved in his death; a widow's hair is shaved off and she must sleep on the ground without a blanket for a month and a week. They stated further that,

> after a man has been buried, the widow is isolated or kept in a secluded place for a period of three months. During this period, she would be observed to know whether she would suffer from emotional trauma or fall sick. If she falls sick, it signifies that she is responsible for her husband's death; and if not, she would be claimed innocent. In this respect, the widow is termed as contaminate and culturally would need purification involving live animals in order to save her life, that of her children and other members of her family. (65)

Quoting Ugwuenze, Aniekan (2011, 72) informs that in Ngwa land, the death of a husband calls for immediate mourning by the widow/widows of the departed victim. The widow is confined to the room where the dead body of the husband lay. There she is meant to sit on the floor, (some even insist that she sits on the cold floor) as long as the body is yet to be buried. After the burial, she is not expected to have free movement for at least ninety-days (in some cases, more than four months). Before entering into the mourning period, her hair would have been shaved to the scalp, dressed in shabby half wrapper. The widow must not wear shoes, slipper, never to trim her nails. She is not permitted to go to the toilet unaccompanied. After the burial of the dead the widow is now expected to enter into another period of mourning which will last for one year during which time she is to be dressed in pure black with no shoes, sandals or slippers.

Amongst the Edo's, especially the Esans, Egharevba (1971) and Okojie (1980) inform that as soon as a man dies, the wife is expected to mourn him publicly for at least seven days. As soon as the body is taken away for burial, the widow is armed with "ikhimin". Ikhimin is a many-sided fruit from a tree which looks like the oil bean tree and believed among the Edos to be much shunned by spirits. She is also armed with a bow and arrows to protect her from the husband's spirit. Earthenware pot with fire glowing from within is left at the door of the room where the widow is. During the mourning period, she is expected to go to the burial ground to have her bath. She will shoot the arrow into the bush requesting her dead husband not to come to her. During this period, she must eat alone with her left hand, sleep on the floor with a mat, because anything she comes in contact with during that period will be thrown away on the seventh day. After she has been through with all the rites for seven days, she now enters the usual three months mourning periods. During this period, she has to use charcoal to smear her forehead and wear black clothes continuously.

Among the Ashanti of Ghana, Rattray (1956) informs that widowhood rites are strictly observed, and wife inheritance is considered the appropriate thing for a heir to do when the father dies leaving a wife and children. If these rites are not carried out it means that the man has not been given a befitting burial. Okoye (1995) concurs that widowhood rites in Ghana can constitute emotional violence on the widow.

There is always a high-level violence against a woman who has just lost her husband. All her husband's properties are eventually taken away from her, without considering her situation and circumstances.

Abdulkareem (2013, 7) informs that in northern Nigeria, death is attributed to God and so the widow is not blamed for death of her husband. The widow goes through a period of mourning for four lunar months and ten days. She can stay and remarry within the family or released to go elsewhere to marry. Although most are neglected during and after morning period, no other physically injurious or degrading practice is inflicted on her. This may be a result of Islamic religious traditions permeating the Northern Nigeria society.

In Cameroon, widowhood is a very painful experience. In the event of the death of a man, the wife is always the suspect and, because of that, she is subjected to harmful and humiliating treatment. Her hair is shaved and, in certain areas of Cameroon, her pubic region hair is equally shaved. This is accompanied with some cleansing or purifying rituals. The mourning period is usually for two years.

BEYOND THE MALTREATMENT PRACTICES

While this chapter argues against what is widely believed to be maltreatment of widows, it is pertinent to take a voyage into some cultural beliefs that does not support this maltreatment. While these gender based cultural practice of treatment of widows is humiliating, we note however, that there are some cultural practices and beliefs upon which such practices are based with the hope these will help to avert certain evil occurrences in the society following the death of the deceased. For instance, John and Maurice (2007, 64) reported that a widow who loses her husband is kept in a closed room and the other widows shave her hairs, from head, eyebrows, and armpit to the public areas. The hair shaved by the other widows is buried in the soil so as to avoid her hair coming into contact with those whose husbands are still living. Particles of her hair touching the body of women whose husbands are still alive are believed to be capable of causing the death of the husband of such women.

Also, in order to sever sexual relationships between a widow and her late husband, John and Maurice (2009, 66) state that "she will be made to lie in the same room with her late husband. Such act guarantees that the husband must have had the last sexual relationship with the woman and as such will never bother her in dreams for sexual matters."

LEGAL AND RELIGION INFLUENCE

Nigeria, as a multicultural and multi-ethnic society is characterised by plural legal systems to preserve the traditional values of her diverse ethnic communities. The frontiers of the legal systems (Common Law, Statutory Law, Customary Law and Islamic Law) are multi-faceted and the customary laws itself are not integrated. Generally, the mystifying plurality of cultures in Nigeria indicates that there is a wide variety of widowhood practices. However, as informed by Iwobi (2008, 79), Nigeria's legal system should be willing to confront these customary laws and traditions with a view to curtailing the operation of contradictory legal frameworks and minimize the adverse effects of these; thereby reconciling them with the provisions of the Nigerian Constitution, which is challenging.

Today's religions, especially Islam and Christianity, had affected the practice of widowhood rites, as well as inheritance traditions in certain societies of Africa. Due to the embrace of the religions and perhaps enlightenment of the practitioners, certain aspects of the widow inheritance is being changed gradually. Before the advent of these religions and modernisation, women went through various gender inflected negative treatment and were even considered to be part of inheritance in some societies. She neither had any right nor was her opinion sought in matters concerning her.

In stark contrast, the period allowed for a man to mourn his dead wife is only three days, while for the Muslim Woman, she must mourn for four lunar months and ten days:

> Thus, if any of you dies and leave widows behind him, they shall wait concerning themselves for four months and ten days, when they have fulfilled their terms, there is no blame on you if they dispose of themselves in a just and reasonable manner. And God is well acquainted with what you do. (Qur'an 2: 234)

This period, in addition to mourning and ascertaining if the woman is pregnant, allows her time to recuperate and prepare for the new life ahead of her. It is also imperative that a Muslim plans for death and to leave at least one year maintenance for the family. If not, the relatives are expected to make provisions for the widow and her children. In the biblical traditions widows and divorced women were looked down upon. The high priest was not allowed to marry a widow, a divorced woman, or a prostitute, for, "The woman he (the high priest) marries must be a virgin. He must not marry a widow, a divorced woman, or a woman defiled by prostitution, but only a virgin from his own people, so he will not defile his offspring among his people" (*Leviticus* 21: 13–15). It can conclusively be suggested that with the advent of the religions and embrace of modern cultures came the liberation and emancipation of women, leading to the condemnation and termination of such acts which victimize bereaved women in their time of grief.

An anecdotal empirical evidence was the death of my brother. After his death, his wife was allowed to mourn him for the required days; after which she was allowed to go out as she wished. During the mourning period, contrary to some beliefs, her hair was neither shaved nor was she barred from taking her bath. In fact, the only thing she did not enjoy was going out the way she used to. She had people coming to visit her, she ate what she wanted whenever she wished, and she was even permitted to wander around the family compound; but was not allowed to step outside it. Even though she was yet to have any child with my brother, all her needs were met and was made not to lack anything, except perhaps the emotional longing for her husband, which we could nothing about. After the mourning period, she was allowed to stay in her former husband's house if she so desired and was allowed to go with all of her husband's property if she wishes. Also, she was not in any way coerced, abused, maltreated or asked to marry any member of the family.

All these were done due to our religious beliefs coupled with enlightenment which were allowed to guide our thoughts and actions. This, I must say has rubbed off on some families within our community, who also followed suit when something similar happened to them. I believe this also applies in Christian communities, if the words of Sossu, as informed by Afolayan (2011, 42), who stated that Christianity and Western influence have reviewed and modernized some of the widowhood practices, is anything to go by.

CONCLUSIONS AND RECOMMENDATIONS

The institution of widow inheritance as informed by religious beliefs and modernisation accords the widow a sense of belonging and continued contractual responsibility and respect for the dead. As it relates to many societies in Nigeria and Africa, it can be observed that some of the traditional customs relegate women to the background and clearly rob them of their rights and privileges. As observed by Samuel (2011, 185), widowhood is a period when a widow is expected to be grieving or mourning the loss of a beloved one, precisely a husband. It involves some rituals and these rituals, as stated by Anugwom (2011, 89) and Agumagu (2007), are inherently gendered, because a widower has no stringent restrictive and punitive laid-down customary laws governing his mourning rites.

   Most of these abuses of women's rights are perpetrated through the patriarchal traditions, and unequal power relations existing between men and women and the greediness of some family members. These then opens the door to all sorts of abuses and violations of the rights of female members of society. The rites, often without disclosure and consent, and of course with the procedural duration of wailing, property dispossession and other hardships, together with food taboos, are a depressing reality of what might even cause widows' deaths in some communities. It is in the light of this that this chapter is arguing for a standardised law or code of ethics guiding widow widowhood, to reduce significantly the maltreatment of widows in society.

BIBLIOGRAPHY

Abdulkareem, Fatimah (2013). "Effects and Implications of Widowhood and Single Parenthood on the Muslim Family." Lecture delivered on July 13, 2013 at the Ramadan Lecture, organized by the University of Ibadan Muslim Community.

Adamu, L. D. (2012). "2 Profs, 17 Others Killed in BUK attack," *Daily Trust Newspaper*, Monday, April 30.

Ademola, John & Maurice, E. O. (2009). "The Politics of Widowhood and Remarriage," in the Catholic University of East Africa's *Journal of the Philosophical Association of Kenya*, Premier Issue, New Series, 1(1): 165–178.

Agena, T. (2008). "The Impact of the Nigerian civil war on Tiv soldiers of central Nigeria". In Armstrong M. Adejo (ed.) *The Nigerian civil war: Forty years after*, Makurdi, Aboki Publishers.

Akinade, E. A., & Ali, Sulaiman. (2005). *Sexuality Education and Couple Guidance*. Ibadan: Olatunji publishers.

Akogun, K., Obi, P., & Sowole, J. (2011). "Police HQ Bombing: Nine Victims Handed Over to Police," *This Day Newspaper*, Sunday, June 19.

Afolayan, E. G. (2011). "Widowhood Practices and the Rights of Women." A paper delivered at Human Rights, Development and Social Justice, The Hague, The Netherlands

Agumagu, J. (2007). "The Nigeria Woman and Widowhood Challenges and Constraints," *Sophia: African Journal of Philosophy and Public Affairs*, vol. 10.

Ahonsi, J. B. (2010). "Widow Inheritance in Bondo District, Kenya: Baseline Results from a Prospective Cohort Study," *PLOS ONE* 5(11). doi:10.1371/journal.

Akumadu, T. U. (1998). *Beast of Burden: A Study of Women's Legal Status and Reproductive Health Rights in Nigeria*. Lagos: CLO.

Alli, Y., et al. (2012). "Boko Haram Strikes Again as Kaduna Count losses," *The Nation Newspaper*, Tuesday, April 10, 2012.

Alubo, O. (2006). *Ethnic Conflicts and Citizenship Crisis in the Central Region*. Ibadan: Eddy Asae Nigerian Press

Aniekan, J. (2011). *Towards a Social Philosophy of the Widowhood Custom.* London and New York: Routledge.

Anifowose, R. (1982). *Violence and Politics in Nigeria: The Tiv and Yoruba Experience.* New York: Nob Publishers International.

Anugwom, N. E. (2011). "The Socio-Psychological Impact of Widowhood on Elderly Women in Nigeria," *OIDA International Journal of Sustainable Development,* 2(6).

Anglophone Africa (2004). *Women of the World: Laws and Policies Affecting their Reproductive Lives,* The Centre for Law and Policy.

Bewaji, J. A. I. (2016). *The Rule of Law and Governance in Indigenous Yoruba Society: A Study in African Philosophy of Law.* Lanham, MD: Lexington Books.

———. and Imafidon, E. (Eds.) (2014). *Ontologized Ethics: New Essays in African Meta-Ethics.* Lanham, MD: Lexington Books.

———. (2013). *Black Aesthetics.* Trenton, NY: Africa World Press.

Emery, K. V. (2003). "Women's Inheritance Rights in Nigeria: Transformative Practices." https://www.semanticscholar.org/paper/Women-%E2%80%99-s-Inheritance-Rights-in-Nigeria-%3A-Practices-Emery/f6868600065f15d0067cb989ddeff4af160eb0c2. Retrieved July 10, 2012.

Heath, D. B. (2001). *Culture and Substance Abuse, Cultural Psychiatry: International Perspectives.* New Horn Press.

Hembe, G. N., and Tarka, J. S. (2003).*The Dilemma of Ethnic Minority Politics in Nigeria.* Makurdi: Aboki publishers

Holleman, C. R. (2007). "Widowhood in the Era of AIDS: A Case Study of Siaya District, Kenya," *Journal of Social Aspects of HIV/AIDS,* Vol.4, No.2.

Malley-Morrison, K., and Hines D. A. (2004) *Family Violence in A Cultural Perspective: Defining, Understanding, and Combating Abuse,* California: Sage Publications.

Merry, S. E. (2006). *Human Rights and Gender Violence: Transnational Inter-national Law into Local Justice,* Chicago: University of Chicago Press.

Nayak, M., Christina, A. B., Mutsumi, K. M., and Anna, G. A. (2003) "Attitudes Towards Violence Against Women: a Cross-Nation Study, *'Sex Roles':Journal of Research,* 49(7–8): 333.

Okoye, P. U. (1995). *Widowhood: A national or cultural tragedy.* Enugu, Nucik Publishers.

Ogutu, G. E. M. (2007). *5th African Population Conference on Emerging Issues on Population and Development in Africa.* December 10–14 , Arusha, Tanzania.

Onojovwo, D. (2012). "Six Killed, 22 Injured as Bombers Hit Media Houses," *National Mirror Newspaper,* Friday, April 27.

Randall, V. R. (2003) "Domestic Violence in the African Context", *American University Journal of Gender, Social Policy and Law.*

Rattray, R. S., (1956).. *Ashanti Law and Constitution.* London: Oxford University Press.

Samuel, G. C. E. (2011). "Emergent Issues on Widowhood Practices in Igbo Culture: Between the Video Screen and Reality. *Unizik Journal of Arts and Humanities (UJAH) .*"

Suberu, R. (1996). *Ethnic Minority Conflicts and Government in Nigeria.* Ibadan: Spectrum Books.

Sossou, M. A. (2002). "Widowhood Practices in West Africa: The Silent Victims". *International Journal of Social Welfare,* (3)5.

Stallion J. M. (1984). "Women and Widowhood: The Suffering Beyond Grief," in *Women: A Feminist Perspective.* Ed. Freeman, Jo. Mountain View, CA: Mayfield Publishing Company.

United Nations (2001). "Widowhood: Invisible Women Secluded or Excluded." http://www.unwomen.org/en/digital-library/publications/2001/12/women2000-widowhood-invisible-women-secluded-or-excluded. Retrieved May 24, 2013.

Breeze Magazine (2012). "Comparison of Widowhood Rituals among the Igbos and Yoruba People in Nigeria," *Breeze Magazine,* January 3. breezemagazine.blogspot.com, retrieved July 4, 2012.

Coleman, J. S. (1975). *Nigeria: Background to Nationalism,* Benin City: Brosburg & Wistrom.

Eweluka, U. U. (2002). "Post-colonialism, Gender, Customary Injustice: Widows in African Societies," *Human Rights Quarterly,* 24: 242.

Nwogugu, E. I. (1980). "Family law," in *Introduction to Nigerian Law*. Eds. C.O. Okonkwo et al. London: Sweet & Maxwell.

About the Editors and Contributors

Listed in order of appearance.

Adedoyin Aguoru is an experienced lecturer with a demonstrated history of working in the research industry. She possesses outstanding skills in administering and supporting nonprofit organizations, conferencing, and conference administration, and has proven skills in analysis, lecturing, editing, and public speaking. A 2007 visiting scholar to Ritsumeikan University in Kyoto, Japan, Doyin is a strong education professional with a PhD in comparative literature, national, and cultural identity (in Japan and Nigeria). Her other other research interests include gender studies, playwriting, and biographical studies for social transformation—on which she has collaborated with the Narrative Enquiry for Social Transformation project at Witwatersrand University in Johannesburg, South Africa.

John Ayotunde Isola Bewaji is professor of philosophy at the University of the West Indies at Mona in Kingston, Jamaica. His publications include *Beauty and Culture* (2003), *An Introduction to the Theory of Knowledge* (2007), *Narratives of Struggle* (2012), *Ontologized Ethics* (edited with Elvis Imafidon, 2014), *Black Aesthetics* (2013), *The Rule of Law and Governance in Indigenous Yoruba Society* (2016), and *Media Ethics* (with Babatunde Adedara, 2017). A recipient of numerous awards, he was Jay Newman Visiting Chair in Philosophy of Culture at Brooklyn College as well as Member of Nigerian Academy of Letters.

Kunirum Osia was, until his transition to ancestorhood, professor in the Department of Applied Psychology at Coppin State University in Baltimore, Maryland, USA.

Moses Oludare Aderibigbe lectures in the Department of General Studies, School of Sciences, at the Federal University of Technology in Akure, Nigeria.

Bosede Funke Afolayan lectures in the Department of English at the University of Lagos in Nigeria.

Michael Achankeng Fonkem I is COEHS faculty at the University of Wisconsin-Oshkosh in the USA.

Michael Olusegun Fajuyigbe lectures in Western art history and art criticism for the Department of Fine and Applied Arts at Obafemi Awolowo University in Ile-Ife, Nigeria. His research interests include aesthetics, art criticism, and sociology of art with an emphasis on contemporary Nigerian art and Yoruba (African) iconography and symbolism.

Elo Ibagere is lecturer in the Department of Theatre Arts at Delta State University in Abraka, Nigeria.

Bifátife Olufemi Adeseye is lecturer in the Department of Theatre Arts at Federal University Oye-Ekiti in Nigeria.

Sandra McCalla is lecturer in the Department of Language, Linguistics, and Philosophy at the University of the West Indies Mona in Kingston, Jamaica.

Babafemi Jacobs is a member of the Nigerian Institute of Public Relations, a media scholar, and lecturer for the Department of Mass Communication at Lead City University in Ibadan, Nigeria.

Margaret Solo-Anaeto, PhD, is a scholar and researcher in the Department of Mass Communication at Babcock University, Nigeria. Her research interests and publications are in the areas of health communication, social mediam, and gender studies. She is also an editor for Babcock University Press.

Fouad Mami is professor for the Department of English at the University of Adrar in Algeria.

Kehinde O. Ola is lecturer at the College of Management and Social Sciences at Samuel Adegboyega University in Ogwa, Edo State, Nigeria.

David O. Oke is lecturer for the College of Management and Social Sciences at Samuel Adegboyega University in Ogwa, Edo State, Nigeria.

Ezinwanji E. Adam is lecturer in the Department of Languages and Literary Studies at Babcock University, Ilishan Remo, Ogun State, Nigeria.

Roxanne Burton is lecturer in the Department of History and Philosophy at the University of the West Indies Cave Hill in Bridgeport, Barbados.

Ifeyinwa Genevieve Okolo is lecturer in the Department of English and Literary Studies at Federal University, Lokoja, Kogi State, Nigeria.

Akinbimpe Akintayo Akinyele is lecturer in the Department of English at the University of Ibadan in Ibadan, Nigeria.

Solomon O. Olaniyan lectures in the Department of English at the University of Ibadan, Nigeria, where he earned his BA, MA, and PhD. His research areas include postcolonial African literature and literary sociology. He has published articles in both local and international journals.

Taofiq Olaide Nasir is lecturer in the Department of English and Performing Arts at Olabisi Onabanjo University, Ago-Iwoye, Ogun State, Nigeria.

Index

www.ingramcontent.com/pod-product-compliance
Lightning Source LLC
Chambersburg PA
CBHW022305280326
41932CB00010B/989